ADVANCE PRAISE FOR

# *Unsettling Education*

"In this political moment and in these palpably perilous times for youth and the adults charged with their care and safe passage—parents, teachers, youth workers—*Unsettling Education* offers both hope and guidance. The dazzling educators gathered together by Brian Charest and Kate Sjostrom are animated by an urgent spirit of resistance to the status quo that they recognize as representing a kind of state of emergency for the oppressed, the exploited, and the disadvantaged. The challenge facing teachers in these troubling times is to resist injustices, unsettle the settled, destabilize the stable, trouble the undisturbed, explore the unknown, and dive into (rather than run away from) the contradictions. The message these teachers bring to their students is generative: you are a full human being; you have a right to be here; you need no one's permission to interrogate the universe. This book shows us what that can look like in real time."

—William Ayers, Distinguished Professor of Education and Senior University Scholar at the University of Illinois at Chicago (retired) and Author of *To Teach*, *Fugitive Days*, and *Demand the Impossible!: A Radical Manifesto*

"From the educational 'standards' being compelled onto students, to the rhetoric of educational 'reform' being sold to communities and educators alike, the problem is not merely the silencing of dissent but the presumption that there is no alternative. What better intervention than the call by Brian Charest, Kate Sjostrom, and colleagues for us all to engage in 'unsettling education.' All who teach and who care about teaching will find sources of inspiration and nourishment in the richly detailed and deeply thoughtful portraits of K–12 teachers and teaching that model for us what this can look like in times, like now, when pressure abounds to settle."

—Kevin Kumashiro, Author of *Against Common Sense: Teaching and Learning Toward Social Justice*

# Unsettling Education

FALL 2019
— FOR DAN & LUCIA

AND SO IT WILL
ALWAYS CONTINUE—

IN APPRECIATION,

BRIAN! KATE!
STUDENTS OF DAVE +
TODD.
LET IT LIVE
ON!

SOCIAL JUSTICE

ACROSS CONTEXTS IN EDUCATION

sj Miller & Leslie David Burns

GENERAL EDITORS

Vol. 11

The Social Justice Across Contexts in Education series is
part of the Peter Lang Education list.
Every volume is peer reviewed and meets
the highest quality standards for content and production.

PETER LANG
New York • Bern • Berlin
Brussels • Vienna • Oxford • Warsaw

# Unsettling Education

## Searching for Ethical Footing in a Time of Reform

Edited by Brian Charest
& Kate Sjostrom

PETER LANG
New York • Bern • Berlin
Brussels • Vienna • Oxford • Warsaw

**Library of Congress Cataloging-in-Publication Data**

Names: Charest, Brian, editor. | Sjostrom, Kate, editor.
Title: Unsettling education: searching for ethical footing in a time
of reform / edited by Brian Charest and Kate Sjostrom.
Description: New York: Peter Lang, 2019.
Series: Social justice across contexts in education; vol. 11
ISSN 2372-6849 (print) | ISSN 2372-6857 (online)
Includes bibliographical references.
Identifiers: LCCN 2019002533 | ISBN 978-1-4331-6350-0 (hardback: alk. paper)
ISBN 978-1-4331-6701-0 (paperback: alk. paper) | ISBN 978-1-4331-6702-7 (ebook pdf)
ISBN 978-1-4331-6703-4 (epub) | ISBN 978-1-4331-6704-1 (mobi)
Subjects: LCSH: Education and state—United States.
Education—Standards—United States. | Educational change—United States.
Education—Aims and objectives—United States.
Educational tests and measurements—United States.
Classification: LCC LC89 .U59 2019 | DDC 379.73—dc23
LC record available at https://lccn.loc.gov/2019002533
DOI 10.3726/b15559

Bibliographic information published by **Die Deutsche Nationalbibliothek**.
**Die Deutsche Nationalbibliothek** lists this publication in the "Deutsche
Nationalbibliografie"; detailed bibliographic data are available
on the Internet at http://dnb.d-nb.de/.

The paper in this book meets the guidelines for permanence and durability
of the Committee on Production Guidelines for Book Longevity
of the Council of Library Resources.

Printed in the United States of America

*For Elizabeth, Charles, and Theodore*
—Brian Charest

*For Andy and Bea*
—Kate Sjostrom

There is no promised land in teaching, just the aching and persistent tension between reality and possibility.

—William Ayers, Kevin Kumashiro, Erica Meiners, Therese Quinn, and David Stovall, *Teaching Toward Democracy*


I began by saying that one of the paradoxes of education was that precisely at the point when you begin to develop a conscience, you must find yourself at war with society. It is your responsibility to change society if you think of yourself as an educated person. And on the basis of the evidence—one is compelled to say that this is a backward society.

—James Baldwin, "A Talk to Teachers"

# Table of Contents

*Acknowledgments*      xi

*Introduction*
    BRIAN CHAREST AND KATE SJOSTROM      1

*Section I: The Promise of Unsettling Moments*

*Introduction*      11

*1. Against Measurement: Making a Case for School Play*      15
    AVI LESSING AND GLYNIS KINNAN

*2. Calculating Justice? Using Mathematical Mindsets for Teaching*
*From a Social Justice Perspective*      33
    ANGELA WHITACRE DE RESENDIZ AND WILL HUDSON

*3. Challenging Misrecognitions Through Reflexive Teacher Education:*
*Knowing and Growing in an Age of Commodification*      53
    NOAH ASHER GOLDEN

*Section II: Pedagogies of Resistance*

*Introduction*      73

*4. Beyond Mandates and Measurement: Imagining a Gradeless Classroom*      77
    SARAH J. DONOVAN

*5. Pedagogies of Resistance: Reflecting on the Successes and Challenges of*
*Humanizing Classrooms in a Time of Standardization and Accountability*      93
    MATTHEW HOMRICH-KNIELING AND ALEX CORBITT

6. *Compulsory Heterosexuality: Unsettling and Undoing the Hidden Curriculum of Heteronormativity in Schools*     111
    MIKELA BJORK

*Section III: Unsettling Education Through Institutional Critiques*

*Introduction*     133

7. *Managing Teachers: Efficiency and Human Relations in Education*     139
    JAMES MCCOYNE

8. *Motivation, Mental Health, and the Eclipse of Social Imagination*     157
    KEVIN CHRISTOPHER CAREY

9. *A Look Into Leaving: Learning From One Equity-Oriented Teacher's Resignation*     179
    SAMANTHA YOUNG AND DEBORAH BIELER

10. *"all schooled up": One Teacher's Path Toward Deschooling*     197
    RUSSELL MAYO

*Epilogue*

*Everyone Knows Whose Side I'm On: Teachers, Students, and the Struggle for Freedom*     219
    JAY GILLEN

*Contributors*     231

# *Acknowledgments*

We thank our series editors, Les Burns and sj Miller, as well as Megan Madden and Monica Baum at Peter Lang Publishing. Thanks, too, to Carolyn Lesnick and Josh Staub for formatting and cover art, respectively.

Our mentors Bill Ayers, Todd DeStigter, Kevin Kumashiro, and David Schaafsma have provided continual guidance and insight.

Many colleagues and friends, too, deserve our appreciation: Chris Bass, Lauren Bell, Mikela Bjork, Jake Burns, Amy McGrail, Sarah Donovan, Angela Gutierrez, Nicol Howard, Abby Kindelsperger, Kate Manski, Russell Mayo, Manulani Meyer, Sarah Rutter, Jennifer Tilton, Beverly Troiano, Andrew Wall, and Christopher Worthman.

Special thanks to this volume's contributors, all of whom challenged us to "unsettle" our thinking on schools and schooling: Deborah Bieler, Mikela Bjork, Kevin Carey, Alex Corbitt, Sarah Donovan, Noah Asher Golden, Matthew Homrich-Knieling, Will Hudson, Glynis Kinnan, Avi Lessing, Russell Mayo, James McCoyne, Angela Whitacre de Resendiz, and Samantha Young. And special thanks, of course, to their and our students, past and present.

Finally, we are grateful to our families for their support and encouragement.

# *Introduction*

Brian Charest and Kate Sjostrom

Last fall, Christopher, a former student of Kate's, entered student teaching excited, but exited unsettled. He documented his development in narratives such as this one:

> This is Freshman English. There are rules here. This is supposed to be the year that we "prepare students for their entire high school experience." These kids are not babies anymore. This is High School. And yet, I am reading "Where Have You Gone, Charming Billy?" [O'Brien, 1975] and all I can think about is how the Vietnam War feels like what we are doing to these kids. The first sentence in the story: *The platoon of twenty-six soldiers moved slowly in the dark, single file, not talking.* Twenty-six soldiers; twenty-six students in a class. Single file lines. No talking. Aren't these elements of the story the things we should dislike about the training that occurs in war? Earlier in the week when doing vocabulary with the sophomores, one of the students says, "School is a *synonym* for prison." The class chuckles and I am left wondering whether I should copy this onto the board and validate the student's contribution. I smile and editorialize: *School sometimes* feels *like a synonym for prison.* I cannot tell if my mentor teacher is amused. I erase the vocab for the day and we move on. Back in Freshman English, our protagonist, Private First Class Paul Berlin, "pretend[s] he [is] not a soldier." I write in the margin of my text: Pretend=Imagination=Childhood. What is this thing that we call childhood, that we need to beat out of people in order for them to "go out into the workforce/go fight for their country"? The students do not wear dog tags on metal chains, but they do wear plastic IDs on cloth lanyards. Straining my eyes throughout the day, I cannot identify the students' faces or names on their plastic IDs. The students do, however, get castigated for not wearing theirs.

Christopher was deeply unsettled by how his host school's practices seemed to erase his students' unique identities, the "faces and names" on students' plastic IDs unidentifiable even up close. He worried that, despite educators' best intentions—indeed, he liked and respected his mentor teachers—schools sacrificed children's imaginations in the name of productivity. Christopher found that he was no longer sure why he was doing work that so blatantly contradicted his understandings of what education was about.

During the weekly seminar that accompanied student teaching, Christopher asked "Why?" a lot: Why must he mark down students for using incomplete sentences in their class notes? Why did his peer spend more time having students label elements of a story's "arc" than engaging students in conversation about the story's meaning? Why? In Christopher's understanding of education and learning, asking this question—Why?—was a fundamental piece of what school was supposed to be about. In this view, schools become spaces where students and teachers engage in a process of critically examining the prevailing orthodoxies. The issue for Christopher, however, was whether or not he would be able to carve out spaces to ask critical questions about the organization of the school, the design of the curriculum, and the need for things like standardized examinations.

During seminar, Christopher also apologized a lot; he could tell he was unsettling otherwise happy student teachers. These happy student teachers, it seemed, were more interested in starting their jobs than in asking the kinds of questions that Christopher wanted to ask about the purposes of education. Eventually, Christopher just kept his questions to himself, but his narratives, such as the following one, show that his concerns only grew:

> We are in an impromptu department meeting. The department head is showing us the new Excel sheet that was made for checking students into "Auburn [school pseudonym] Hour," the school's new RTI period. In the first column is a list of students' names highlighted in red, signifying that they have not been checked in today, because there is no Auburn Hour today. The department head demonstrates how students are checked in to Auburn Hour. There is a handheld scanner like one would find at a checkout line that will be placed on every teacher's desk for use during Auburn Hour. At the beginning of the period, the teacher is supposed to scan the barcode on the students' ID card that is hanging from their necks, and then the students' names will go from being highlighted in red to being highlighted in green on the Excel sheet. This is supposed to streamline the attendance-taking process. There is a new student teacher at the meeting who is enthusiastically nodding at everything that is said about the new streamlined spreadsheet. After explaining other logistics to the new attendance-taking process, the department head brings up the topic of "Won't" students. The department head says that if the students who keep getting assigned to Auburn Hour are "Won't" students that teachers should remove those students from the attendance sheet and assign them to a study hall instead. A teacher asks what the study hall is like. Someone says it is silent and the students just sit there. Auburn Hour, the department head says, is for "Can't" students, not "Won't" students. In this school, there are "Can't" students, and there are "Won't" students.

Christopher is clearly attuned to the ways that schools dehumanize the young people in their care, reducing them to scannable bar codes and to "'Can't' students" and "'Won't' students." Again and again throughout his student teaching, Christopher zeroed in on moments of opportunity—a class period devoted to supporting struggling students, a student's critical (if flippant) inquiry into the purpose of prison-like schools—when humanizing students was possible. Why did these missed opportunities seem so discomforting to Christopher, while many of his peers—including the "new student teacher … enthusiastically nodding"—seemed willing to ignore or gloss over them so quickly? How was it, in these instances, that schooling became "settled" in ways that allowed the participants to, as Maxine Greene notes, "accede to the given" of the institution and leave so much unsaid and unchallenged (1998, p. 7)?

We believe that *all* of us—educators, administrators, parents, and community members—should be uncomfortable when students, teachers, and learning are objectified. We also believe that to counteract such objectification, we need a conscious and deep ethical commitment to the work of schools, as well as a political analysis to go with it. Enthusiasm for kids (or spreadsheets) isn't going to be enough to wade through the contradictions and challenges of education without sacrificing our young people's humanity. This book tells the stories of those who have worked to articulate a humane understanding of the role of schools in society and worked towards solidarity with students, colleagues, and community members. Their stories are not heroes' tales. Indeed, sometimes these stories leave us to confront more questions—questions that unsettle our understandings of teaching and schools. That's okay by us; we believe education is in need of some unsettling right about now.

\*\*\*

When Kate last observed Christopher student teach, he used discussion of *Brave New World* as an opportunity to invite students to consider what they think education should and could look like. Though he tried to remain buoyant throughout the class period, his spirits steadily sank; though he finally coaxed ideas out of a handful of students, they were narrow in scope ("teachers should explain directions more") and, ultimately, uninspiring. Worse yet, when Christopher tried to offer an alternative vision of education, he struggled to paint it in any particularity. It was as if the purposes and practices of schools had been settled, even for Christopher. This collection of stories, we hope, can help teachers like Christopher—teachers who intuitively understand that education can be so much more than test scores—to develop a political analysis and a voice to articulate a new vision for schools.

## What's Supposedly Settled

The last two decades of reforms have tried to reduce education to the teaching and learning of that which can be measured on standardized examinations. Education becomes "settled" precisely when there is some agreed upon "stuff" that we call the curriculum (and standardized examinations to go with it) that we import into our schools. The curriculum and the examinations are developed, packaged, and then disseminated to our schools, neatly wrapped in the perceived efficiency and neutrality of scientific language. We are told that all teachers in all schools should simply implement this curriculum using the "best practices" defined by those elsewhere. Students who fail are either the victims of "bad" teaching or, worse, lack sufficient grit or have yet to embrace a growth mindset.

The examination has, in many ways, become the single most important factor in many schools today. Not only does it inform and produce the need for future testing, but it also informs teacher training and licensing, provides or denies access to further education, and influences instruction and curriculum development. There is currently a national movement underway (and this is already happening in many states) to link teacher evaluations to student performance on these exams, raising the stakes even higher for both teachers and students.

This scheme to link teacher ratings and salaries to student test scores has been euphemistically termed "merit-based" pay. The seduction of these common sense reforms is undeniable, because the logic of these reforms appeals to deeply held beliefs about rewarding those who work hard to raise test scores (good teachers) and punishing those who do not (bad teachers) (Kumashiro, 2015).

Standardization in this system comes to mean fairness and equity, though, interestingly, these terms are never used in relation to community investment, school funding, or extracurricular or economic opportunities. In the latter realms fairness, equity, and standardization are irrelevant. The neighborhood or community from which a student comes, in fact, becomes irrelevant, too, since what matters here is access to curriculum, a good teacher, and the individual's self-discipline and work ethic. We are compelled to understand, through the logic of neoliberalism, that where you are from has nothing to do with where you might go.

Suggesting that the purposes of school and the role of the teacher are settled (i.e., uncontestable and immutable) is precisely how neoliberal education reformers have framed the remaking of public schooling as a market-driven proposition. Wrapped in the logic and efficiency-speak of science, technology, and business, the rhetoric of neoliberal reforms helps to mask the problems and contradictions inherent in neoliberal policies—ones that diminish the work of teachers, decrease funding for social services in urban areas, privatize public schools, and ignore the political, economic, and social conditions affecting schools and their surrounding communities (Harvey, 2007). The effects of the misleading but powerful narrative of neoliberal education reform continue to ripple outward, reshaping the way we understand the work and preparation of teachers, the responsibilities of students and our responsibility to them, the nature of learning, the value of schools and communities, and, of course, what counts as knowledge.

## *Unsettling the Roles of Teacher and Student*

The purpose of the teacher in the neoliberal framework is to implement the curriculum which has been aligned to the state-mandated, standardized examination. The student's job is to learn the tools and tricks to perform well on these standardized examinations. This scenario ignores the contribution and potential of students and teachers to collaborate as fully human agents capable of defining their needs and interests. Teachers are never explicitly told *not* to attend to the complex humanity of students and their lived experiences, yet the entire accountability apparatus looms in ways that compel teachers to do just that.

In his book, *Educating for Insurgency*, Jay Gillen notes that "imagining that the purposes of schools are settled is a way of hiding the political role of young people" (2014, p. 50). We might add to Gillen's analysis that such an approach also neutralizes the role of teachers in paradoxical ways—both underscoring teacher agency and denying it simultaneously—since once the goal of school is made clear, isn't it the teacher's job merely to make sure that students reach it? Gillen tells us that this understanding "misrepresents the sociological and political problem," and that "the problem is that the social and political purposes of the country are contested, and young people are already participating in working toward a settlement of the contest, even while their political role remains unacknowledged" (p. 50). In this way, too, the role of teachers in public schools is also contested. Teachers, like students, continue to push back and resist efforts to standardize curriculum and learning outcomes. Teachers, like the ones in this collection, suggest that there are, in fact, many ways to organize schools, design curriculum, and understand the purposes of education.

What makes a good teacher and how should one approach working with young people? What are the purposes of schooling and how do our practices reflect these priorities? We believe schools should be spaces where these questions are explored openly and honestly with all participants.

## *Why Now's the Time to Unsettle Education*

As Christopher's narratives at the beginning of this introduction show, some schools are not sites of such questioning. We find this of urgent concern given recent research findings that education reforms are effectively producing a new kind of teacher—one that conceives of herself in the seemingly incontestable terms of scientific validity embedded in the assessment technologies now being used to evaluate both teachers and students. What happens—and what does it mean for students—when teachers are interpellated through this new framework for understanding the work of teaching? What happens when this new teacher subjectivity emerges—one that essentially denies the full humanity of students and teachers?

In their article, "Making accountable teachers: the terrors and pleasures of performativity" (2017), Jessica Holloway and Jory Brass suggest that the neoliberal education policies of the last several decades have resulted in a "shift in the construction of teachers' … subjectivity" (p. 1). After comparing teacher interviews that coincided with the implementation of No Child Left Behind (NCLB) and those concurrent with Race to the Top (RTTT), Holloway and Brass determined that the increase in accountability mechanisms (including the addition of value-added measures) in the intervening decade effectively "fabricat[ed] a new kind of teacher" (p. 20):

> While teachers of the first accountability stage positioned NCLB's (self-) disciplinary mechanisms as external intrusions on their autonomy, professionalism, and practice, the second group positioned RTTT's accountability mechanisms as the very modes by which they knew themselves and their quality. (p. 2)

To illustrate: whereas teachers in the earlier study complained that NCLB expected them to "'Produce. Produce a test score. Produce on the AP exam. Produce diplomas'" despite their conviction that standardized tests were not "'any measure, whatsoever, of what [students] learned,'" teachers in the later study questioned neither the drive to production nor the assessment of that production. As one teacher said, "'all you have is what you produce, and you have to produce the best product that you can, which is who can perform on a test'" (p. 10). In this way, there has been a "normalization of the marketized teacher [and] the managed teacher" (p. 1), as well as what Holloway and Brass call a "collapse" between the "governed" (teachers) and the mechanisms of governance. The "accountability apparatus" is no longer external; one is a score determined by constant surveillance (Foucault, 1977).

It takes a concerted effort to resist the particular pressures of this heavy, neoliberal surveillance, but without resistance, we face what Marx (1844) described as the inevitable alienation experienced by a worker in a market-based culture: alienation from the product of labor (from students); from the act of labor (resulting in the de-professionalization of teaching); from our "species-being" (our "own bod[ies], as well as … [our] spiritual aspect, [our] human aspect"); and from others (colleagues, students, school and neighborhood communities) (pp. 31–32).

When a teacher must operate in such a system of commodification, no interaction is spared from alienation. How, then, can we thrive—not just survive—as teachers? How can students thrive—not just survive—in schools? In this volume, we share stories of how teachers have resisted state and local mandates to teach to the test in dehumanizing ways, how such teachers have sought to de-commodify educational spaces, how they have enacted their ethical commitments to students and communities, and how they have theorized such practices, sometimes even reconsidering their role as teachers and the very purposes of schooling.

We get in close to the work that teachers do with students and unmask not only the ways that teachers resist, but also the contradictions and failures that teachers work through each day as they struggle to negotiate the spaces between their ethical commitments to their students and the work they are told they must do to keep their jobs.

Given Holloway and Brass's findings regarding the insidious and corrosive effects of market-based reforms on teachers' identities and goals, the need for such stories and theories has never been more urgent. All of us are implicated when we allow policies and procedures to push us away from our ethical commitments to students, to justice, to equity, and to humanity. This book, then, seeks to reveal the ways in which teachers and teacher educators struggle to resist education policy of the last two decades—policy that has distorted the work of teaching, undermined the work of teachers and teacher educators, and obstructed the progress and potential of students, especially in our most underserved communities.

Whether you relate to Christopher or even to the other student teacher he describes—the one "enthusiastically nodding" at the "new streamlined spreadsheet"—we encourage you to let the following stories first unsettle you. Then, we invite you to *use* these stories to ask questions about what it would mean to find ethical footing wherever you walk in our educational landscape.

## References

Foucault, M. (1977). *Discipline and punish: The birth of the prison.* New York, NY: Vintage Books.

Gillen, J., & Moses, R. P. (2014). *Educating for insurgency: The roles of young people in schools of poverty.* Oakland, CA: AK Press.

Greene, M. (1988). *The dialectic of freedom.* New York, NY: Teachers College Press.

Harvey, D. (2007). *A brief history of neoliberalism.* Oxford, NY: Oxford University Press.

Holloway, J., & Brass, J. (2017). Making accountable teachers: The terrors and pleasures of performativity. *Journal of Education Policy, 33*(3), 361–382. doi: 10.1080/02680939.2017.1372636

Kumashiro, K. (2015). *Against common sense: Teaching and learning toward social justice.* (3rd ed.). New York, NY: Routledge.

Marx, K. (1959). *Economic and philosophic manuscripts of 1844.* Moscow: Progress. Retrieved from https://www.marxists.org/archive/marx/works/1844/manuscripts/preface.htm (Original work published 1932)

O'Brien, Tim. (1975). Where have you gone, charming Billy? *Redbook, 145*(1): 81, 127–32.

# Section I

# The Promise of Unsettling Moments

# *Introduction*

It seems that everywhere we turn these days we encounter the claim that feeling unsettled is essential to growth. In education textbooks, we read of the disequilibrium integral to Jean Piaget's theory of cognitive development. At Curriculum Night at our children's schools, we hear references to Lev Vygotzky's Zone of Proximal Development as teachers preview the necessary discomfort students will feel as they stretch their brains. Friends send us links to TED Talks about how important it is to get comfortable with discomfort.

So why does so much within our public education system feel *settled*? In the following chapter, "Against Measurement: Making a Case for School Play," high school teachers Avi Lessing and Glynis Kinnan suggest that it is difficult to make schools safe for students' intellectual experimentation and failure—and thus eventual innovation—when "external ... performance metrics trump all." In other words, teachers pressured to continuously document linear student growth and students pressured to continuously achieve high scores will find it difficult to linger in the unsettling moments necessary for authentic development. Kinnan and Lessing propose that students' processes and present should trump a preoccupation with students' scores and future. Moreover, they insist on the value of "nonachievement, rupture, spontaneity, nonconformity, uncertainty, puzzlement, nonclosure, and tentativeness" in the classroom. As they show through stories of both planned classroom projects and unanticipated classroom moments, such "immeasurables" can "enrich the experience of all the people who inhabit schools."

Like Lessing and Kinnan, elementary school teachers Angela Whitacre de Resendiz and Will Hudson suggest that unsettling classroom moments hold great potential for both students and teachers. In their chapter, "Calculating Justice: Using Mathematical Mindsets for Teaching from a Social Justice Perspective," Whitacre de Resendiz and Hudson recount a moment so unsettling it would have been easier to sidestep than face head on: the moment when a white first grader naively suggested that her black schoolmates "dance for us" for Martin Luther King, Jr. Day. Indeed, Whitacre de Resendiz and Hudson and their colleagues weren't able to address the inadvertently offensive comment in the moment—shocked, they "brushed over it"—but they were sufficiently unsettled by this inability that they undertook "a reexamination of privilege, racism, and the inadvertent perpetuation of systems of thought and action that marginalize and, in many ways, dehumanize students and teachers alike." Identifying one of the problematic "systems" as the hurried drive for production in schools, Hudson and Whitacre de Resendiz worked to create time and spaces for the "questions, uncertainties, and mistakes" that lead to stronger communities and lasting learning. In the process, they found a framework for their efforts within current conversations around developing mathematical thinking. "Regardless of content area," they suggest, "challenging discussions and deeper understandings all require a willingness to ask questions, think creatively, look for patterns, and take chances." Through many classroom examples, Whitacre de Resendiz and Hudson show how they have used Jo Boaler's "Positive Norms to Encourage in Math Class" to facilitate "deep, analytical, and honest discussions related to historical and justice-related topics" in hopes of "lay[ing] the groundwork for empowerment."

The unsettling moment that prompted former high school teacher and current teacher educator Noah Asher Golden to find a new framework for teaching for social justice was when a "harmless interaction" between him and his high school student was "'misrecognized' as a drug deal" by undercover detectives. With a new, visceral understanding of one way his minority students were "misrecognized," Golden became committed to understanding and dismantling the misrecognitions that occur on multiple levels, up to the national level where social systems and accountability measures "misrecognize the strengths and talents of so many people." In this section's final chapter, "Challenging Misrecognitions through Reflexive Teacher Education: Knowing and Growing in an Age of Commodification," Golden suggests that "understanding misrecognition … is key for those of us who dare to take up the role of educator." Recognizing that race- and class-based misrecognitions are not the daily experience of most teachers, he proposes a teacher education grounded in critical reflection and engagement so that teachers will be less likely to unwittingly enact misrecognitions of their own. Drawing on the work of Paolo Freire, Golden calls on educators to "continue being curious to know, and expand this knowledge so that we can grow." His experience has shown him that by growing out of "reductive framings of success and opportunity," we can "work with our students to challenge the misrecognitions that can shape opportunities and outcomes."

All of the chapters in this section highlight how much growth is possible, for students *and* for teachers, if we let ourselves be unsettled. To be sure, when we slow the rush to production in favor of stopping to ask questions when discomfited, we make ourselves more present to our and our students' humanity.

# 1. *Against Measurement: Making a Case for School Play*

AVI LESSING AND GLYNIS KINNAN

Where are you going? How are you going to get there? How do you know when you're there?
> —Professional Development Session on Writing Teaching Objectives

Being able to be comfortable with vulnerability is a really important inter-personal skill, as well as being good for self care. I guess for me becoming a person is about figuring out that everyone else matters.
> —Excerpt from a letter from Sam, a former student living and working in China

I do not expect to enjoy high school.
> —Anonymous statement from an incoming freshman, class of '22

The sixth-grade teacher assigns the students to research a topic of their choice under the general subject of health, and then to present their findings in a talk to their classmates. One boy, whose father is a dentist, gives his report in front of the class on how to care for teeth. He has a model of a mouth that he borrowed from his dad. He speaks well and he is in command of his material. Another child, a girl, gives her report on wolves. Clearly deeply invested in the topic, she talks passionately without using notecards and maintains consistent eye contact. She plays a record of wolf vocalizations and presents a chart of wolf body language. She ties her presentation to the topic of health because she says that wolves are being unfairly slaughtered, that people wrongly fear wolves as dangerous.

The boy receives an A for his presentation; the girl gets a B because she did not hew closely enough to the directive to research a topic on *human* health.
> —Memory from grade school

We are veteran public high school English teachers. Our well-funded school of 3,200 students serves an economically and racially diverse community close to the border of Chicago. Both of us have been around long enough to have borne witness to the ways in which educational practice has been influenced by the advent of technology that facilitates the accumulation of data.

Like many teachers in the nation, we were horrified to watch as Al Franken pressed Betsy DeVos to delineate her views on the merits of a proficiency versus growth model of assessing student achievement and it became ever more clear that the then candidate for Secretary of Education had no acquaintance with the debate that Franken was referencing. Certainly, anyone under consideration for the nation's top education position should have been sufficiently familiar with the educational zeitgeist to have known what Franken was talking about. Our dismay, however, strikes deeper: indeed, we refute the premise underlying Franken's questions that the two models, proficiency and growth, are appreciably different, based as they both are on a belief in the value of measurement, certainty, and closure, and we worry about the notion of school that is implied by both the proficiency model and the growth model, which reduces school into a sorting machine.

The proficiency model sets standardized benchmarks and then evaluates students on the basis of how well they achieve these fixed markers. In comparison, the growth model also establishes a fixed point of competence that students are expected to meet, but it differs from the proficiency model in that it requires a baseline assessment of each student and then evaluates not only whether or not the student meets the benchmark, but also how significant the student's growth is relative to where she started. Under current educational practices, the growth model also has a corollary: 25% of a teacher's evaluation is based on her ability to demonstrate via an established metric that her students have improved over time in her classroom. In other words, the growth model is pressed into service to establish that the teacher has "added value" to the student's profile.

While it may be true that a growth model represents a more inclusive way of recognizing student achievement than a proficiency model allows for, we question the premise that the primary function of school is to measure and quantify narrow aspects of students' and teachers' performances. It is our purpose here to flush out some hidden drawbacks to a growth-model incarnation measuring student performance and then to further interrogate the assumption that measurement itself is an unqualified good. Finally, we conceive of ways we might complicate notions of education to emphasize relationship, non-achievement, rupture, spontaneity, nonconformity, uncertainty, puzzlement, non-closure, and tentativeness, which may enrich the experience of all the people who inhabit schools. In sum, we suggest that the emphasis on measurement is antithetical to a spirit of play and playfulness, which should more properly inform the practice of education.

## *Interrogation of Measurement*

### *The Growth Model and Fetishization of the Metric*

Even if we leave aside for a moment the more fundamental question of whether we can feasibly measure learning and teaching, we can still notice some problematic aspects of a growth model of student achievement. Indeed, the act of measurement may function to constrain what it purports to measure. This is especially true when student growth is tied to teacher evaluations. For example, in our classrooms, if we were not obliged to submit proof of student growth to administrative overseers via metric evaluation, graphs, etc., we would design writing assignments that build in complexity so that students would actually grow by grappling with new challenges. But a growth model requires that we give students the identical task at least two times so that we have an accurate comparison. In this respect, the metric itself assumes more importance than the learning. Indeed, in a classroom that is not focused on proving growth, a test itself can be an instrument of learning. A test, for example, might be used to challenge students beyond what they had previously done. But tests that are designed to serve a growth agenda have a different, more overtly utilitarian function because they exist to make a case to an administrator who needs to make a case to a board or a district or a state.

Moreover, if the teacher's own performance evaluation is based in any significant degree on her students' ostensible growth, she will have strong incentive to make sure that the students register on the metric as having grown. In other words, instead of being free to attend to students' actual needs, which could certainly involve challenging them at a level slightly above their zone of comfort, she will be compelled to design a post-assessment that will graph well. For the teacher, the project of learning must take a backseat to the project of proving the learning.

In some cases, moreover, time that teachers could be using to enrich their own practice must be devoted to the designing of baseline instruments that only establish what was already known. For example, in Glynis's classroom, students and teacher focus a lot on vocabulary. If Glynis were to measure student growth on vocabulary acquisition, she would first have to design a baseline quiz, which is to say, a quiz that students would take before they had been exposed to the words in class. Predictably—and this has been borne out by experience—students would do poorly on this quiz. Students could legitimately decry as busywork the experience of taking a quiz for which they were not prepared, for which the outcome was virtually certain, and for which the raison d'étre was bureaucratic convenience divorced from student welfare.

These shortcomings, though, would perhaps be quibbles if the underlying premise that measurement itself is an unqualified good could stand up to scrutiny. In our view, however, the emphasis on measurement is fundamentally misplaced because it forestalls so much of what we value about education.

## Measurement: The Negation of Play and the Disavowal of the Now

In his TED Talk, psychiatrist and play researcher Stuart Brown (2008) argues that play is essential to human and other animal development. He notes that there are many kinds of play—body play, imaginative play, object play to name a few—but he says that the quality that distinguishes play from other activities is that it has no reason to exist other than itself. Play is done for itself rather than for a goal or some ulterior objective. Brown claims that, "If its purpose is more important than the act of doing it is, it is probably not play." His research suggests that play is good for the brain, that indeed it is essential for optimum development of humans and other animals, and that play deprivation results in neurological deficits. Interestingly, Brown also suggests that the opposite of play is not work but depression.

When students are trained to care about their performance on a metric or to regard that performance as the point toward which they are striving, they are schooled against play. When they are taught that the teacher knows what the outcome of their learning should be and that they will be measured by how close they come to that ideal, they are being denied the opportunity to simply engage in intellectual play for its own sake. Pondering, imagining, wondering, speculating—modes of intellectual play—are forestalled when students are driven toward a predetermined goal.

In such a paradigm there is no room for valuing experiences that have intrinsic meaning; instead, thinking, being, and experiencing are subordinated to the production of the score on the metric. This is why students raise their hands when a classroom discussion appears to have veered "off track" and ask if what they are talking about will be on the test. They have been conditioned to believe that value derives from performance on a metric or a rubric and that anything outside of that laser-focus is extraneous. Moreover, the rigid definition of the goal that the teacher must provide in order to ensure the accuracy of the assessment acts as a constraint on both the teacher's and the students' opportunities to be creative, to envision learning in novel ways. The teacher is not free to create an open-ended project for students in which she might be surprised by their responses, nor is she free to regard students as co-creators of learning. Instead, the emphasis on measurement inscribes a hierarchical relationship between teacher and student.

At the famous-among-teachers Westtown seminar, in the summer of 2004, Fran Norris Scoble, a head of an independent school, started her talk with the following question: "Is school good for our souls?" That question bowled us over. It threw into stark relief the fact that most schools do not ask that question, and because they don't, the answer is too often no. Perhaps Scoble's question is another way of asking whether or not schools are places that authenticate the value of play; the soul, if nothing else, is suggestive of good-in-itself. Too often, even as schools preach growth and growth mindset, they act from a place of deficit and not-good enough.

In Charlotte Brontë's *Jane Eyre* (2002), the character Miss Scatcherd is the type of teacher who is so determined to make her students conform to her definition of achievement that she fails to recognize the extraordinary intellectual and spiritual gifts of Jane's friend Helen Burns. Miss Scatcherd focuses on how Helen misses the mark she has set for her, not how invested Helen is in moral questions or how she is guided by her religious principles. Jane says, "Burns wore on her arm 'the untidy badge'; scarcely an hour ago, I heard her condemned by Miss Scatcherd to a dinner of bread and water on the morrow because she had blotted an exercise in copying out. Such is the imperfect nature of man! Such spots are there on the disc of the clearest planet; and eyes like Miss Scatcherd's can only see those minute defects, and are blind to the full brightness of the orb" (p. 64). Indeed, we know that many students find school to be a stultifying, creativity-crushing experience that seems to have little relevance to them as human beings, and that many of them regard school as a hoop they must jump through to get to the next hoop, which is college. School feels neither playful nor soulful to them. We both worry how the full brightness of our students' orbs dim in the way we narrowly conceive teaching and learning.

As Avi's student Jennie wrote in her final reflection:

> I'm so exhausted but I have no reason why. Maybe it is because I have no real passion or true reason to keep up with this routine. I know I do all of this, keep up with grades and extracurriculars, for college. But do I even want to go to college? If it is just more of this meaningless misery—why even bother? It's not like I even know what I want to do. I have no real passions or strengths, and I'm running out of time to figure something out.

One source of Jennie's dismay is that she has been given no sense that the present is important and meaningful in its own right. She has been encouraged to train her focus on the future, specifically on what she wants to do (presumably what job she aspires to) rather than to regard the present as an opportunity to safely explore and play around with her possible interests and passions. In fact, she cannot explore her personal growth in a way that she finds meaningful because she feels compelled to attend to quantifiable markers.

In one of his lectures, the Buddhist scholar Alan Watts makes a comparison between the creative act of engaging with music and the conventional notion of school. Watts says of school,

> It's all graded. And what we do is we put the child into the corridor of this grade system with a kind of "come on kitty kitty kitty," and now you go to kindergarten. And that's a great thing because when you finish that you get into first grade, and then come on; first grade leads to second grade and so on, and then you get out of grade school. Now you're going to go to high school, and it's revving up—the thing is coming. Then you've got to go to college, and by Jove then you get into graduate school and when you're through with graduate school you go out and join the World! (Lindberg & Watts, 2016)

In Watts's view, such a mindset misses the point as the present is subsumed by the future. As he puts it, "it was a musical thing and we were supposed to sing or to dance while the music was being played." In a classroom where measurement metrics predominate, there is no room for singing and dancing in the moment because the now is merely that which must be overridden by the future. It is no wonder then that students like Jennie feel discouraged about more school on the horizon when in the present they have not had the opportunity to discover what makes them happy and curious about life.

## Limitations of Instruments of Measurement

As teachers, we live inside a powerful contradiction: we succumb and abide by the system and simultaneously fight to subvert and transform it from within. In 2004, shortly after returning from the Westtown seminar, Avi developed a senior year rite-of-passage English class dedicated to being good for students' souls.

He was adamant that seniors should have a class that presses the proverbial pause button before they leave compulsory education for college or gap year programs, before their childhood, in effect, would end. The field of Social and Emotional Learning (SEL), which is now ubiquitous, had just established state standards in Illinois. The standards' language was language school administrators could understand. Avi didn't mention the word soul to sell the class; he used language around student targets like "will become more self-aware." Of course, that *was* the goal, just not one that could be easily measured, let alone described.

In Avi's senior class, students write personal essays, develop oral history projects, practice mindfulness, and play theater games to build their social and emotional ability to empathize with their classmates, develop self-awareness, and expand their capacity for attention. As part of their oral history study, students do a project inspired by MacArthur genius grant awardee Anna Deveare Smith's "On the Road" work. Smith travels around America interviewing people whose words she transcribes exactly and then renders as verbatim monologues to create one person plays. One of her essential questions is the following: If we cannot or refuse to embody someone who is different from us, how can we possibly have empathy for them? (2001). She's been called the most empathetic person in America (Smith, 2018).

For his most recent evaluation, Avi attempted to measure students' growth in empathy. While he remained dubious of the requirement to measure growth, he decided to try and make it a worthwhile exercise. But even when a teacher has the best intention to design an instrument to measure student growth specific to his class, the challenge is appreciable and hidden limitations of the measurement tool may emerge.

On the surface, Avi's project seemed tailor-made for measuring growth in empathy. He was thrilled to teach students the skills they would need to become more empathetic, by training in listening and attunement, reserving judgment, and understanding another person's life circumstances. After assigning each student a partner who they did not know well, Avi gave them a pretest asking them to measure how much empathy they felt for their partner. Then, five weeks later, after the students had participated in activities meant to make them more connected, gone to Storycorps (a national oral history organization) to learn to conduct oral history interviews in one another's homes, and transcribed and edited their partners' words into two-minute monologues that they then memorized and performed for one another, he gave them a questionnaire as a post-test to see how much their empathy had grown.

That night, Avi visualized spectacular graphs with lines angled sharply upward, perhaps bearing the heading *Extraordinary Growth*. He knew the power of graphs because for months he had been meeting with the superintendent to emphasize the results of a yearlong study in SEL, which were mostly ignored until a colleague's husband, who led a prominent Chicago sports team's marketing department, organized all of the information in a few graphs, and the superintendent banged his hand on the table and said, "Now this is what I've been waiting for, Avi." Avi was confident that the data would show that students had gained more ability to be empathetic; indeed, he fantasized that now they were perhaps the most empathetic kids in the whole school, and he hoped that their newly cultivated empathy would correlate with higher GPAs, fewer absences, and more incentive to finish college.

The actual graphs were more shocking than merely disappointing, with several of the lines not bound for the sky but diving towards the dirt. Many of the students reported growth, but, strikingly, a number of students too large to dismiss reported that they went down in empathy. A teacher's nightmare: after five weeks of training in empathy using the methods of the most empathetic person in America, Avi's students had become *less* empathetic. And this was the instrument Avi was to use for his own evaluation!

Avi tracked down some of the students, curious about their reactions and concerned about his professional rating. Their responses all amounted to different versions of the following feedback: "You see, Mr. Lessing, when you partnered me, I thought my empathy was pretty high because why wouldn't it be? I'm an empathetic person. That's why I think I gave myself sevens across the board. But when I interviewed my partner and found out about their lives, I realized I didn't know anything about them. In some of those exercises you did in class where we had to repeat back what people said, I couldn't do it, because I was spacing out all of the time. Empathy is hard, which is why I lowered myself to 4's in my ranking."

Avi talked to several students whose scores went down but who grew tremendously—though not exactly in a way that could be captured between the perimeters of a pre- and post -test. In this case, the baseline assessment, which was an exercise in self-reportage, proved not to be a waste of time, but also not to be accurate. In fact, its value was precisely its inaccuracy: it helped illuminate for the students what they had not understood about themselves. Undoubtedly, students did become more empathetic despite the fact that this was not represented on the graph; moreover, they became way more aware of themselves and how much future growth they could achieve if they could only be more present now.

Empathy wasn't a skill you learned once forever more. It wasn't even a goal to reach, because why would you want to finish being empathetic? It was like Alan Watts said: more of a *musical thing*.

A linear, objective, numerical tool to measure what happened was inadequate to the task. Avi understood his students by talking to them, and they understood themselves through their relationships with others and their reflections. They were practicing the three R's that neurobiologist Daniel Siegel (2009) re-envisions for schools beyond reading, writing, and arithmetic: reflection, relationship, and resiliency—all things that resist numerical representation. Indeed, Avi's students having taken a step backward on the metric was really a step forward in their becoming more empathetic people.

How would the system of professional evaluation, also represented numerically, accommodate this extraordinary moment in Avi's career? It couldn't, and he was downgraded from "excellent" to "proficient" on the student growth segment of his evaluation. Apparently, he added less value to his students' growth in empathy than the year before.

### Alternative Conceptions: Making Space for Relationships, Pleasure, Uncertainties, Personal Experience, Connections, and Wonder

While we think that there is a place for evaluation of student growth—and indeed we are especially enthusiastic about it when it is used to help students self-reflect, as it was in Avi's class—we think that school should mostly be a place that's good for the soul, where students play, which is to say, school and the classroom should value the act of wondering, of free thinking that is not conscripted to a tightly prescribed goal; it should value experimentation, including the failure that is an inevitable aspect of risk-taking; it should value pleasure that arises in the present and in the context of others. It should be a place that supports Keats's (1970) notion of negative capability, where one is "capable of being in uncertainties, mysteries, doubts, without any irritable reaching after fact and reason" (p. 43).

### Relationships

When we conceive of education as something that is valuable in the moment, that is in fact happening right now, rather than as something that is simply preparation for a future circumstance, we recuperate a recognition of the importance of relationships. When we privilege the present, relationships—between students and teachers and students and one another—can be seen for the significant aspects of school experience that they are. The emphasis on measurable outcomes tends to devalue both student and teacher in that it attempts to reduce that which is complex, nebulous, or subjective to discrete, clearly locatable data points in the past and in the future, whereas a recognition of the value of relationships in the moment confers dignity on both students and teachers.

When Glynis was in high school in the seventies—the same high school in which she now teaches—one experience stands out far above the rest. Her sophomore English teacher, James Berkley, a preternaturally cheerful middle-aged man with a buzz cut, dressed in a perpetual tweed jacket, sometimes read short stories to the class. He did not offer any pedagogical justification to the students for these endeavors. They were simply presented as pleasurable experiences, where the only obligation was to enjoy oneself.

Berkley read the stories because he loved them and he believed the students would too. These were the most moving moments of Glynis's academic life as an adolescent. She can still conjure Mr. Berkley's voice as he read the final devastating sentence of "The Scarlet Ibis." There was no test, no assessment of the experience, no metric for capturing Glynis's growth as a student. But she was affected in a way that spoke to her soul; she went on to get a Ph.D. in English literature and obviously to become a teacher herself. School was rendered meaningful for Glynis because James Berkley gave her a no-strings-attached gift simply through generously sharing and celebrating the joy of literature.

When we recognize that relationships between and among teachers and students are central to the experience of school, important in their own right, we value the whole human and we recognize that pleasure is rightfully a component of school. When we look through a relational lens, students' stories, mishaps, wariness, enthusiasms, and concerns are not something we dismiss, deny, or shirk. In the process of valuing a student's life, and students' lives together, we seek meaning in their presence, in the present, without regard always to the immediate task, or how we may show immediate measurable growth. Paradoxically, an education that lingers in the present, that makes space for play, that nurtures relationships, may lead to the more meaningful and sustaining growth in the future that we wanted all along: the kind to which we refer when we talk about lifelong learners, or college persistence rates, or increased happiness and satisfaction in life.

## Risk and Uncertainty

We maintain that school should be a place where students can feel free to experiment, mess around, try things on a whim, and fail, without dire repercussions for them or the teacher. In Glynis's classes of seniors she works with the students on their college application essays. The greatest challenge is to get the students to tap into their unique voice in order to write lively, distinctive pieces. Indeed, many students will say that they feel they were quite creative and imaginative when they were little kids, but that their experience in school has diminished their ability to think outside the box. In this respect, schools' emphasis on metrics undercuts the purported aim of preparing students for success in the marketplace, since the ability to think innovatively is one of the characteristics potential employers most demand. But students will not be able to develop their creativity if it is not safe for them to fail, or if they have been conditioned to believe that external, potentially irrelevant, performance metrics trump all. When Glynis works with the students on their essays, the students are willing to experiment in their writing because they know in advance that they will all receive full credit for their work, and they know they can rework their material as much as they want to. Some students volunteer to have their essays workshopped by the whole class precisely because they are having problems with their material. They know that the idea is not to receive praise but to spark inspiration, not just for themselves but for others too. Their failures may provide rich opportunity for innovative revision for others as well as themselves.

In general, educators don't have a language that truly values mistake-making, failure, falling apart, not knowing, being wrong, reconsidering, second-guessing, screwing up, going the wrong way, getting triggered, getting in over your head, all of the challenges that truly make up so much of living, and of course, school. These nonlinear aspects of life deserve our attention as educators, and not just because educators should be normalizing rather than pathologizing self-doubt, but also because these moments that first appear as regressions, or irrelevant pleasurable digressions, have the potential, especially with mentorship, to stimulate great growth. The growth we seek is not the transitory, fabricated kind revealed in pre- and post-tests, but the kind that transcends school per se and entwines people's academic skills and their personal experience.

While we sympathize with the desire to be sure that all students are learning, we suggest that high stakes testing, monitoring, and tracking may be having adverse psychological effects on students. In the *New York Times Magazine*'s article "Why Are More American Teenagers Than Ever Suffering From Anxiety?" (Denizet-Lewis, 2017), two alarming statistics emerge. One is that the American College of Health Association found a significant increase in the number of undergraduates reporting "overwhelming anxiety." The other is that since 1985, when the higher institute at UCLA began asking freshmen if they were overwhelmed by all that they have to do, the percentage of students reporting feeling overwhelmed has risen sharply. In 1985, it was 18 percent. In 2016, it was 29 percent. Last year, it surged to 41 percent. The number of young people who have been hospitalized has more than doubled. In our school, 32 percent of the sophomore class (well over 200 students) reported feeling so sad or hopeless almost every day for two weeks or more in a row that they stopped doing some of their usual activities (Center for Prevention Research and Development, 2016).

These statistics suggest that our emphasis on a narrow notion of academic success may be backfiring, and that we pay a price for neglecting students' social and emotional learning. In his TED Talk on success, Alain de Botton (2009) lays out the classic situation that creates anxiety all across America. "It's Sunday night and just as the sun is starting to set, and the gap between my hopes for myself and the reality of my life starts to diverge so painfully that I normally end up weeping into a pillow." That scenario is of course amplified for school-aged children and doubly amplified in adolescence, because young people face significant instability and change because of the way their brains develop (Siegel, 2015). As clinical psychiatrist Richard Friedman (2014) writes in the *New York Times*,

> Adolescents, on average, experience more anxiety and fear and have a harder time learning how not to be afraid than either children or adults. It turns out that the brain circuit for processing fear—the amygdala—is precocious and develops way ahead of the prefrontal cortex, the seat of reasoning and executive control. This means that adolescents have a brain that is wired with an enhanced capacity for fear and anxiety, but is relatively underdeveloped when it comes to calm reasoning.

When schools emphasize measurement and judgment they inadvertently foster a climate for anxiety through the implication that worth must be continually re-established on the basis of performance metrics. One corollary of students' high anxiety is a reluctance to experiment or deviate from a formula that has proven successful in the past. If we do not privilege a student's social and emotional experience of school, we do nothing to help students cope with their particular challenges, and we undermine their potential for creativity.

## Personal Experience

In Avi's class, self-care and getting to know others aren't merely feel-good sprinklings of fun or play that he gets to once he's taught the important material. Writing narratives, for instance, is one of the most real and substantial intellectual pursuits capable of capturing a students' own process in making sense of their lives, in thinking about their own thinking. In fact, researchers who listened to the stories of young people who had recovered from a psychiatric illness, "came to recognize personal narrative as a resource and a tool, a way of grasping how people maintain meaning over time ... They found that those who were able to process difficult material had richer and smoother narratives" (Apter, 2006). But there's an inherent risk in telling a story, or processing difficult material, which brings up fundamental questions about the nature of school and what is and what's not supposed to happen there.

For instance, this year, Avi's student, whom we will call Tonya, was triggered by a story that another student, whom we will call Miranda, shared.

Tonya spoke to Avi before the next class, asking to share her experience with the whole class. When she did, she made a request for trigger warnings for stories in the future. Another student objected, saying that trigger warnings could make the process of telling stories even more fraught, since a trigger implies that there's something potentially troubling about one's story. The back and forth raised all sorts of questions from the students, ones that Avi didn't have answers to in the moment. The conversation also became racialized as a student of color asserted, "No one ever gave me a trigger warning for any of the experiences I was about to have. It's a guarantee that I will walk into triggering situations left and right." The conversation was rich and bold; students spoke who had never before uttered a word in class; the learning was authentic and suddenly real, neither abstract nor abstruse; students were dealing with some of the most difficult material in their own lives. They were grappling with how and whether to share their own stories, how to react to others' stories, how to be honest without being hurtful, how to be triggered but stay in the room, how to recognize and validate difference and its impact and still maintain faithful communication.

That day, all the students were present, engaged with the problem of those questions, but not all of them had revelations. Their growth was all over the map. Some students may have felt that was the deepest learning of the entire year. Others may have felt it was far too intense for a high school English class in the middle of the day. Avi didn't deliberately create an experience that would send the students into a dizzying 48-minute bell-to-bell conversation, but, once it began, he didn't try to shut it down and divert the class to his planned lesson. He recognized that what was happening was a form of the most serious kind of play, with all its attendant riskiness, and he was a participant in its unfolding. Life, whether it's work, relationships, or even one's free time, rarely follows our expected script. Falling off track then in school sometimes provides the most rewarding moments of all.

While schools can purport to value openness and transparency, the safer bet for the teacher is to maintain strict control of the classroom. When things are unpredictable, in-process, or in a state of becoming, we are in unfamiliar territory where we don't know what we don't know. Students may discover the teacher to be at just as much of a loss as they are. Once, much earlier in his career, when Avi sought to begin a teacher group that would focus on what to do when you—the teacher—get triggered in the classroom, the head of the counseling department, with great exasperation, said, "Well that shouldn't happen!" The counselor's point was that teachers should not ever be in a situation where they feel challenged on an emotional level, that they should structure the class to obviate such a possibility. But when teachers authentically share leadership of the class with their students, the teacher is no longer the sole determiner of what happens in that space. When we conceive of education through the narrow lens of measurable growth, students are denied the capacity to grow in important life skills that cannot be measured. They don't learn how to step back, or engage in difference, or sit stunned in their seats, or lean how to process what is happening. That ability also erodes for the teacher. Conversely, an experiential learning environment creates space for the unplanned, the unknown, the unmeasurable, and the previously unexperienced.

## Connections

At first glance, the idea of welcoming mistakes, growth that involves stepping back, and working with resistance seems counterproductive and inefficient and bodes poorly for teacher accountability. But by embracing a pedagogy that includes mistake-making and doubt, where growth is the goal but not the guarantee, we may have the power to enliven what we're teaching, break down barriers between us and our students, and connect our and our students' personal and academic lives together. A pedagogy that welcomes intrusiveness, impediments, and obstacles makes the classroom more like life, infinitely more complex to navigate, and thus correspondingly more valuable to experience.

In 2015, Avi initiated a Social and Emotional Learning Coaching Pilot at our school. Fifteen teachers participated in the program in which the goal was to integrate social and emotional learning with academic learning. The idea was to take some of the tools that were used in different classes—such as project-based learning, mindfulness, and partner exercises—broaden their use, and observe the impact. The evaluation, designed by a professional evaluator, and conducted by multiple parties inside and outside the school, involved interviewing teachers, organizing focus groups, and conducting observations. We coded the interviews and wrote multiple reports of our findings. Administrators listened politely, but that was the extent of it. It was qualitative research, and there were no graphs to support our work. We couldn't make correlations to the bottom lines to which all administrators seem beholden—GPA, SAT, attendance statistics.

But you can't truly understand the impact of a teacher, a class, or school, unless you actually go see and talk to the teacher, observe the class, walk around the school. For instance, two teachers at our school, John and Lindy, teach a new leadership class which is designed both to develop junior and senior leaders and to provide mentoring for freshmen and sophomores. By conventional evaluation, the program has not met some of the performance metrics that schools typically equate with success, like correlations to higher GPAs, better test scores, and other things that can be counted. And yet, according to the participants, the class has been wildly successful in its own terms. Students have had the opportunity to practice techniques that enhance their social and emotional learning, and then to reflect on the effectiveness of those techniques. Students themselves say: "I'm more compassionate"; "I'm more patient because I've learned to work with people younger than me. While my freshmen are getting work done, it motivates me to get work done, so I'm more diligent"; "I feel like I can talk to different people in the school now."

The most important student responses are sometimes, at first glance, the ones that are tangential, idiosyncratic, even obstructionist. The format of school discourages potentially useful interruptions; instead, we tell our students "to get back to work." Long before they reach our classrooms, students have internalized that being a good student means handing in the work, getting through the day. Sure, completing things is important, as is the ability to set and meet goals and be held accountable, and even to measure certain types of growth. But not at the expense of everything else. If we are going to bemoan our students' lack of creativity or drive, we should look for offbeat opportunities to spark and engage that are unplanned.

Avi's student Asha took his senior rite-of-passage course first semester. She was a smart and artistically gifted young person, who could sometimes be overwhelmed with her life. Even as she completed the work for the class, and had a great rapport with her partner, Payton, she also dealt with a tremendous amount of anxiety. One day, months after the class ended, Avi exchanged hellos with her in the hallway, aware of the looming hall clock that was counting down the minutes until the start of the next period. Asha looked pale and like she wanted to say something more, so Avi lingered, though a part of him was anxious to move on to class. But Asha wasn't moving. She took a couple of deep breaths. And then after 30 seconds, she said thank you, smiled, and went off happily. This little, delicate moment recalls a scene from Natalie Goldberg's (1994) memoir *The Long Quiet Highway* which reveals how worthwhile experiences come sometimes from doing less, not more, from being off the track, not on it. She relates her only memory from high school, the time her teacher took her to watch the rain fall by the window. She writes: "Thank God for that rain out the window and for Mr. Clemente who allowed us in ninth grade to listen to it for no reason, in the middle of the day. That one moment carried me a long way into my life. I didn't know it then. At the time, I think, it made me a little nervous—it was too naked, too uncontrolled, too honest. I thought it odd. In those days I was watching my step, making sure I knew the rules, keeping things in control … here was Mr. Clemente who asked me to listen to the rain, to connect a sense organ with something natural, neutral, good. He asked me to become alive. I was scared, and I loved it."

## Wondering

In his book *The Art of Wondering*, William A. Covino (1988) argues for reconceiving of the teaching of writing as a form of wondering. Though his work specifically focuses on writing, we extrapolate his remarks to apply in general to the project of education. Covino identifies the epistemological crisis of our era as "the failure of objectivity, Cartesian rationality, and detachment to account for our complicated perception of a world in flux where matters are never settled" (p. 121). He argues that students "should trade certainty for ambiguity, trade preservative writing for investigative writing, trade conclusions for 'counterinduction'" (p. 130). We propose that schools should do something similar themselves, and should train students accordingly.

Our students are disserved by the notions of certainty and closure that a reliance on performance metrics inscribes. They need the ability to understand multiple perspectives, to be comfortable with ambiguity, paradox, and uncertainty. They need strategies that help them regulate their experience of the present; they need ways of relating with others in and through similarity and difference, ways of understanding, as Sam implies at the beginning of this piece, that one person's personhood is intimately connected to another's personhood. They need to feel that pleasure in school is an expectation, not the exception.

The narrative we related at the beginning of this chapter, the one about the girl who did her report on wolves, was Glynis's experience as a child. How do we understand that story? What is more important, following directions or following passion? Students' personal experiences or the nation's mandates for accountability in public education? The way we as educators wonder about things matters, as does the way we frame our answers. What if, to the questions: Where are we going? How are we going to get there? How will we know when we are there, we answer more tentatively, more provisionally, in ways that allow for us to revise, adapt, linger in a space of uncertainty, confusion, and doubt? What if we value a spirit of wonder rather than an ethos of conviction that we already have the answer? What if schools could accommodate ostensible failure so that Avi's empathy growth experiment could be recognized as a success? What if we include in our curriculum as guiding questions: Who are you? How are you? How do you relate to others? What if we ask Jennie not what she wants to do with the rest of her life, but about her hopes and fears in the present? What kind of curriculum and pedagogy would be inspired by the pressing dilemmas she presents?

## References

Apter, T. (2006, July 21). The bounce: What we can learn from troubled teenagers who get back on track. *Times Literary Supplement*, 3–4.

Brontë, C. (2002). *Jane Eyre*. Mineola, NY: Dover.

Brown, S. (Director). (2008). *Play is more than just fun* [Video file]. Retrieved October 21, 2018, from https://www.ted.com/talks/stuart_brown_says_play_is_more_than_fun_it_s_vital?language=en

Center for Prevention Research and Development. (2016). Illinois youth survey. Retrieved October 21, 2018, from https://iys.cprd.illinois.edu/

Covino, W. A. (1988). *The art of wondering: A revisionist return to the history of rhetoric*. Portsmouth, NH: Boynton/Cook.

de Botton, A. (Director). (2009). *A kinder, gentler philosophy of success* [Video file]. Retrieved October 21, 2018, from https://www.ted.com/talks/alain_de_botton_a_kinder_gentler_philosophy_of_success?language=en

Denizet-Lewis, B. (2017, October 11). Why are more American teenagers than ever suffering from severe anxiety? Retrieved from https://www.nytimes.com/2017/10/11/magazine/why-are-more-american-teenagers-than-ever-suffering-from-severe-anxiety.html

Friedman, R. (2014, June 28). Why teenagers act crazy. *New York Times*. Retrieved from https://www.nytimes.com/2014/06/29/opinion/sunday/why-teenagers-act-crazy.html

Goldberg, N. (1994). *Long quiet highway: Waking up in America*. New York, NY: Bantam Books.

Keats, J. (1970). *Letters of John Keats: A new selection*. R. Gittings (Ed.). Oxford, England: Oxford University Press.

Lindberg, D., & Watts, A. (Directors). (2016, July 26). *Music and life* [Video file]. Retrieved October 22, 2018, from https://www.youtube.com/watch?v=qHnIJeE3LAI&disable_polymer=true

Siegel, D. J. (2015). *Brainstorm: The power and purpose of the teenage brain*. New York, NY: Jeremy P. Tarcher/Penguin, a member of Penguin Group (USA).

Siegel, D. (Writer). (2009, November 12). *The power of mindsight* [Video file]. Retrieved October 22, 2018, from https://www.youtube.com/watch?v=Nu7wEr8AnHw

Smith, A. D. (2001). *Talk to me: Travels in media and politics*. New York, NY: Anchor Books.

Smith, J. (2018, March 5). Opinion: Anna Deavere Smith is the most empathetic person in America. Retrieved October 22, 2018, from https://www.huffingtonpost.com/entry/opinion-smith-anna-deavere-smith-empathy_us_5a905997e4b01e9e56bb8287

# 2. Calculating Justice? Using Mathematical Mindsets for Teaching From a Social Justice Perspective

ANGELA WHITACRE DE RESENDIZ AND WILL HUDSON

### "Maybe They Can Dance for Us"

Each week, all the students in our school meet in one room for discussion, problem-solving, or students' presentations of their ideas for the school. During one such meeting, a teacher explained that Martin Luther King, Jr. Day was approaching, summarized who Dr. King was and why we celebrate him, and asked students to think of ways we could mark the holiday. Some students suggested reading books about the Civil Rights Era; some thought creating a bulletin board or display was a good idea. And then it happened. A rather precocious, white, first-grade girl, who we learned later had discussed in her classroom that some schools and community events feature African music or dance for Black History Month, suggested that some of the Black students could present a song or do a dance for us. Teachers' faces went into shock as we looked at each other. Did a white student just suggest that Black students ("They") should sing and dance for non-Black students ("Us")? Yes, yes she did, and several kids, their brows furrowed and mouths agape, seemed to have gotten what just happened.

We teachers were suddenly faced with a litany of internal questions, none of which had easy answers. How could we address this comment without crushing this child? How could we explain the weight of the historical and polarizing racist imagery she had just conjured? How could we make clear to all present that this was hurtful? How could we do it in the thirty minutes available without stirring up more confusion or unresolved harm? How could we protect those students who were offended, angry, or confused? How could we unpack this in the moment as a multi-age group?

Well, we didn't. We let the comment sit there a few moments and then brushed over it thinking that those students who got what happened "got it" and those who didn't hear the offense wouldn't need any further discussion. And so we moved on. We were not prepared. As a faculty, we were fairly well-versed in history, racial inequity, and activism. We were well-spoken, vocal, and "good" at navigating nuanced conversation. But, in this moment, we failed. How did this happen to us? And how were we to pick up the pieces and make sure it didn't happen again?

## Angela's Response

A student in my third-grade class went home deeply affected by the all-school meeting, so I spoke with her mother about her and her sister's reactions at home. The younger sister cried about dancing for the white kids, and my student was angry. The following day we discussed as a class what went wrong, how teachers should have reacted, and why what was said was so upsetting to some of us.

In discussing the incident as a faculty, it became clear that we had not done the work to know how to call someone's racism out in a productive way. We knew how to agree with other adults that leaned in the same direction, and we knew how to impart facts and ideas. We did not know how to really open ourselves up and be completely present, engaged with children in difficult, open dialogue about sticky topics where we might not have all the answers. I am haunted by that all-school meeting, and always will be, because I know that my inaction, even if only delayed by a day, will be a story that lives in several children's memory.

These are the moments that make teachers, particularly white teachers, afraid to open discussions about race, gender, sexuality, class, and social justice. Indeed, some of our faculty later suggested we should simply avoid discussing such potentially unpredictable topics in mixed-age settings. It can be easier to do nothing, because if we do nothing, we can feel as if we have caused no harm. But not knowing what to do is not an excuse for inaction.

The discussion I and my students had the day after the all-school meeting was deep, honest, and meaningful. I cried, and students cried. We talked about our discomfort and opened up to each other in a way that wasn't about saying the "right" thing, but about using the right tools. We stopped excusing and protecting ourselves and started explaining and asking questions.

As a facilitator of that discussion, I used a lot of "I statements" to guide students through how I analyzed my thoughts and actions. More importantly, however, I started asking the group open-ended questions like,

"What were you feeling? Why do you think you felt that way? Does anyone have something to say about that? What are you wondering about now as we're talking about this?" Asking such questions allowed students to talk about a full range of emotions both related to that moment and to racism in general. Several comments were about wanting to understand racism and what it was, where it came from, and how it worked but not knowing how or when to ask. One child spoke about wanting others to understand how racism felt but not wanting to always be the person having to explain it or point it out.

And here I made a conscious choice not to always just nod and thank, not even to rephrase and reaffirm, although I believe these to be effective discussion tools. While acutely aware of the risk of exploiting the existing power imbalance between teacher and students, I did not want to facilitate a feel-good talk about everyone being right in their own way. I chose to say so when I thought some comments lacked context, history, truth, or respect. I analyzed and unpacked bias, and I talked openly about *why* such analysis and unpacking were important. We discussed how even unintentionally racist comments are still painful and that when our friends are oblivious to their racist behavior it can hurt more. We talked about the importance of saying what we really felt and not what we assumed was "right," even at the risk of being critiqued, because it gave everyone a chance to learn to recognize and combat racist ideas in a safe space. We talked about not liking what someone may say but still being able to like them as a person. And this conversation carried on well beyond that day. We created a working definition for racism. We began referring to *racist behavior*, distinguishing between the actions and the person. Reframing the conversation allowed us to be critical of each other and hold each other accountable, without alienating each other or suppressing genuine expression.

Because I have the privilege of working in a private, progressive school that is based on democratic, project-based learning, our class chose to start a new project on racism. The project involved several activities where we explored racism not as "hatred" of a group of people, but as the systemic "othering" of one people and the privileging/centering of another. I learned in this project that, while the content was important, the way in which we learned to discuss the content was equally so. We weren't trying to have definitive answers; we were trying to understand better this complicated thing called racism, get comfortable exposing our discomfort, and ask better questions. Furthermore, we were trying to do it in a room full of eight-year-olds and one grown-up. I knew we weren't going to replicate this project every year, but surely we could replicate something about the process. There was a familiar framework evolving that would not formulate clearly in my head until many projects and several years later.

## Will's Response

I spent the first ten years of my career as a public school teacher. In the schools where I taught, racism and bias were common and pervasive. From hearing white teachers telling students of color that they weren't speaking "correctly" to observing students struggle with biased standardized test regimes, I witnessed low-income students, immigrant populations, and students of color be marginalized and penalized. At the time, my efforts at pushing back against this system were sporadic and ineffectual; I had yet to develop a sense for myself of how to teach for justice and equity. However, beginning my first year as a sixth-grade teacher in a new middle level program at a small, progressive, and independent school, I quickly understood that I was no longer in a situation where I could hide behind systems that silenced important and challenging discourse. On the contrary, my very privilege and ability to make an impact within this school community required me to begin the process of interrogating and addressing my own shortcomings, biases, and even fear.

Looking back on the morning described above, I realize my inaction in that situation set me on a trajectory towards developing a deeper understanding of what it meant for me, a white heterosexual male, to teach for social justice and anti-racism. When the student made the suggestion that Black students dance for us, I remember feeling uncomfortable and slightly embarrassed. I wasn't shocked or mortified. Rather, I saw this as a young child whose choice of words had uncomfortable implications. In the moment, we glossed over the comment and moved on. But that was the beginning of a reexamination of privilege, racism, and the inadvertent perpetuation of systems of thought and action that marginalize and, in many ways, dehumanize students and teachers alike. The process has been challenging. It has been difficult and painful as I have had to reconcile my own past actions, or inactions, with who I am and want to become personally and professionally.

Social justice and anti-racist work is ongoing, and I have found that, for me, there are no easy answers, no ready-made solutions. In fact, it's quite the opposite: questions, uncertainties, and mistakes define my efforts more than solutions and comfortable outcomes. To be sure, so much of learning is about being comfortable with mistakes, with not knowing exactly what to say or how to approach a topic or problem. As a teacher, I take this to heart and encourage my students to become more comfortable with discomfort as it is an integral component of growth and learning. Big problems, or real-world problems as we like to call them, do not come with an ordered set of steps or predetermined solutions. They can often be approached from a variety of angles and always require one to struggle and to grapple with uncertainty.

Maybe it goes without saying that a change in one's thinking is a critical component of deeper understanding and growth, but I didn't internalize this truth until I began thinking about math differently while working with K-2 students who were learning English as a new language. We were working on counting and learning numbers when I unexpectedly developed a deeper number sense for myself. Most notably, I grasped the different representations of number and the series of abstract leaps that take place between them—from quantity of objects, to the words we use to name that quantity, to the symbols we use to represent the quantity. As a young student, I had often struggled with mathematics, but suddenly, with a small group of young students from around the world, I began to think about mathematics in a new way.

What was interesting about this case, in particular, was that the change in my thinking was *fundamental* to how I viewed and thought about number. I would argue that similar fundamental shifts are necessary in the way we approach teaching history and working for social justice within our classrooms and institutions—namely, that this kind of work requires a reconsideration of the rudimentary context of our own thinking. Moreover, I would argue that much of what we consider best practices in mathematics can also be applied to teaching for justice and equity.

## *The Framework Was Already There*

We, Angela and Will, have come to believe that social justice teaching is more than stories of struggle with happy, victorious endings of freedom and civil rights. Social justice teaching requires that we provide students with the analytical toolbox that allows them to be active in their own education, develop agency within the classroom, and transfer their empowerment to self-advocacy and democratic action against the larger social and economic structures they will encounter in their own lives.

We are privileged to teach in a context that, by its very existence, is an act of resistance against the dominant educational system currently enforced by policy makers who often have little to no experience in education or child development. Nevertheless, while we are afforded a level of autonomy not always available to teachers in other settings, our ability to create, curate, and even reject content does not make us immune to the larger social context in which racism, sexism, heterocentric thinking, religious biases and marginalization occur. Though the context of our teaching may be different, our efforts to offer social justice-oriented curriculum present challenges similar to those encountered by teachers in other, more conventional, educational structures.

It was through one of our many discussions about these challenges that we realized that the existing conversations around math instruction and developing mathematical thinking in children can be applied across disciplines, specifically to history and social justice-oriented teaching. Regardless of content area, challenging discussions and deeper understandings all require a willingness to ask questions, think creatively, look for patterns, and take chances. Indeed, mathematical thinking used as a framework for deep, analytical, and honest discussions related to historical and justice-related topics provides a safe vehicle through which teachers in conventional settings can use the existing standards-based guidelines to create a model of real "critical thinking" that lays the groundwork for empowerment. To this end, social justice teaching and learning is a habit of mind that opens doors to a more comprehensive view of the world and society, one that fosters community and whole-child, whole-teacher development.

In addition to Common Core and National Council of Teachers of Mathematics standards for mathematical practice and processes, we have found Jo Boaler's book, *Mathematical Mindsets* (2015), to be a useful resource for framing an approach to mathematics that can be applied to the teaching of history for social justice. Boaler sets out the following tenets for creating a mathematics classroom rooted in inquiry, creativity, and discourse:

*Positive Norms to Encourage in Math Class*

- Everyone Can Learn Math to the Highest Levels
- Mistakes are Valuable
- Questions are Really Important
- Math is About Creativity and Making Sense
- Math is About Connections and Communicating
- Value Depth Over Speed
- Math is About Learning Not Performing (p. 277)

Boaler's framework has helped us consider curriculum and instruction generally and also specifically address some of the challenges of teaching history and engaging in social justice topics. We hope that having a framework will help other educators and those who work with children feel more comfortable engaging in social justice topics as well, understanding that all good teaching and all good learning is about developing strategies, experience, and understanding, not about following a program.

## Everyone Can Learn Math to the Highest Levels

This tenet pushes back against the idea that there are some people who can do math and others who cannot. Boaler writes at great lengths about this misconception and its dangers. It gives students and teachers an excuse for not understanding math, which limits their development as mathematicians. In the realm of history and social justice, we see a similar dilemma: many teachers feel unqualified to teach around topics of justice such as race, class, gender, sexuality, religion, and historic and systemic inequalities. They fear so much saying the wrong thing that they say nothing at all. Similarly, when we found ourselves faced with the uncertainty of how to respond to a child's suggestion to have the Black students in our school dance for "us," we did not know how to respond. And so we didn't.

As teachers, we all have strengths and weaknesses, and sometimes those fall along subject lines. It is commonly accepted that to be well-rounded we teachers must train ourselves in our weaker areas. Social justice is another area where we can grow. It requires dedication. It requires extra reading, workshops, seminars, and all the things other subjects require. But it also requires that teachers, particularly white/male/hetero/privileged teachers, accept that it is hard work to allow oneself to be vulnerable and to recognize when we inadvertently perpetuate and fail to recognize the benefits of privilege that many of us enjoy in a systemically unjust culture.

Those of us who do receive privilege in multiple aspects of our lives need to recognize that it can be tiring and painful to keep explaining one's own experiences to others and justifying one's very self to those who have always been recognized and justified by the dominant culture. All teachers benefit from honing their skills as discussion facilitators and mastering the subject matter, but in the case of teaching for social justice, this is work that needs to be done especially by privileged educators—particularly those privileged in multiple aspects of intersectionality.

As educators, "I just don't get it" and "It's not my thing" are unacceptable barriers to learning, be it in math or social justice-oriented history. These types of mindsets perpetuate the myth that some can do the work and improve while others don't have it in them and just can't. This is a disservice to the teacher, the learner, and ultimately to all of us who are vulnerable to injustice. Developing a greater sensitivity to and understanding of different perspectives on race, gender, culture, class, sexuality, and ability changes us all for the better and helps to mitigate the fear to broach these topics.

When mathematics provides opportunities for open-ended exploration, practice, and creativity in problem-solving, then all students can learn to the highest levels. We've seen this in our classrooms whereby students willingly persevere through challenging mathematical scenarios, ask questions, explore ideas, and engage with others in mathematical discourse. We foster these same mindsets in ourselves and our students when it comes to history: What happened? Who is telling this story? What perspectives are most dominant, and which are being left out? How can we think about this in a different way?

After that morning meeting, many of us went back to our classrooms and began the dialogue, stating how what was said made us feel and encouraging students to share their thoughts. We then began to do the work of unpacking and exploring racism and stereotypes, historical hurts that linger to this day.

Everyone can engage these subjects if they bring their humanity and humility. Doing so will make for better teaching, a better classroom experience, and a better world. Just be prepared to struggle, and recognize that learning is not always comfortable. To learn is to challenge oneself to push beyond the known, to compromise one's own comfort to gain a deeper understanding.

## Mistakes Are Valuable

Learning is a precarious business, fraught with peril. Creating a space that feels safe is essential and, in this space, we must learn not to fear mistakes but to recognize them as critical components of growth and learning. In math class, valuing our mistakes may mean modeling interest and excitement when mistakes present opportunities for discussion and deeper understanding. Indeed, mistakes are valuable because they can help us discuss and understand our assumptions, our perspectives, and even our metacognition. They are valuable because to err is human and we want to keep our humanity alive in a classroom, not stifle it in order to memorize right answers.

Often, students and teachers do not value mistakes. We tend to value product over process. When we overemphasize the product—the correct response—we lose sight of the value in trial and error, in just trying to figure something out. The right answer becomes the goal, and anything that falls short of that goal is felt as a demoralizing failure.

While miscalculating a division problem might generate negative feelings about one's aptitude in mathematics, mistakes made when talking about gender, class, or race can hurt at a much deeper level. This means the teacher and the students need to have open and clear conversations not only about how to welcome mistakes, but also about how to respectfully and productively call out others on mistakes. This is one of the most difficult aspects of classroom culture to create. People of privilege are generally very responsive to the idea that they get to make mistakes. It is letting that mistake get analyzed in a way that is honest and productive that students (and teachers) don't often like, but where true growth and learning occur.

Following the morning meeting when the student asked for an MLK dance, the faculty felt some degree of discomfort with both that child's statement and our failure to adequately respond. Looking back, it would have been very easy to shrug our shoulders and say, "Oh well, that was awkward. Better luck next time." The reality is such that, within the classroom, there is always a next time. This is why we have to do the work now so that we can be better prepared when the time comes, because it will. This child was not intentionally making a racially prejudiced comment with the intent to hurt others. However, this child was speaking from within a larger cultural and historical narrative where various forms of systemic oppression have been normalized and woven into the fabric of our society.

Doing the work means recognizing that mistakes are essential to teaching for social justice. We want our students to learn to analyze their words and behaviors, to understand historical contexts, and to develop awareness of institutionalized injustice, systemic misrepresentations, and cultural influences that engulf and confuse them every day. We want this so that they may build better relationships and a stronger resistance to a culture of oppressive norms and social marginalization. To accomplish this goal, we must do this work ourselves and recognize the value of the mistakes that we will make along the way.

## Questions Are Really Important

Students tend to ask fewer questions as they get older. Afraid of being seen as inept or contrary, they may not seek the help they need to understand. But students need to ask questions to think through their work from their own perspective; otherwise, they are memorizing and parroting, not learning. In math, it is important for students to ask why they should perform a specific step or why they should apply an operation to solve a word problem. Math teachers may explain why students should "carry the one" in an addition problem such as $15 + 27$, but are often confused when a student "carries the 2." The student has understood that $5 + 7 = 12$ and that one of the numbers stays and one gets moved over. It may take several times before the student really understands the relationship between "carrying" and place value. They need to ask the question, "Why do I move the 'one' and not the 'two'?" The forming of the question is part of the learning process.

Within many settings, stepping aside and placing students' questions at the forefront of learning remains only an ideal because educators are also expected to show results in the form of standardized test scores, which then impact student advancement and teacher evaluations. As a consequence, many of us find ourselves in a nearly impossible situation where we cannot, without great risk, enact the type of teaching that we know to be best.

That being said, the importance of questions cannot be overstated. It is through their questions that students are able to take ownership of their learning. In addition, the questions that we, as teachers, ask of ourselves form the basis for own learning and growth. Taken together, the questions that we ask can serve to provide direction for the learning that takes place within our classrooms and to help us better understand the world and our place in it.

What types of questions should we ask? How do we structure our questions so as to get the most impact, the biggest bang for our buck? There are countless resources on classroom questioning structures, but the process should not be that complicated because we ask questions all of the time, and children are geared towards asking questions. It's a part of their programming.

One of the most powerful questions we can ask is, "Why?" It is a good question to ask about history, the world around us, and our own conceptions. Teachers often use this question to mean, "Why are you saying this or giving this answer?" Other versions of "why" that can be easier for children to engage are: How so? What do you mean? Tell me about that.

In many cases teachers are asked to follow the classic Bloom's Taxonomy when asking questions—ask lots of questions that test basic comprehension/ regurgitation and move into some higher level questions involving synthesizing or analyzing information in order to arrive at a unique conclusion. The problem is those higher level questions are not really meant to question the material itself. When studying history, we have found the following questions to be helpful for examining historic and current events. Who was/is involved? Whose perspective is being included and whose version is being excluded? Who are you identifying with? What might others think or feel about this event? Who benefited from this? Who did not benefit? How were people affected? Who made this decision? What effects might be connected to now? How does this connect to you?

Ask questions. Encourage and engage questions. Understand, though, that the work is not about finding facts for the sake of facts, but about asking questions that will help both you and your students arrive at deeper understanding. We should strive for understanding, all the while recognizing that our understanding will be imperfect, that we will always have to be seeking, rearranging, and reorganizing what we think we know, as well as the methods and pedagogies we employ in our work. If we arrive at the point where we think we've got it all figured out, then we've reached a creative impasse, a point where we are no longer learning, and where our effectiveness as educators will begin to diminish.

## *Math Is About Creativity and Making Sense*

Math is about creativity and making sense, and so is childhood, and so is life, and so should be our approach to history. The traditional algorithm in mathematics is a tried and true formula, and sometimes it is the easiest and best way to arrive at a solution, but we should recognize that the algorithm was arrived at through creativity, by working through problems in a variety of ways to arrive at a point where accuracy and efficiency meet. Creativity in problem-solving suggests that there is not a single approach to solving a problem. Moreover, though long division and rounding and regrouping are helpful and important skills, complex problem-solving and the deeper understanding and processes contained therein cannot be arrived at through a prescriptive approach. Students need space and time to create sense of situations and circumstances. This presents significant challenges within any classroom, but especially the classroom held hostage by the dictates of predetermined content and curriculum.

Though not easy, providing students with open-ended situations that require them to develop and apply creative strategies is more cut and dried when we are dealing with mathematics than with historical narratives and perspectives. There is a wealth of resources for presenting young students with engaging, open-ended mathematical situations, but what about for history? How can we approach history creatively, and what kind of sense are we trying to make?

We posit that a great deal of the creative and sense-making work of teaching history must be done by teachers themselves. There are no easy solutions, and historical timelines are often more significant in the information they leave out than what is included. We are all victims of misinformation, of bias, of a failure to recognize our position within a wider continuum of privilege, oppression, and resistance. As history teachers, we must inquire deeply into our own preconceptions and misconceptions. The creativity in teaching history comes from how we contextualize and present the information that students are expected to learn as well as from modeling creative sense-making for students to emulate.

*Angela's Example*

In my third-grade class, we often have small groups or individuals studying different topics or subtopics. I try to sit and read with each group as they're researching. It morphs into a bit of a storytime-like lecture, with ample time for questions and discussion. Usually nearby students begin listening in, and I let that happen.

On this particular day, I am finally sitting down with my Aztec group who has been asked not to read or look at images on certain pages until I can sit with them. In almost every children's book on Aztec culture we have gotten from the library there is an explanation of the importance—and a large, gruesome illustration—of human sacrifice in Aztec culture. My own child is in the group and is highly invested in this project. She knows her own ancestors were Aztecs. She is already sad that much of the reading has focused on war and not on math like the books on the Maya. My blood boils for the hyper-inclusion of this aspect over many other aspects of culture that are not included in these simplified books.

It is tempting to ignore the racism of reducing a culture to shocking "savagery" and to simply tell the students what is on the page quickly or keep pages discussing sacrifice off limits. But this is actually a great opportunity to talk about cultural bias and historical sources. I talk to my students about how most information about Aztecs was written by the invading Spaniards:

> If you came across this culture that was new to you, and on Monday they took care of some plants and went to the market and paid some taxes, and on Tuesday the same, and Wednesday the same … and on Saturday there was a sacrifice. What would you be most interested or surprised by? What would you write about? Would you write about the fact that they had extensive botanical gardens? Would you write that botanists from every area of the empire studied the medicinal qualities of plants and the emperor valued scientific health studies? Would you write that the Aztecs had a complex mathematical system to calculate farmland boundaries? Or would you write about that crazy human sacrifice at the temple?

They get my point right away. And the conversation takes off with much of the rest of the class listening. We go deep about how we read history with caution, knowing who wrote it and looking for the many angles that always exist. I could have just printed out some articles about the medical and mathematical advancements I know the Aztecs to have made, but doing so wouldn't have had the same effect. The students needed to make sense not only of the Aztec world, but also of the Spaniards of the time and the book publishers of today. Why would bias seep in? Because human sacrifice is awful and yet fascinating. Why does the over-representation of this aspect of their culture continue? Because if we don't try to see the humanity of others, if we don't learn to be creative in making sense of history, we will only see the awful and the fascinating, thus reinforcing the prejudices and stereotypes that we need to dismantle.

## Math Is About Connections and Communicating

Mathematical understanding is more about identifying the connections between different concepts, or ways of representing quantities and relationships, than memorizing facts or being able to follow the steps of an algorithm, such as long division. We should encourage our students to see the relationship between fractions and ratios, for example, or how multiplication and division are repeated addition and subtraction. We want students to see the connections between quantities, discover patterns, make generalizations, and communicate their thinking and observations. The goal in history, as in math, is for students and teachers to see beyond isolated facts and events to the connections and relationships that tie them together.

Accomplishing this goal can be a daunting task. As educators, we must push ourselves to approach the subjects we teach with a wide and encompassing lens. In the same way that helping young learners develop a strong number sense prepares them for the rigors and abstractions of algebra and beyond, providing students with a sense of the interconnectivity of history prepares them to look more deeply and with a critical eye at the world and contemporary society.

### Will's Example

At the beginning of every school year, students go through an extended process of exploring and sharing their interests and concerns. We make lists, find connections, and identify themes. This year, my sixth-grade students chose "History and Identity" as the theme for our first project. As so often happens, events that were being reported in the news began filtering into the classroom. With the increasing media attention on the protests against the Dakota Access Pipeline (DAPL) at Standing Rock, students were angry and confused about what was going on and wanted to know more.

Students asked questions and researched the history of the region and the indigenous peoples' ongoing struggle with the United States government and private companies over land and water rights. They learned about the various iterations of the Treaty of Fort Laramie, the systematic reduction and appropriation of native land, and the partitioning of the Great Sioux Reservation through trickery, dishonesty, and violence. Students were able to develop a deeper understanding of how the contemporary conflict over sacred land

and water rights is an extension of events and trespasses extending back to the 1800s. In so doing, students came to see that this was not a new struggle, but one that has been ongoing for generations.

But once we begin to see patterns and make connections, how do we communicate our thinking? In the case of our group meeting, what could we have communicated that would have made the connections and implications of the first grader's comment more visible and tangible? In the DAPL project, how could we communicate our learning in some way that would rise above an undercurrent of "us and them" or a sense of feeling sorry for "those" people?

In the context of teaching and learning history, one of our primary objectives is to help students develop a sense of empathy. By developing empathy, we are all able to better relate to and communicate feelings of struggle or marginalization. There is a danger in this, though; we must always be aware of privilege, in whatever way it presents itself, and not assume that the experience of being picked on, excluded, or betrayed by a friend is the same as systemic oppression and discrimination. To do so runs the risk of devaluing the lived experience of those who have endured treachery, injustice, and atrocity.

As part of our DAPL project, students chose to write letters of support to the council at Standing Rock. I encouraged them to incorporate what they had learned about Lakota history and culture to communicate a connection to their own lives. One of the most compelling letters came from a student of Palestinian descent. He spoke of studying the Battle of Little Bighorn and how this reminded him of stories that his mom would share of growing up in Palestine. Another student wrote of the discrimination directed towards her sibling with special needs and the unfairness of how she was treated. Yet another student spoke of indigenous language and how her twin struggles to speak, and how she is one of the only people that can understand her.

Connecting their own experiences to the past does not automatically link students to others, but it creates an opening where students can begin to understand how their personal stories are complex and play a role in the development of their own perspectives. Making connections is about learning to uncover patterns and recognize cause-and-effect relationships. It is also about seeking out ways to make history relevant to our own lives. Communicating our observations and emotions around something we have learned or the connections we have made can change how we are able to hear others speak. We can come to listen and learn without assuming we have the answers, instead knowing we are working to better understand.

## *Value Depth Over Speed*

Even in our teaching situation, we feel the pressure to do more, to move more quickly. This is a mindset that is pervasive throughout the whole of society and something that we need to push back against in all areas of our lives. In mathematics, the prevailing attitude is that speed is synonymous with being good at math and that slower students have a lower aptitude than their peers. We tend to focus our attention on the students who find answers quickly, or who always have their hands raised to offer solutions. The slower, deeper thinkers can easily be ignored. Even worse, these students can develop negative and self-limiting attitudes about their own competency in mathematics that can have long-lasting consequences.

We must make time to take time, to do the work of deep learning and community-building. This is what much of this chapter is really all about—the importance of orienting ourselves towards the development of community. Building a community with members who are willing to struggle and challenge one another in order to emerge stronger and better is one of the most stalwart forms of resistance there is.

It takes time, commitment, and hard work to build community. In order to do this work, we must take the time to ask questions, search for patterns, and make connections. When we look deeply into our own lives and the lives of others, we take the steps towards community-building. Our work as progressive educators is rooted in democratic ideals; we bring questions and issues to the table, we discuss, we vote, and often we have to go back and vote again. This is a time-consuming process, and it flies in the face of prevailing attitudes around the importance of quickly accomplishing tasks and meeting curricular goals. However, it is imperative that we look for ways to model these processes and look deeply into the world, our place in it, and how we relate to one another.

### *Will's Example*

Unfortunately, even within a democratic classroom where dialogue is a key element of the decision-making process, some student voices may not always be heard. One year in my sixth-grade classroom a group of students encountered a difficulty in how they were having discussions and debates. I observed that certain students were consistently silent while others dominated the conversation. I brought this up with the class and students quickly identified the problem as a tension between the fast/loud and slow/quiet talkers. The fast and loud talkers were usually the first to get their ideas out there and tended to dominate the conversation, and this was causing friction and some hurt feelings among other students. In the discussion that followed, the "slow talkers" explained that they didn't feel like they were being given an opportunity to speak and share their ideas and opinions. The more outgoing students countered by stating that they felt as if they were trying to give space for other voices, but that some of their peers weren't stepping up and making their voices heard.

As this conversation continued, it became clear to everyone that there were different perspectives at play, but that both sides had valid points that needed to be taken into consideration. The more effusive students were able to step back and really hear how some of their peers needed more time to order their thoughts and to figure out how to communicate their thinking. They were also able to understand how their peers were often feeling left out, slighted, and even ignored. Likewise, the quieter students came to understand that their peers were not being intentionally overbearing, which helped to mend some hurt feelings. In the end, all students were able to agree on new rules for discourse where the loud and fast talkers would focus on stepping back while the slow and quiet talkers would concentrate on stepping forward and making their voices heard.

## Math Is About Learning Not Performing

Much as many teachers often think that the younger years are for memorizing math facts rather than learning to become thinking mathematicians with number sense, analytic skills, and a bit of wonder, we often hear that social justice topics are for older students or even adults. But we believe that if our students are not too young to experience injustice, they are not too young to learn the vocabulary to express its harm and the tools to dismantle its source.

### Angela's Example

I know giving my third graders the skills to battle injustice to be a moral imperative, and I also know they are capable because my eight-year-old students constantly amaze me with their abilities. We are currently undertaking a study of maps, graphs, and infographics. I found several books that were cultural atlases of some kind or other, but, as typically happens when looking for books for our research, I found that many books focused primarily on North American and European cultures, countries, or cities. I expressed this disappointment each time I brought in a new book and let the class know that if I tossed out every Eurocentric book I found, we'd end up all sharing one or two books. We agreed that we could use the books but needed to be aware of this bias and of subtle misrepresentations in order to be less susceptible to their marginalizing effects.

Not long after, we were looking at some infographic examples and discussing scale representation and a white boy raised his hand to ask, "Isn't that a racist infographic though?" "What do you mean?" I asked. "Well," he replied, "it is showing the size of a human for comparison, but the human is a light-skinned man. Aren't most humans in the world dark-skinned women? So isn't it racist to make that the average human?" This student is not performing a set of skills in order to impress the teacher. He is not attempting to regurgitate facts in order to get a right answer. Our focus at the moment was not on recognizing racism, nor on over-representation. He was genuinely contemplating what he understood about bias and applying it. He was asking the question because he needed to engage his thoughts in dialogue with the group in the moment. This is learning.

Just as we want our students to develop a mathematical mindset, to recognize math all around them, to engage math as a useful tool, and to enjoy the mental exercise of math, we teach them to develop a justice-oriented mindset. We want them to develop the skills of analysis and vigilance to understand, deconstruct, and reconstruct the world around them. We want them to question whether a given fact or representation or social norm is truly as it is presented or if it has been shaped by the many -isms and pitfalls of our educational system and the systems beyond. We want them to take this seeing and questioning with them when they leave the classroom. Real-world analytic skills are the foundations for change. Students need to be encouraged to think, not to perform. We have got to stop teaching overt, historical discrimination as a series of events with memorized dates and names and start giving students the tools from early on to recognize and come to terms with the enormity of privilege, implicit bias, and subtly imposed power structures.

### *Frameworks Become Foundations*

As educators, we are on the front line of a critical endeavor, which is to harness and direct the energies of our students towards cultivating the fullest expression of their own humanity. In so doing, we strive to help our students learn to value themselves and others, and to believe that everyone can learn and participate to the highest levels. As teachers, we work to build resilient and inclusive communities where we are able to recognize the value in our own mistakes, struggles, and shortcomings so that our students can do the same. This is challenging, relentless work, but it's not without its rewards. The struggle for justice and equity in our schools, homes, and society is ongoing, with no end in sight, but we are invigorated by the successes in our own classrooms and the relationships we build with others in our profession who aspire to do the best work possible under what are, unfortunately, increasingly challenging circumstances.

We must continue to ask questions, and we must encourage our students to do the same. Working within a social and educational paradigm that values answers and ready-made solutions over open-ended exploration means that we will often find ourselves swimming against the tide of mainstream thought and the status quo. However, it is through the questions we ask of ourselves, and the questions that our students ask about the world around them, that we are able to take ownership of our learning. As we pursue these questions, we engage in creative exploration and interrogation of our world, its systems and institutions, and we begin to make sense of how the different parts fit together and impact our lives.

Be it in mathematics, history, or in teaching for equity and social justice, our work is to discover what is meaningful for us as individuals and for our students. In the process, we open ourselves to different perspectives and experiences. For many of us, this questioning and creative exploration can reveal and help us understand how privilege, the words we use, or even the things we fail to say impact other people, oftentimes in negative ways. Even though this can be painful and challenging, we can identify our mistakes and begin to rectify our errors, to understand where we went wrong and how to do right. Therefore, we must strive to take our time, even when faced with the expectation to do more, always faster.

Learning is not about performance; it is about process. The emphasis on learning as that which can only be revealed through an artifact, measured with a grade or test score, or somehow quantified as data fails to discern the complexity and richness of what learning entails. Learning as performance is a destructive notion that undermines the joy and excitement of childhood. As teachers, we understand implicitly that kids are full of questions and curiosity, and they are relentless when set on the trail of something that they are interested in. Children and young people also have a deep and innate sense of justice, fairness, and equity. Our role then is not to point out to students what they don't know, or how to do something right, but to cultivate the habits and tendencies already inherent in children who are made to run, play, and learn.

## A Concluding Story From Angela

I am at the kitchen table. My children, a third grader in my own class and my younger first grader, come in. They are still acting out a game from outside. My youngest is using her accented speech that she uses for most of her pretend characters; it's a mix of her dad's heavy Mexican accent and the British of almost all the audio books we listen to.

"I will have your meal prepared soon, madam."
"Ok, and then I'll need to go out."
I ask what they are playing.
My younger pipes up. "Oh, we're playing Ancient Africa in Mali."
The third grader adds, "I'm not the Mansa, but I live in the palace and she's my servant."

We had studied Ancient through Medieval African kingdoms earlier in the year, a topic suggested and voted on by the students themselves. We learned lots of facts and geography and read and researched. All that straight academic work. Then we wrote a play. We talked a lot about multicultural-ism, and religions coexisting, and female militaries, and looking at history with modern bias, and slavery, and bicameral male/female governments, and plenty of other important topics. But as I watched my own children act out their game at the table, I thought about how important this project was to the students in our class and also to those who came to see our play. When our class references the Medieval time period the students don't first think knights and princesses. They think of the time of Mansa Musa and the librar-ies of Timbuktu. It is our historical reference point in a small group that is now learning about the Aztecs. And this, as I watch my kids in my dual role as teacher and parent, is what I am most proud of in our work together. We are not simply learning formulas and the "right" way to talk about injustice. We are not glossing over our doubts to make things easier or to get along. We are learning to see ourselves in other people, at other times, across differences.

I and my third graders are in ongoing conversation about all the sticky stuff that comes up, and we are able to dig deep in a way that, after a very short while, becomes so second nature that it's not just me modeling this mindset. The kids share their thoughts and critiques and questions every day. Through their play they are proving to me that we can break with academic canon and reshape our world. We took the most classic Eurocentrically taught time period possible—the Medieval period—and we shifted our center. These children started from Africa as their norm and saw how other cultures related to and differed from it. They will not always look at the world in comparison to Africa specifically, but they now have the understanding that our "norms" are constructed, and can be deconstructed. This internalized, non-performa-tive re-centering is true resistance that guides us toward being more humanly connected, and we did it with honesty and joy and genuine curiosity.

And much like for the mathematician, there is no end to understanding and learning here. We can solve a single equation, even a rather large, com-plex one without being "done." The highest end of mathematics becomes a form of philosophy. The individual skills (addition or multiplying fractions) and the sub-disciplines (algebra or geometry) only give way to an enhanced mathematical mindset, one able to further delve into inquiry at a more complex level. There are small victories that help us grow our social justice mindset and allow us to pick up specific and necessary skills, but only in the service of further inquiry. My children and students have not solved the problems of racism or the centering of the white experience, but they have begun to recognize and question those problems' existence. It is vital that we as teachers allow ourselves to celebrate small victories and their relevance while we continue to be critical and reflective. There is much work to be done.

## *Reference*

Boaler, J. (2015). *Mathematical mindsets: Unleashing students' potential through creative math, inspiring messages and innovative teaching.* San Francisco, CA: Jossey-Bass.

# 3. Challenging Misrecognitions Through Reflexive Teacher Education: Knowing and Growing in an Age of Commodification

NOAH ASHER GOLDEN

## Pulling Down the Veil

When I was a high school English teacher at Franz Fanon Academy[1] (FFA), my colleagues and I worked hard to recognize our students' strengths and accomplishments in an educational system that seemed designed to frame them as walking deficits. This framing is based on test scores, which can perhaps tell an educator what a student does not know or cannot yet do but often falls short when assessing what a person does know or can do. This way of measuring success and academic potential are particularly problematic for working class and poor young scholars of color, who are routinely denied educational opportunity and must contend with reductive stereotypes as they grow up in a society that routinely dehumanizes black and brown people. FFA is an alternative transfer high school designed for students who have not (yet) been successful in formal education. The stories that FFA students, the overwhelming majority of whom are students of color, would tell about why they chose to come to the school are as unique as each learner, but some common themes included the desire to attend smaller classes, to call teachers by their first names and feel valued by them, and to no longer be lost in the large urban, bureaucratic educational system within which FFA is situated.

One example of our attempts to honor students' strengths: our February graduation dinner. Our goal was to recognize these adolescent scholars' growth and contributions to our community, as these young people were often those assumed to be the ones who would not graduate. This recognition was an undertaking meant to counter the dominant perception that our students could not succeed in secondary or tertiary education, or that they could not support each other in determining their own life trajectories. We had a budget for a graduation each June, but given our students' non-traditional paths, many students met the criteria for graduation after the fall semester. These students were invited to wear the cap and gown at the commencement in June, but we wanted to honor them and all they had accomplished before then. For this reason, we had an annual winter graduation dinner, but with our commence-ment budget being what it was, we had to ask each graduate to contribute $40 to cover the costs of the dinner for themselves and their guests. We teachers would make a speech about the accomplishments of each graduate and share an anecdote or two about their contributions to the school community. The February Graduation Dinner was an event that highlighted the importance of relationships and connection in the educational processes of FFA.

During my fifth year as a teacher at FFA, one of my students, Rafael,[2] was on track to graduate in February but did not immediately have the money for the celebratory dinner. He shared that he did not want to have to ask his mother for the graduation funds, that he would be getting his paycheck for his part-time job the following week, that he wanted to feel like a grown man and invite his mother to his graduation dinner without having to ask her to pay for it. He asked if I would lend him the money, and I agreed. He prom-ised that he would have it to me the Friday following the dinner. The grad-uation dinner was beautiful, Rafael hosted his guests, including his mother, and the following Friday school day (which Rafael no longer attended as a graduate) came and went without my seeing him. I prepared for my bicycle commute home (and I should share that this was February in New York City, so heading home entailed changing into winter cycling gear, covering myself head to toe to ward off the cold). I trusted (and trust) Rafael implicitly, and knew that there must be a reason that he hadn't made it in time … and that reason was that he was running late.

As I walked outside into the frigid air, carrying my bike down the steps in front of the school, I heard Rafael shout my name from down the block, and break into a run. What happened next was the unsettling moment that shifted my thoughts on my teaching and, eventually, my role as a teacher educator. Rafael and I met a short distance from the front of the school, and he gave me a pound, a handshake/hug. When I pulled my hand away from his, in it were small bills, the $40 graduation dinner repayment, which I started to put in my front jacket pocket. Before I could thank him and crack a joke about his being down to the wire with his timing, just barely honoring his word to get the funds to me by Friday, a tan SUV pulled up alongside us. Two men got out of the vehicle and pushed us up against the wall demanding to know what was in my hand. I imagine that the men, who pulled their badges, hanging on chains from beneath their coats—and a moment later identified themselves as undercover detectives—thought that what they had observed could only have been the sale of illegal narcotics.

Amidst the shouted requests, I pulled the small bills from my pocket. I imagine the bundle of ones and fives confirmed the biases of the detectives. But their manner changed as soon as I pulled down my winter bicycle-commuting facemask, called the officer "sir," and spoke a dominant form of English. After asking if I had identification and if the school security agent just inside the school would verify that I was, indeed, a teacher, the officers vanished. They neither took the time to look at my ID, nor talk to the NYPD school safety agent. The detectives silently walked back into their vehicle and melted away.

This event—a harmless interaction between a high school graduate and his teacher being "misrecognized" as a drug deal—may be a regular occurrence for some readers, or something that has never happened for others. This kind of "misrecognition" is made possible, however, because how we read, relate to, recognize, or understand any interaction depends on our own social locations and lived experience—the positions we occupy as "readers" of text and experience (Freebody, Luke, & Gilbert, 1991). It is beyond doubt that my social location as a so-called[3] White person and my use of particular linguistic resources led to the immediate dismissal of any suspicion without verification. If I looked like Rafael, who is Garifuna,[4] or teacher colleagues who are of color, would the detectives have walked away without further questions, automatically assuming that I (and, by association, my former student Rafael) were upstanding citizens? This unsettling moment was an interaction that made me reflect on the work of philosopher John Rawls and his (1971/2009) notion of the veil of ignorance, the idea that a just society can be measured by whether justice is meted out without recognition of who is behind the veil. The shift in power, in position, the moment I pulled down my facemask brought to (my) life racial profiling and structured inequities in a way that the previous seven years of listening to my students had not. Experiencing the briefest of moments before Whiteness and class privilege protected me from discrimination and possible violence contributed to my learning as I worked to better hear and support my students.

## *Misrecognitions*

As much as any of us would wish to live in a society in which benign interactions are not misrecognized, with potentially severe consequences, we are far from that ideal. Some young people get to be seen as students who have strengths and may sometimes make mistakes; other people are positioned as deficient or perhaps deviant before they utter a word. Based on one's actual or perceived identity, basic human rights or dignity are proffered, withheld, or violated. This happens in life-or-death situations involving law enforcement as well as classrooms taught by well-intentioned people (like those of us who were teachers at FFA) from pre-kindergarten to graduate school. The extent to which a teacher or student realizes this depends on our/their own lived realities. After the unsettling moment in front of the school, I questioned what I had been taught (and had experienced) about how schooling and success work. I became more aware of what is for many people (though not for me) the everyday occurrence of being misrecognized in ways that can have significant material effects, including physical violence and death. This, for me, shattered myths about how our society works. These myths are still prevalent in our society, and include the myth of meritocracy and schooling as a surefire vehicle of social mobility, opportunity, and access.

Understanding misrecognition and the ways it interrupts opportunity is key for those of us who dare to take up the role of educator. By misrecognition, I mean two ways that opportunities for social participation are shaped, hindered, or shut down: (1) individual uses of designs are not recognized when used by marginalized people (Fraser, 2007); and, (2) the ways social fields are structured to value forms of capital that reproduce existing power relations (Bourdieu, 2000). An example of the first sort of misrecognition would be if Rafael had spoken to the undercover officers exactly the same way I had. Rafael is certainly capable of employing the same "designs," social or cultural tools, including linguistic ones, employed for a particular purpose, but they may not be read in the same way. When I call an officer "sir," it is likely heard (and, in fact, was heard in the incident described above) as an indicator that I am being respectful, that I am accustomed to being treated with respect by law enforcement officials, and so on. This way of being read is grounded in my social location as a so-called White, cisgendered, middle-class man. If Rafael called the undercover detective "sir," he may (as he later shared when we discussed this incident) have been accused of being "smart," or disrespectful to the officer. (Rafael and several peers, who are also of color, shared after the fact that, regardless of the energy they put forth, they experience negative treatment and are assumed guilty of something by law enforcement.) This process of misrecognizing obscures Rafael's full humanity, and requires him (and many other people) to have to constantly work to mitigate misrecognitions. No matter how Rafael chooses to present himself, dress, or speak (the fallacies of what are often termed "respectability politics"); he will be "read," or misrecognized, by many in our society based on his perceived racial, class, gender, or other identity.

Misrecognition also occurs in a second, broader sense: the linguistic tools that I employed, and that are related to my primary discourse (Gee, 2015), are in no way intrinsically better than any other code or dialect of English (or any other language for that matter). The linguistic forms that are valued in a social space carry the weight of history in the present; they are legacies and perpetuations of colonization, imperialism, and domination (Flores & Rosa, 2015). As a result, (some of) Rafael's literacy practices may not be valued in social spaces and positions he desires to enter or occupy. To work towards a society in which peoples' strengths and competencies will not be misrecognized, one must recognize the contingency of socially-constructed hierarchies of linguistic resources and literacies. As educators, it is important to enact a literacies education (and, as a literacy researcher and teacher educator, I understand all forms of education to be grounded in literacy, as will be explored in what follows) that not only provides access to literacies that may be considered desirable, but also critique the social systems, and circulations of power that ground current social arrangements. In doing this, we can acknowledge how schooling has been and remains part of and complicit in producing these systems. In what follows, I lay out the ways that teacher learning might engender such knowing and growing.

## *The Importance of Critical Literacy*

For the reasons referenced above, we need a critical literacies perspective. By literacy, I mean the reading and writing of texts, a social practice embedded within other social practices. We do not read or write in neutral isolation from the world; our literacies are always about doing something in the world (whether that be writing out a shopping list to assist us in the buying of groceries, writing a letter to a supervisor to request a cost-of-living raise, or some other text that serves some purpose). All disciplines and all levels involve literacy, as they all engage language and involve reading and writing in particular genres in disciplinary-specific ways. Here is where the "critical" comes in: teaching and learning can play a central role in de-naturalizing that which is considered to be natural, or rendering truths about our social worlds contingent—truths that are assumed to be necessary, fixed, or settled. By critical literacy, I mean the analysis and potential transformation of social processes involving representation, which include not only traditional and new reading and writing practices, but also the ways that people are misrecognized (i.e., written or read in negative or undesirable ways). The goal of education is not to produce students who only know what other people have done, or students who are subsumed by the weight of other people's knowledge (what Freire (1970/2007) has called the banking model of education), but to create the conditions for students to create new possibilities and representations, build knowledge themselves, and be and do things in the world beyond the classroom.

These critical literacies work in multiple disciplines and can take many forms. Education can be thought of as preparation for democratic civic participation (Garcia, Mirra, Morrell, Martinez, & D'Artagnan, 2015). Learners can be invited to study social issues in their own communities, and employ different disciplines to contribute to solutions. Rafael and his peers, for example, were invited by their Environmental Science teacher to study the ecology of the Bronx River, and, in collaboration with university researchers, utilized scientific instruments to contribute to data sets that monitored the health of the river. They then used these data to explore current environmental policies and associated health effects. This is an example of a place-based pedagogy (Comber, Thompson, & Wells, 2001) in which learning is not a series of decontextualized skills or abstract principles, but the building of toolkits to engage the world around us (Luke, 2013). Students like Rafael can be invited to take up and analyze issues that matter in their lives and communities (e.g., the assumption of criminality by law enforcement). This sort of critical literacy in action demonstrates adolescent scholars taking on new positions, participating in new practices, and questioning their social worlds. Developing these and other toolkits may help students experiencing marginalization to (re)position themselves when facing misrecognitions.

When engaging a critical literacies approach, it is important to recognize that not all of this work is born out of the classroom or the teacher. Rafael, like his peers and all other learners, comes to classroom learning with organic critical literacies (Campano, Ghiso, & Sánchez, 2013), modes of questioning outside of formal academic space, and there is much for us educators to learn from these funds of knowledge and experience (Golden, 2017a, 2017b). Broadening what counts as teaching and learning (i.e., the production of new knowledge and not simply the transmission of existing knowledge) is central to unsettling education, for this critical approach can align our work with the desires and needs of community members. But in order to take up these goals of critical literacies practice, it is necessary for us educators to engage our own responsibilities, and to critically examine the cultural stories surrounding our work and profession.

Both educators and students can engage the process of questioning current social arrangements, and wonder why (as examples) some schools have so much more funding than others, why some linguistic resources are valued in schools and others are often not, or why climate change is not accepted by many in our society despite abundant empirical evidence showing otherwise. Literacy is key here, as social arrangements are built, in part, through reading and writing and the force of interpretations and representations of reality. Students can be invited to take up powerful positions through a disciplinary literacies perspective (e.g., Moje, 2008; Smagorinsky, 2015), and do the work of historians or scientists rather than simply learn what past historians and scientists have done. Within these critical disciplinary literacies approaches, students can use the tools of each discipline (e.g., analysis of water quality in environmental science, or a reading of a primary source or historical artifact) as they evaluate and examine readings and representations of reality. In this way, students are invited to take on new social identities and participate in practices that, due to the weight of continuous misrecognitions, may be difficult for some learners to access. This is an important countering to continuing discourses that assert that certain careers or pathways are not for people "like them."

## *Our Responsibility as Educators*

Educators simply cannot subscribe to (sadly) still-prevalent views on the relationships between education, merit, and outcomes. The myth believed by many in our society is that where one ends up and what one achieves is simply a matter of effort. This account is a colossal misrecognition, one that persists because it validates what many would like to believe about how and why they occupy certain social positions. It is also a broad misrecognition with substantial consequences for our work. We know from decades of research (e.g., Anyon, 1981; Luke, 2009) that stark opportunity gaps and inequities shape outcomes when analyzing data in aggregate. The notion that minoritized[5] people are somehow to blame for the opportunity gaps they experience is the "culture of poverty" framing, the misguided sense that people experiencing economic poverty share a common culture that is grounded in deficit and causes material lacks (Gorski, 2012). A more generative framing is to understand our society in terms of systems that produce privilege and oppression, and to acknowledge the role that one's social location plays in educational access, outcomes, and ease with which one's talents are valued, recognized, or misrecognized within these social systems.

This is not to say that minoritized learners cannot and do not succeed; it is to say that they have to overcome much in order to do so. The current educational reform movement has seized on research investigating the role of low expectations in producing poor educational outcomes (e.g., Beady & Hansell, 1981), and focuses solely on the need for standards and an understanding of accountability that reduces what should be a multi-directional concept to high-stakes tests. What has been termed the "income achievement gap," that is, the correlation between family income and educational achievement, has only grown in the past three decades (Reardon, 2013). Reasons for this widening gap include growing inequality, diminishing access to mobility in a shifting economy, and the reduction of educational success to unitary measure such as high-stakes tests. Talking about these contributing factors, though, has been framed within the current educational reform movement as "the soft bigotry of low expectations" (Bush, 2000), an attempt to silence those who are, with significant empirical evidence, calling for needed changes beyond the classroom. Acknowledging the role of these multiple contributing factors is seen as taboo, or somehow construed as a belief that not all learners can achieve.

This political shift has occurred through a co-opting of the languages of critique and equity. In the 1970s, research on the importance of high expectations (e.g., Rist, 1970) demonstrated that a lack of belief in learner capability could contribute to poor educational outcomes. The current educational reform movement has seized on this important research but willfully ignored, and sought to delegitimize, bodies of empirical scholarship that investigate other significant contributing factors. It is easy to throw a test at educational inequities (and particularly easy when a test can create profit and new markets); it is far harder to distribute resources, access, and opportunity equitably. For these reasons, we see reform grounded in standards documents like the Common Core and accountability measures like high-stakes tests along with punitive measures for educational communities that do not demonstrate growth via these measures. These reforms avoid looking at the income achievement gap, and eschew analysis of the material and symbolic resources, social locations and positions, and access that are important contributing factors (along with merit and effort, though these are often vastly overemphasized) to success for those who experience it. Copies of books on "grit" and "growth mindset" continue to proliferate in teacher professional development spaces, offering convenient framings of why some students fail with easy answers for teacher praxis. This is not to say that hard work and belief in one's potential is not important, but to argue that there is nowhere near enough dialogue around the privileges of the few that are the flip side of the oppression of the many, and what this means regarding educational opportunity, attainment, and associated life paths. For readers who may doubt the existence of these processes and systems, I point to a statement by

Beverly Tatum: "it's hard to critique a system when it's working pretty well for you" (as quoted by Rich Milner, personal communication, March 22, 2015). Working for an educational system and broader society *not* grounded in such misrecognitions means critiquing the privileging of the few at the expense of the many in terms of access and resources. As Hilary Janks has said, "social justice means something different when you have to give something up" (personal communication, IFTE/CEE July 7, 2015).

The current educational reform movement avoids these analyses by design, a gross misrecognition. The reality is that these approaches to reform have not worked to significantly improve outcomes, and there is no reason to believe that they will start working through continued repetition. We have had decades of experimentation with new standards documents and testing and they have not lead to significantly better outcomes (Luke, 2009). School reform has indeed "failed the test" (Rose, 2015). Unsettling education means that we need new generations of educators to understand how and why we have the outcomes we have, and what we can do to create meaningful opportunity through education. The key to understanding why misrecognition in the form of a simplistic school reform persists is in the politics. In the 1960s, there was a genuine attempt to understand and address the gross inequalities in school funding and other social systems that were (and continue to be) grounded in race and class in our society. The Great Society reforms were an initial step to addressing funding inequities and creating social programs that offered opportunities to those who were not already receiving materials benefits from social arrangements.

As I have written elsewhere (Golden, 2017c), these reforms acknowledged the importance of the inputs, financial and otherwise, to public education and related social systems. The political winds of the 1980s brought a hyper-focus on outputs, and accountability for these outputs. This continues in the current educational reform movement, in which accountability is only one-way. There is little discussion of accountability to learners and communities in terms of providing the necessary resources and opportunities to achieve excellence. This is what Gloria Ladson-Billings (2006a) writes of the "education debt" owed many learners. To fulfill this education debt and create greater opportunities, we need to work for an educational system and society in which people's strengths and talents are not misrecognized, but valued, supported, and enriched. For this reason, our current educational and life trajectory outcomes are better understood as an "opportunity gap" rather than an "achievement gap." If we are serious about supporting all students, we need to recognize that lack of meaningful opportunity shapes outcome data far more than any lack of drive, determination, or growth. Data tell a story, and a far more generative narrative to build from current outcome data is that we need to work to create opportunities for all learners.

So, my unsettling moment leads me to argue this: our responsibility as educators involves an awareness that much more is needed for educational opportunity than standards documents and high-stakes tests. While high expectations for all learners and accountability for educational communities are undoubtedly a piece of the puzzle, there are broader analyses that must ground our reform. Our responsibility as educators means that we need to work to create the conditions for excellence in multiple temporalities, including short-term needs, medium-range approaches, and long-term activism. Short-term needs might be the creation of lessons and units for tomorrow morning's class, the building of engaging co-produced critical literacy activities that ground learning in local communities and knowledges. Medium-range approaches might be collaborative work to create new democratic practices or restorative justice policies in a school. And long-term activism might include the fight for more equitable funding streams, new understandings of student or family rights, and better ways of assessing learners that acknowledge, value and sustain community and cultural ways of knowing and being. Long-term activism also requires the awareness that schooling alone cannot be the great equalizer in a grossly inequitable society in the way it is often assumed to be, and that we have a responsibility to fight to make other social systems (e.g., health care, housing, etc.) equitable as well. Each of these involve challenging misrecognitions through civic engagement and the building of knowledge.

## *Positionality and Responsibility as Educators*

If we accept as a premise that so much of where students end up is due to opportunity gaps and education debt rather than an "achievement gap," and that these inequalities are largely grounded in misrecognitions associated with race and class, then we have engendered an ethical responsibility to go beyond the preparing of learners for high-stakes tests or the skill sets needed to write an essay (though these are undoubtedly necessary endeavors; they are simply insufficient for the sorts of social transformations we need to work towards). We educators have a choice: we can continue and deepen existing misrecognitions at multiple levels, or we can actively work to dismantle them.

When thinking through our axiological responsibilities as educators, it is important to reflect on our own positionality as well. As my unsettling moment shows, our social locations reflect and engender our experiences and knowledge in relation to systems of privilege and oppression. They can obscure the lived realities of people with different social locations, making us either complicit or actively engaged with the misrecognitions of other people or their social worlds. Beyond this, though, is the important realization that our social locations shape the ways we engage our work for meaningful and equitable education and other social systems. Our own racial, class, gender, and other identities position us in relation to the work of social transformation, and there are times when we educators have the responsibility to step up and lead, and times when we need to sit and listen.

Let me share a story that highlights my emerging thinking about these issues. Several years ago, I attended a talk given by Ruth Wilson Gilmore on her research on racial capitalism and the prison system. She detailed the ways that capitalism requires inequality and the impacts of this on criminalization and mass incarceration (Gilmore, 2007). After discussing the relationships between capitalism, racism, and inequality, she took questions from the audience. A woman, so-called White like me, stepped to the microphone and posed the questions: "What can we in the White community do about these issues? What is being done in the Black community, and how can White people get involved?" The implication was that these are "Black issues," that the locus of solutions to these problems was the Black community. Well-intentioned White people, sensitive to issues of race, the thinking might go, should be sensitive to issues of race and follow the lead of Black folks and other people of color.

Ruth responded with something along the lines of: "These aren't issues located in the Black community; these are things being done to people of color overwhelmingly by White people. What do *you* think needs to be done about it? What are *you* going to do with the research I have just shared with you?"

I share this vignette not to denigrate the questioner, for I am certain that I have posed similar questions and made similar statements. I share it as preamble to an exploration of how we educators reflect on what our role is in justice-oriented work. If we educators must get involved with (messy) justice-oriented work beyond the classroom, we need to be reflexive so that we can think through where, when, and how we might advocate with our students, or engage in activism to work for social transformation. In my case, as a former secondary-level educator who is identified as White and worked with learners of color, many of whom were experiencing poverty, I needed to (and need to) know when to stay in my lane and when to step up and try to engage or lead on an issue. Having said that, there is a tendency (as evidenced by the above vignette) to see issues of race and class as important only for those people experiencing negative outcomes related to them. How might we be reflexive in this way, and work to mitigate misrecognitions in and beyond our classrooms?

Regardless of our various identities and social locations, there is a need for us to learn with and from our students so that we can work *with* the communities we serve. There will be times when this means being leaders in our own communities, and times when this means that we have to listen and learn from those with different life experience. We need to recognize that this work is a choice for some of us and a matter of survival for others. For those of us, who are, like me, identified as White, there is a need to critically examine our own identities so that we do not make this work all about us. This can happen if Whiteness is seen as normative or culturally-responsive and sustaining pedagogies are enacted in limiting ways that effectively maintain the status quo (Alim & Paris, 2014; Matias, 2013). When teachers do come from the communities they serve, they may have first-hand experience and knowledge of these issues. The reality of our current teaching force, though, is that misrecognitions grounded in race and class are not the daily lived reality for most teachers—though many teachers' lack of awareness may lead to them enacting misrecognitions. Recent studies show that 82% of all educators and 80% of all administrators are White (though educator diversity is slowly rising), while 49% of America's students are of color (U.S. DoE, 2016, pp. 3–6). Contrary to the widespread belief that post-Civil Rights desegregation efforts led to expanded opportunity for students and teachers of color, there were severe setbacks, particularly for the then-growing middle-class of Black students, teachers, and administrators (hooks, 2003). America's schools continue to be segregated, particularly for Black and Latinx students (Orfield, Ee, Frankenberg, & Siegel-Hawley, 2016). Gloria Ladson-Billing commented in 2009 that she would prefer a "real Plessy to a fake Brown," meaning that separate schooling systems that are truly equal would be preferable to de facto segregation and continuing inequities. Despite the reality of hate being on the rise (Center for Hate and Extremism, 2017), popular discourses locating all class bias and racism in the past continue to be perpetuated. While we need to diversify the teaching workforce, this cannot be seen as a panacea (Pabon, 2016), and additional social transformations are needed so that learners' strengths are not misrecognized. In short, educators of all identities and experiences would do well to consider moving from allies of learners, understood as people who stand with others, to accomplices *with* learners, understood as people who work to dismantle the structures and processes that create inequalities and inequities (Clemens, 2017). How might all educators engage this work?

## *The Knowing and Growing We Need*

It is helpful to recognize that we live, and work, in an age of commodification. Teaching and learning are often reduced to commodities within neoliberal education reform, with effects that reduce and limit what it is to learn. Neoliberalism can be understood as "a theory of political economic practices that proposes that human well-being can best be advanced by liberating individual entrepreneurial freedoms and skills," and operates through a framework that "seeks to bring all human action into the domain of the market" (Harvey, 2005, p. 2). This makes our work of challenging misrecognitions and transforming opportunity structures that much more difficult, as educators' roles within this "marketplace" are widely understood to be only concerning the transmission of a set of skills and competencies that allow students to participate in the knowledge economy labor market (Brass, 2015). To challenge misrecognitions of people, including Rafael and other students positioned in similar ways, we need to both know and grow in our work.

Paulo Freire distinguished between knowing and growing in a way that is invaluable. He wrote that knowing is the result of our mundane, conscious moving throughout the world but also our reflection on lived experience. Growing, though, goes beyond these two forms of knowing: growing entails "an object of our restlessness, of our epistemological curiosity … growing is a process in which we can intervene" (Freire, 2005, pp. 168–169). This is not the knowing of the natural world, but a deeper way of recognizing that, while "we are indisputably programmed beings … we are in no way predetermined" (p. 169). We educators need to embrace the unsettling moments that help us to grow in these ways. My unsettling moment leads me to argue that, through critical reflection and engagement, we can and must grow in ways that will make us better teachers, people, and accomplices as we challenge social arrangements that misrecognize the strengths and talents of so many people.

This requires an ongoing and dialogic teacher education practice that can catalyze knowing into a necessary, reflexive growing. Rather than service learning or student teaching opportunities grounded in colonial and deficit-oriented frameworks (Cann & McCloskey, 2017; Rost-Banik, 2018), the goal in our work as educators must be to create generative dialogue across contexts. If we ground our growing in listening with the communities we serve (Kinloch, Larson, Orellana, & Lewis, 2016), we have the possibility of stepping outside of reductive framings of success and opportunity to learn ourselves to value multiple funds of knowledge. Indeed, Gloria Ladson-Billings has argued that the first thing future educators might do is spend time in spaces where young people are successful outside of school (2006b). So much of our work as educators is predicated upon the belief that learners are deficit-laden or "damaged" (Tuck, 2009), and that our role is to "fix" them. Regardless of whatever credentials or licenses we hold, continuing on a path of knowing can engender further growing through racial literacy (Sealey-Ruiz, 2011), challenging pre-existing biases (Kirkland, 2014), and working to build cultural competence to value and recognize learner strengths (Milner, 2011).

My unsettling moment led me to reflect on my own social location and that of Rafael (and my other students) in ways that made me a more responsive teacher and teacher educator. I encourage you to do the same as you work to unsettle education and reflect on your relationships with students and your teaching/learning praxis by engaging the following questions:

- In what ways are you recognized or misrecognized?
- What obstacles or challenges have you had to overcome, or perhaps are in the process of navigating? In what ways are these similar to or different from those of your students?
- How has opportunity played a role in your successes and growth? How is this similar to or different from your students?
- How are your students positioned in your/a classroom, school, or broader society? Do these positionings involve misrecognitions? How so?
- How might listening to and with students help you to learn how they, as individuals and as members of perceived groups, experience the world? How might this knowledge help you to create and enact meaningful learning projects?

To challenge the misrecognition of people in our society, we educators must continue being curious to know, and expand this knowledge so that we can grow. This unsettling of education can allow us to work with our students to challenge the misrecognitions that can shape opportunities and outcomes.

## Notes

1. This name is a pseudonym.
2. This, too, is a pseudonym, and this narrative is shared with Rafael's permission.
3. I say "so-called" to in no way deny the extremely problematic benefits and privileges of Whiteness, but to highlight the constructed nature of these benefits and privileges, which are grounded in social arrangements that can and must be changed. My decision to describe myself in this way is indebted to personal communication with Dr. Johnny Eric Williams in April 2018.
4. Garifuna people are the descendants of West African, Central African, Island Carib, European, and Arawak people. Many Garifuna people live in Central America, including Honduras, where Rafael spent his childhood before coming to the United States.
5. I say "minoritized" to call attention to the fact that social processes and arrangements create majority and minority communities.

# References

Alim, H. S., & Paris, D. (2014). What are we seeking to sustain through culturally sustaining pedagogy? A loving critique forward. *Harvard Educational Review, 84*, 85–100.

Anyon, J. (1981). Social class and school knowledge. *Curriculum Inquiry, 11*, 3–42.

Beady, C., & Hansell, S. (1981). Teacher race and expectations for student achievement. *American Educational Research Journal, 18*(2), 191–206.

Bourdieu, P. (2000). *Pascalian meditations.* Palo Alto, CA: Stanford University Press.

Brass, J. (2015). Standards-based governance of English teaching past, present, and future? *English Teaching: Practice and Critique, 14*(3), 241–259.

Bush, G. W. (2000). *Soft bigotry quote.* Retrieved from https://www.c-span.org/video/?c4629748/soft-bigotry-quote

Campano, G., Ghiso, M., & Sánchez, L. (2013). "Nobody knows the … amount of a person": Elementary students critiquing dehumanization through organic critical literacies. *Research in the Teaching of English, 48*, 98–125.

Cann, C., & McCloskey, E. (2017). The poverty pimpin' project: How whiteness profits from black and brown bodies in community service programs. *Race, Ethnicity, & Education, 20*, 72–86.

Center for Hate and Extremism. (2017). Hate crime analysis and forecast for 2016/2017. Retrieved from https://csbs.csusb.edu/sites/csusb_csbs/files/Final%20Hate%20Crime%2017%20Status%20Report%20pdf.pdf

Clemens, C. (2017). Ally or accomplice? The language of activism. Retrieved from https://www.tolerance.org/magazine/ally-or-accomplice-the-language-of-activism

Comber, B., Thompson, P., & Wells, M. (2001). Critical literacy finds a "place": Writing and social action in a grade 2/3 classroom. *The Elementary School Journal, 101*(4), 451–464.

Flores, N., & Rosa, J. (2015). Undoing appropriateness: Raciolinguistic ideologies and language diversity in education. *Harvard Educational Review, 85*(2), 149–171.

Fraser, N. (2007). Reframing justice in a globalizing world. In D. Held & A. Kaya (Eds.), *Global inequality: Patterns and explanations* (pp. 252–272). Malden, MA: Polity Press.

Fraser, N. (1999). Social justice in the age of identity politics: Redistribution, recognition, and participation. In L. Ray & A. Sayer (Eds.), *Culture and economy after the cultural turn* (pp. 25–52). Thousand Oaks, CA: Sage.

Freebody, P., Luke, A., & Gilbert, P. (1991). Reading positions and practices in the classroom. *Curriculum Inquiry, 21*(4), 435–457.

Freire, P. (2005). *Teachers as cultural workers: Letters to those who dare teach.* Boulder, CO: Westview Press.

Freire, P. (1970/2000). *Pedagogy of the oppressed.* (30th Anniversary Edition). New York, NY: Continuum.

Garcia, A., Mirra, N., Morrell, E., Martinez, A., & D'Artagnan, S. (2015). The council of youth research: Critical literacy and civic agency in the digital age. *Reading & Writing Quarterly, 31*(2), 151–167.

Gee, J. P. (2015). *Social linguistics and literacies: Ideology in discourses.* New York, NY: Routledge.

Gilmore, R. W. (2007). *Golden gulag: Prisons, surplus, crisis, and opposition in globalizing California.* Berkeley, CA: University of California Press. Golden, N. A. (2017a). "In a position I see myself in": (Re)positioning identities and culturally-responsive pedagogies. *Equity & Excellence in Education, 50*(4), 355–367.

Golden, N. A. (2017b). There's still that window that's open: The problem with "Grit." *Urban Education, 52,* 343–369.

Golden, N. A. (2017c). (Re)framing education for equity: Acknowledging outputs and inputs in literacies education. *English Journal, 106*(4), 86–88.

Gorski, P. (2012). Perceiving the problem of poverty and schooling: Deconstructing the class stereotypes that misshape education policy and practice. *Equity & Excellence in Education, 45*(2), 302–319.

Harvey, D. (2005). Spaces of Neoliberalization: Towards a Theory of Uneven Geographical Development: Hettner-Lecture 2004 with David Harvey (Vol. 8). Franz Steiner Verlag. Retrieved from http://books.google.com/books?hl=en&lr=&id=Z7sS53uq-TJoC&oi=fnd&pg=PA3&dq=harvey,+david+2004+neoliberalism&ots=JEAmr HBe7-&sig=IUOzikc-t__UU3LmtR6qh4dCjTc

hooks, b. (2003). *Teaching to transgress: Education as the practice of freedom.* New York, NY: Routledge.

Kinloch, V., Larson, J., Orellana, M. F., & Lewis, C. (2016). Literacy, equity, and imagination researching with/in communities. *Literacy Research: Theory, Method, and Practice, 65,* 94–112.

Kirkland, D. E. (2014). "They look scared": Moving from service learning to learning to serve in teacher education—A social justice perspective. *Equity & Excellence in Education, 47*(4), 580–603.

Ladson-Billings, G. (2006a). From the achievement gap to the education debt: Understanding achievement in U.S. schools. *Educational Researcher, 35*(7), 3–12.

Ladson-Billings, G. (2006b). It's not the culture of poverty, it's the poverty of culture: The problem with teacher education. *Anthropology & Education Quarterly, 37*(2), 104–109.

Ladson-Billings, G. (2009). *The dreamkeepers: Successful teachers of African American children.* Hoboken, NJ: Wiley & Sons.

Luke, A. (2009). Documenting reproduction and inequality: Revisiting Jean Anyon's "social class and school knowledge." *Curriculum Inquiry, 40,* 167–182.

Luke, A. (2013). Regrounding critical literacy: Representation, facts and reality. In M. Hawkins (Ed.), *Framing languages and literacies: Socially situated views and perspectives* (pp. 136–148). New York, NY: Routledge.

Matias, C. E. (2013). Check yo'self before you wreck yo'self and our kids: Counterstories from culturally responsive white teachers? ... to culturally responsive white teachers! *Interdisciplinary Journal of Teaching and Learning, 3*(2), 68–81.

Milner, H. R. (2011). Culturally relevant pedagogy in a diverse urban classroom. *The Urban Review, 43,* 66–89.

Moje, E. B. (2008). Foregrounding the disciplines in secondary literacy teaching and learning: A call for change. *Journal of Adolescent & Adult Literacy, 52*(2), 96–107.

Orfield, G., Ee, J., Frankenberg, E., & Siegel-Hawley, G. (2016). Brown at 62: School Segregation by race, poverty, and state. *UCLA Civil Rights Project.* Retrieved from https://www.civilrightsproject.ucla.edu/research/k-12-education/integration-and-diversity/brown-at-62-school-segregation-by-race-poverty-and-state/Brown-at-62-final-corrected-2.pdf

Pabon, A. (2016). Waiting for black superman: A look at a problematic assumption. *Urban Education, 51*(8), 915–939.

Rawls, J. (1971–2009). *A theory of justice.* Cambridge, MA: Belknap Press.

Reardon, S. (2013). The widening income-achievement gap. *Educational Leadership, 70*(8), 10–16.

Rist, R. (1970). Student social class and teacher expectations: The self-fulfilling prophecy in ghetto education. *Harvard Education Review, 70*(3), 257–301.

Rose, M. (2015). School reform fails the test. *The American Scholar,* 18–30. Retrieved from https://theamericanscholar.org/school-reform-fails-the-test/#.XFE7HRLhXIU

Rost-Banik. C. (2018). Racial melancholia: The post/colonial work of service-learning. In T. Mitchell & K. Soria (Eds.), *Educating for citizenship and social justice* (pp. 113–125). Basingstoke, UK: Palgrave Macmillan.

Sealey-Ruiz, Y. (2011). Dismantling the school-to-prison pipeline through racial literacy development in teacher education. *Journal of Curriculum and Pedagogy, 8*(2), 116–120.

Smagorinsky, P. (2015). Disciplinary literacy in the English Language Arts. *Journal of Adolescent & Adult Literacy, 59*(2), 141–146.

Tuck, E. (2009). Suspending damage: A letter to communities. *Harvard Educational Review, 79*(3), 409–428.

United States Department of Education (2016). The state of racial diversity in the educator workforce. Retrieved from https://www2.ed.gov/rschstat/eval/highered/racial-diversity/state-racial-diversity-workforce.pdf

# Section II

# Pedagogies of Resistance

# *Introduction*

Edward Said (1996) says that the role of the intellectual is to challenge the status quo, to upend prevailing orthodoxy, and to be wary of received dogma. In this section of the book, the authors not only challenge orthodoxies, but also expose the contradictions embedded in official ways of knowing and doing in our schools. Revealing and then facing these contradictions helps shape the way that these teachers resist official policy pronouncements about the role of educators, students, and the purposes of educational institutions. At the heart of this resistance is a belief in the ability of educators to clarify, question, and then challenge the limits of official mandates—mandates developed and foisted upon educators by outside authorities. The stories that follow show us ways that we can recognize the full humanity of our students and resist the pressure to succumb to processes and procedures that reduce students to a set of numbers or a score on an exam. At the same time, these stories show us the limits of individual actors and the need for broad coalitions in order to reinvigorate a commitment to the public good. How, then, can teachers find ways to be bold and ask questions about the received wisdom in our institutions, particularly when that supposed wisdom pushes us away from notions of community toward an embrace of hyper-individualism? The authors in this section take up these questions in different ways and examine what it means to challenge and resist such dogma in the work they do.

Henry Giroux (2001) notes that resistance pedagogy gives us a way to examine the everyday practices in schools and universities in order to make them strange—to queer them up in ways that reveal the social relations they too often conceal. In other words, a pedagogy of resistance takes the basic assumptions that structure the day-to-day work of schooling and then exposes the institutional rationality that supports these often oppressive frameworks. The role of the teacher, then, is not simply to resist these frameworks, but

rather to be bold and to take risks in the classroom by exposing the contradictions we encounter. This risk taking involves examining our work in
schools in ways that help our students better understand how ways of knowing, doing, and being are produced, enforced, legitimated, and contested
through schooling. Of equal importance, perhaps, it means revealing the connections between our schools and the political, social, and economic realities
that shape how we understand our place in the world.

In her chapter, Sarah Donovan shares the moment in her teaching when
she says, "I thought back to all the other books I had taught with this narrow
packet-based approach, all the student-written essays I had labeled right or
wrong, all the conversations I had dismissed with a swipe of a pen, all the
complexities I had reduced to something neat and measurable." The epiph-
any Donovan describes here leads her to other realizations, and, perhaps, of
equal importance, to a surprising change in her practice. Interestingly, Donovan's insight occurs while she's teaching a unit on genocide. It's during this
unit that Donovan sees most clearly the horror that is made possible when
we reduce people to numbers. She notes that "the way state mandates are
written and implemented in schools carries on the collective desire of state
systems to make things legible by reducing ideas and people to that which
can be quantified, checked-off, covered." As teachers, we are made complicit
in this process of dehumanization. But, through her refusal to reduce students to numbers or grades, Donovan also offers us a chance at redemption.
She shares with us the importance of the human interaction between student
and teacher—an interaction that defies measurement or quantification. Donovan reminds us that "a live encounter invites transformation—not standardization—of both teacher and student because the outcome is unknown and
open to becoming."

In the next chapter in this section, Matt Homrich-Knieling and Alex Corbitt, teaching in Detroit and the Bronx respectively, share with us some of the
challenges they faced when teaching for justice—challenges brought on by
"the disempowering impacts of education policy that pushes schools to prioritize standardization and test preparation over creativity and inquiry." However, Homrich-Knieling and Corbitt don't give up. They continue to resist
the disempowering impacts of education policy, and they find "strength and
direction by collaborating with each other, listening to [their] communities,
and reflecting on the work of many esteemed educators, particularly educators
of color." The authors share their process of un-learning—a process that takes
place for them when they are willing to listen to their colleagues of color—that
leads them to recognize that in order to center and see the full humanity of
students, teachers must be radically de-centered. For the authors, this work

involves embracing a pedagogy of healing while seeking out new avenues for student and teacher agency. These two authors also grapple with the contradictions that emerge from who they are and where they work. They note that as "White cis-men who are not from the communities of color in which we teach, we are constantly negotiating how to employ justice-oriented pedagogies that do not reproduce oppressive dynamics and unconscious biases." Rather than providing easy answers, the authors remind us through their stories that tension, complexity, and paradox saturate our work.

Mikela Bjork, in her essay about the hidden curriculum of compulsory heteronormativity, explores teacher and student resistance through stories about schooling. While the stories in this chapter are about schooling, they are also about what happens to us in school. Or, more precisely, the stories in this chapter explore what schools do to those who do not fit into dominant frameworks. Bjork's chapter encourages us to confront questions about how schools traumatize queer students and to see how "queer women in AA come to understand themselves through their schooling stories of resistance, so that [we] might glean from firsthand experiences how to educate and proactively support young women and girls of varying class, race and ethnic backgrounds." The stories of the women in this chapter call out to us to change how we organize our schools—to open safe spaces for different ways of knowing, doing, and being.

Bjork outlines for us how "the institution of heterosexuality is alive and thriving in schools" and also reminds us that our schools "are populated with more and more students who do not relate or identify with the gendered boundaries with which they are positioned." The chapter challenges teachers to confront the trauma caused by the hidden (and not so hidden) mandates of compulsory heteronormativity. Once confronted, teachers might better see and understand their own complicity in the oppression of queer students. This, in turn, may lead all of us to use our privileged positions in schools to become better allies and accomplices working for justice alongside our students. Developing these new networks of resistance can help teachers to see their work differently and take up new positions in schools to create space at the center for all students.

Each of these authors in this section, in their embrace of different pedagogies of resistance, seeks to decolonize educational spaces from market-driven mandates and to rehumanize the work of teaching for both teachers and students. These authors remind us that as educators we are locked in a political fight to resist dehumanizing mandates and to define our work in our own terms, including our working conditions and what's worth knowing and doing with students. This fight involves more than creating better standardized tests, or increasing motivation, or improving teachers; it involves actively challenging oppressive structures and supporting the rights of our most marginalized community members; it means taking back control and determining what "doing well in school" means; and it means working with others to best leverage the resources of our communities in ways that honor the knowledge, diversity, and aspirations of students and families. Resistance, these authors show, often starts with an individual teacher in a classroom, but they remind us, too, that resistance is always and already outward looking, seeking connections to others and to social movements for a more just and sustainable world.

## *References*

Giroux, H. A. (2001). *Theory and resistance in education: Towards a pedagogy for the opposition.* Westport, CT: Bergin & Garvey.

Said, E. W. (1996). *Representations of the intellectual.* New York, NY: Vintage Books, a division of Random House.

# 4. *Beyond Mandates and Measurement: Imagining a Gradeless Classroom*

Sarah J. Donovan

In 2005, after my first year teaching junior high English, Illinois passed a mandate to expand the required Holocaust unit to include other acts of genocide. Like most new teachers, I turned to colleagues for help, but found very few knew much about genocide beyond the Holocaust, so I began researching and reading genocide literature appropriate for junior high readers.

The first book I found was *Tree Girl* by Ben Mikaelsen about the genocide of nearly 200,000 Maya in Guatemala in the early 1980s. I bought a class set with my own money eager to "meet" the standard and further explore this atrocity alongside students. I approached this reading the way our English department had taught the Holocaust unit, mandated in the early 90s: with a packet of guiding questions, discussions, quizzes, research, and a multiple-choice/short-answer final exam.

As we read *Tree Girl*, students filled out the packet, which I used to assess their reading. I marked wrong answers with a slash; I awarded right answers with a smiley face or a "Good job!" I continued like this until we got to chapter five, when the main character, fifteen-year-old Gabriela Flores, witnessed a massacre. The graphic nature of the scene prompted a discussion about the "truth" of this event and how Mikaelsen, the author, had access to the facts. Students wanted to know what *really* happened. We discussed how much "truth" was necessary in a young adult novel, and we discussed why, if the novel is based on a true story, did the real Gabriela Flores not write her story for us. The "answers" we uncovered did not fit neatly into the blanks and spaces on that packet. The answers were neither right nor wrong. The process of uncovering *was* the learning.

I was in over my head and incredibly uncomfortable being in this position of ignorance, unable to speak with any authority about "what" happened in Guatemala. Clearly, I should have studied more about how to approach genocide literature rather than simply seek out titles, but there was something about not knowing, not having answers that shifted my perception of "teacher" as a co-learner, as an inquiry partner of students.

I thought back to all the other books I had taught with this narrow packet-based approach, all the student-written essays I had labeled right or wrong, all the conversations I had dismissed with a swipe of a pen, all the complexities I had reduced to something neat and measurable. Implicit in this approach was the reduction of people to numbers, the reduction of ideas to "right" or "wrong." The way state mandates are written and implemented in schools carries on the collective desire of state systems to make things legible by reducing ideas and people to that which can be quantified, checked-off, covered. Indeed, this is most clear when we look at genocide education. To teach about genocide means to call attention to (1) the question of how much power a state should have; (2) the responsibility to prioritize human concerns over political and economic ones; and (3) the way that each institution contributes to the development of a nation. If schools contribute to the development of our nation, what is that contribution if schools consistently reduce human complexity to neat, quantifiable measures? Specifically, labeling and sorting students by test scores and grades perpetuates a system of conflating learning into symbols and students into easily sorted and ranked tokens within the system.

To know *about* is one way of knowing, but to uncover, confront, and question in the classroom is something quite different. This insight led me to spend the next decade researching and writing about genocide instruction in *Genocide Literature in Middle and Secondary Classrooms: Rhetoric, Witnessing, and Social Action in a Time of Standards and Accountability* (2017). And what I learned is that what we do in English language arts (ELA) classrooms when we read literature of times and places within and beyond our own is to bear witness to lives represented. Students and teachers have to be literate in how stories represent humanity in all its forms, and that does require certain skills (e.g., summarizing, citing text evidence), but reading also requires a certain stance—one of responsibility for understanding how narratives are constructed and what one is to do with new literacy experiences. An ethical reading stance does require understanding plot structure, but it also takes into account who is telling the story, how it is written, and why. Again, this defies neat methods of assessment and grading, yet so many of our classrooms continue to measure learning by points and percentages even when the content, like genocide and other literature of human rights violations, critiques systems of categories.

To sit alongside a student as she is reading and say, "Tell me about what you are reading. What do you think about it?" is different from standing in front of the class and saying, "Write your name on this worksheet, answer these questions, and turn it in. It is worth 10 points." The identity of the teacher—one who knows, who assigns, who grades—is superfluous in the first encounter. In the learning conversation, the teacher is careful not to coerce the student into saying what the teacher wants. When a student has misunderstood a key component or skill, what do we do? Subtract points, cross out the error, write "awkward" or "do over"? That is easier. That is controlled. That is standardized because it minimizes diversity, marginalizing the students' individuality and humanity in the process. A live encounter invites transformation—not standardization—of both teacher and student because the outcome is unknown and open to becoming. And isn't learning about becoming?

The experience of trying to meet a mandate about genocide education illuminated for me not only the failed promise of "never again" and the gaps in my education, it confronted me with the discrepancy between *what* we read in ELA and *how* we assess and evaluate reading.

Traditional grading practices undermine authentic learning and constrain the relationships among and across content, students, teachers, parents, and the school. A rubric is a neat table for measuring success on an argument essay. A letter grade conflates a semester of learning to one letter. How can teachers align the complexity of the content to evaluation practices (i.e., resist conflation), so that conversations about learning processes and outcome are as rich as the reading and writing experiences?

This chapter tells the story of what I learned when I stopped putting points and letter grades on every assignment and made space for more conversations about what we were learning and why. The year that I committed to aligning *what* I teach with *how* I assessed and evaluated learning. I will show how I tried to minimize grading in order to subvert discourses of measurement and shift evaluation toward assessment, a distinction that is essential if we are to nurture in students an appreciation for and understanding of English that embraces discovery and self-discovery. Shifting my evaluation practices has prompted a shift not necessarily in *what* I teach, as I am mandated to follow the state standards, but certainly *how* I teach and *how* I organize the use of class time, homework, and the process of coming to the required term grade has shifted dramatically. The changes have not only impacted how students think about reading, writing, and grades, but also the culture of the classroom.

## *Imagining a Gradeless Classroom*

It began at the end. It was the final month of the school year. Our suburban junior high of close to a thousand students was facing a long list of students with low GPAs, in danger of not graduating. The time and energy spent in meetings and over emails talking about low-GPA students was staggering, and while the list lead to conversations about often-marginalized students, the conversations also pointed out problems with grading practices: zeros, homework, late work, rubrics, and absences. While our school district had outlined grading policies, teachers weighted assignments differently; some teachers offered extra credit while others did not, and accepting late work was up to the discretion of teachers. Instead of talking about what students learned, we were arguing about points and percentages. I wondered what would happen if we eliminated grades:

- What would motivate students?
- What force would move them to "comply"?
- Could we get them beyond compliance toward involvement?
- How would they then celebrate and be celebrated?
- What might they discover about themselves, learning, school, and the world?
- How might the conversations among teachers and administrators change?

Clearly, these are broad questions, and eliminating grades is a great undertaking, requiring cooperation from many teachers and administrators, but I wanted to propose a "no grade classroom" to pilot for the next school year.

Of course, many teachers in our school already resist grades by not putting a grade on everything, by doing more conferencing, by weighting results over process in their grade book. However, I wanted to be more explicit by removing zeros, resisting points for assignments, and stopping the ranking of assignments according to letters. I was not sure what I would say when a student asked "how many points is this worth" or "will you take points off if it's late." I wanted those moments to prompt a conversation. What would replace numbers and letters? What was our purpose? Why is this worth doing? How would we prove learning?

## Preparing for the Pilot: Research on Grading

The first step was to write a pilot proposal for my principal. My principal was open to the idea, but I would have to give a final grade on the report card if I could develop a plan for assessing learning between grading periods.

Why pilot a year without grades when it is not school policy or when we still have to enter midterms and report card grades? In *Assessment 3.0*, Barnes (2015) writes, "You just do it because our greatest responsibility is to kids" (p. 6). Perhaps the teacher next door will use grades, and it is likely that the teacher in the next grade will use grades, but it is not a good enough reason to abandon what is "right" for the human beings with whom we are entrusted. Barnes suggests grades "stunt" the growth of our students. Even if we provide narrative feedback, if we also assign a grade, "students ignore comments when marks are also given" (p. 19), which is what I found in my own experiences.

According to Tomlinson and Moon (2013) in *Assessment and Students Success in a Differentiated Classroom*:

> [A grade] misrepresents the learning process to students leading them to conclude that making errors is cause for punishment rather than an opportunity to improve. Second, it focuses students more on getting good grades than on learning. Third, it makes the classroom environment seem unsafe for many students—and would make it seem unsafe to more students if classwork were appropriately challenging for the full range of learners. (p. 62)

In other words, grades distract students from exploring what is valuable. Daniel Pink in *Drive* (2011) writes, "Good grades are a reward for compliance but don't have much to do with learning. Meanwhile, students whose grades don't measure up often see themselves as failures and give up trying to learn" (p. 176). When it comes to a test that includes multiple skills—comprehension, analysis, application—a single grade conflates all the skills and tends to signal the end of learning. What, then, is the alternative?

In *Rethinking Grading: Meaningful Assessment for Standards-Based Learning* (2015), Cathy Vatterott offers a framework for standards-based grading to reflect student progress and learning, and she provides examples from elementary, middle, and high schools. While still "grading," standards-based grading can make visible the writing process, parts that make a whole, strengths in thinking, concepts that need review. Vatterott suggests we start with a standard (e.g., write narratives to develop real or imagined experiences using effective techniques, descriptive details, and clear event sequence). The standard then drives learning tasks, which drives learning activities that can be evaluated separately.

The standards set learning goals that guide learning and provide language for teachers and students to engage in conversations about what is happening in the classroom. A standard such as "writing an engaging lead" can start conversations about what students are creating and the sort of thinking that is happening as students demonstrate learning or discover they need more resources. Standards could make this process of shifting learning away from "grades" more meaningful if teachers can resist assigning points and letter grades to the process and product.

Thus, I adopted a standards-based *instruction* framework as a way of making clear to the principal, students, and parents what I was teaching and assessing and then used narrative feedback instead of points to keep the learning conversation going. In other words, even though I would focus on standards as a way of framing instruction, I still had to resist measurement-based feedback. I was worried that evaluating standards would result in language like "exceeds" replacing letters like "A." If we were going to focus on learning, we had to focus on feedback and revision, which meant resisting any language of evaluation.

## Assessment vs. Evaluation

Teachers use formative assessments every day and know the importance of quizzes, anecdotal evidence, checking notebooks to assess learning in-progress so that they can adjust instruction. Teachers may or may not assign grades to those formative assessments but likely assign grades to the end-of-unit assessments or final exams: summative assessments.

But isn't it all formative? All meaningful assessment should illuminate what students know and can do, but also why it matters and implications for future learning. After a "summative" exam, teachers and students can glean the extent of learning and establish new goals; however, when a student completes an exam but has clearly missed a key component or can't quite do the skill, what do we do (if we are using traditional grades)? Subtract points, put a slash over the error, write a phrase like "awkward" or "do over." This doesn't seem kind, helpful, or ethical, does it? And, such an assessment does not make space for revision or reflection on why the misunderstanding or awkward phrasing matters.

How many times are teachers "grading" and realize the problem was the instructions on the exam or that they—the teacher—in fact, did not teach a key concept that students needed in order to complete the exam or do an activity? How many times is the reason the student has a zero in the gradebook is because he or she was absent or needed more time?

In developing the no-grades pilot, I knew that I had to define assessment, and in doing so, I extract assessment from evaluation (e.g, grading) for purpose, focus, tone, agents, form, and scope. See Table 4.1.

Assessment is daily and frequent. It is an interactive process of collecting evidence, noting the process and elements of the process, and using information to revise, improve, and learn. Evaluation should happen rarely, if ever. What is the purpose of comparing or ranking? When would learning ever be finished?

*Table 4.1.* Assessment vs. Evaluation/Grading.

|  | Assessment | Evaluation/Grading |
|---|---|---|
| **purpose** | to give feedback about how approaches, skills, lines of think-ing, risks are working (formative, ongoing) | to judge quality (summative, specific point in time) |
| **focus** | a process: cyclical and reflective including the *how* and *why* of choices and outcomes | a product: final and prescriptive, conflates multiple skills, outcome quality, accuracy |
| **tone** | observational notes on artifacts, experiences, performances | passing judgment on a specific products or collection |
| **agents** | teacher, students, peers assessing, reflecting, adjusting | evaluator determines the extent to which the objectives are achieved |
| **form** | written and verbal questions, com-ments, observations, compliments, suggestions among agents | letters, numbers, scores that symbolize the conclusion of learning on a project, test |
| **scope** | absolute: viewed as existing inde-pendently, personal | comparative: making a distinction between better and worse based on a standard |

In the first term of the pilot, agents (the teacher and students) practiced on the form of assessment, learning how to offer written and verbal feedback with an observational tone. Our feedback included conversations about the *how* and the *why* of the product.

Students submitted an artifact—blog, essay, slides, presentation—on our class blog where everyone could have access to their ideas. The teacher and students could write narrative feedback or give verbal feedback based on standards *and* the larger purpose of the artifact during daily conference time (which they write in their notebooks).

Using feedback, students typically revised some aspect of their work during class when they had support and resources. The focus is on the process of critical feedback and revision rather than an outcome.

When students struggle with a standard or concept, we talk about what they *are* doing and how they *are* approaching the work to illuminate opportu-nities for growth. We talk about specific strategies and moves they *are* making in their writing and thinking, then learn or review alternatives. The process of feedback and revision is messy, complex, and ongoing. To assign a "grade" ends this conversation (or, at minimum, changes it).

However, not every student attended to my feedback or used the pro-cess to grow. Some students just saw an assignment or project as a task to be completed. I had to reframe my thinking about compliant students. I had not done a good job making the purpose relevant to every student, or, better yet, supporting students in making the process or product their own, relevant to them. I considered avoidance, refusal, and apathy about English as schooling's failure to inspire and make relevant learning to all students.

## An Example of Assessment in Reading Literature

For seventh-grade reading, we adopted a reading workshop model where students read self-selected books while I conducted reading conferences. In mini-lessons, we worked on reading standards, and then once a week, students wrote about their reading experiences on their blogs using the standards we practiced. In the example below, Katrina is focusing on how the setting impacts the character and using text evidence to support what the text explicitly says. The asterisk at the end of the post is Katrina responding to my feedback from the previous week, which is different for each students depending on what I am noticing about their reading experiences.

Here is an excerpt from Katrina's blog:

> The title of the book that I am reading is *Girl in Translation* by Jean Kwok. Today in my post, I am going to talk about the setting and how this impacts the character. The setting in the story starts briefly in Hong Kong, China—Kim's home. Her mom and her make a tough journey from there to America. The setting impacts Kim and her mother because this is unknown territory ... They are also in New York, a very fast-paced city which can be very overwhelming. Anybody who has moved can understand the hardships, but in Kim's case there is a language barrier. Her and her mother speak little to no English. Kim and her mother live in an old and worn down apartment. This was the only thing they could afford. For example, there are roaches, rats, and other nasty creature living in what they now call home; the windows are all broken and have to be covered with garbage bags, and they have little to no food. This is all falling on Kim. Since she is narrating the story, we get to see how she is handling all of this, and she seems to be doing well. I have noticed since reading this that when people move to America at first, it isn't all sunshine and roses; it is actually really tough. For example, Kim's mom works days and nights at a clothing factory just to be able to provide for Kim. I am also noticing that the subjects of all the books I have read this year talk a lot about the hardships of characters such as language, war, culture ... thousands of immigrants who come to the U.S. each year, and this books gives me an idea of what the process of that transition might be like for some people.
>
> * Dr. Donovan, what I did differently in this response was that I added some of my own ideas about how I felt that they impacted humans more generally (beyond the text). I also tried to connect to the subjects of other books that I have read this year.

This post shows how Katrina and I were in an ongoing conversation about her reading, which goes beyond mere standards. Of my 150 reading students, about half responded to my feedback similarly and weekly; the others responded intermittently, so I conferred daily with students about their reading and, once a week, I met with small groups to guide them in the process of reading and responding to feedback. Because assessment includes agents beyond the teacher, students also responded to one another on the blog and in book groups, so that reading is not about a "right reading" but about nurturing a community of readers.

## An Example of Assessment in Writing

For seventh-grade writing, one piece of writing we took through the writing process is a comparison article. Writers took on the role of a blogger for an online magazine and wrote a point-by-point piece about something they knew well. We worked with the informative essay standards in our writing workshop, and they published their work on their blogs.

As a class, we offered verbal feedback during the writing process—from pre-writing to revisions—but once students published their work, it was up to me to evaluate how well they were meeting the standards. Instead of a grade or percentage, I wrote each student a letter inspired by Mark Barnes' SE2R (summarize, explain, redirect, resubmit). Below, I summarized what Stefanie did in her essay using standards language and explained its function/purpose; then, I make a suggestion for revision.

Dear Stefanie,

You start with a lead that helps the reader know who you are, why you care about this topic, and why you are an expert (ethos).

You include a thesis statement early in your article, which helps readers understand how you will organize your article; then, you follow that promise in the body of your essay.

Each paragraph explores the items in the topic sentence with details and language (jargon) to show you know what readers need to know, understand, and consider.

You use transitions (conjunctive adverbs, subordinating conjunctions) that create a flow of ideas and signal the reader that you are moving from point to point—on one hand, first, in conclusion, because.

Your conclusion summarizes your article well and leaves the reader thinking about the importance of your topic. To improve this, I think making a connection to your reader or asking your reader to take action will make them feel like you wrote this to help them be more informed about seafood and even try it. Can you offer some suggestions for beginners? Can you recommend a restaurant or give a tip what to avoid?

Stefanie read my feedback and then revised her conclusion. Even though I was "evaluating" the final product, passing judgment on each part/standard, I viewed the tone of my feedback as observational. After reading classmates' essays, their feedback, and mine, she decided that revisions would improve her piece. The most important "evaluator" is the student.

The above examples offer a glimpse of how I used standards-based instruction and assignments with narrative feedback in lieu of rubrics, points, and grades for the first eight weeks of the no-grades pilot. Knowing I would have to assign a grade to each student at the end of the quarter, I set aside week nine, the final week of the quarter, for conferences—five days—and managed to conduct 150 conferences during class time. It is here where I am wondering if I failed. What does a final grade do for learning? Does a final grade continue, wrap-up, change, or just end the learning conversation? How does a final grade validate a student's self-image as an "A student" or "bad at writing"? What happens when students internalize and then narrate themselves through these grades as a teenager? And even later as an adult and parent?

## Collection and Reflection Letters

As the end of the quarter approached, I knew that I would ultimately have to conflate an entire quarter of learning to a letter grade. So, during the final week of the quarter students looked over artifacts of their learning, including feedback from me and their peers. As students collected evidence of learning, some wanted to revise blog posts and essays once again, having gained a new perspective on their work that only time permits.

To reflect on the learning and come to some evaluation of what students knew, could do, and why it mattered, we resisted the letter grade (e.g., A, B, C) and embraced letter-writing. Students wrote letters about their learning to their families, summarizing with evidence what they learned. The letters with links to and pictures of evidence function as a portfolio, a beautiful story of learning from the learner. In the process of collecting, revising, reflecting, and telling the story of their learning, students discover who they are as writers and readers and members of a community.

The process of composing these letters opened up fissures to explore. For example, this assignment asks students to look through their paper notebooks and online blogs for evidence of learning the standards. For writing, this included a biographical narrative, conventions, and short-term writing assignments. For reading, this included making claims about literature with text evidence, reading poetry, and engaging in small group discussions. During the letter composition process, some discovered a note I had written to them a week prior with a suggestion for revisions, so, at last, they make that revision or called me over to talk about reworking a lead or connecting evidence to a claim.

Students emailed or mailed their letters to their families, and I used these letters to inform our final grade conferences and future unit and lesson plans. Here is an excerpt from a letter one student wrote about her writing:

> Dear Mom,
>
> I have just finished the quarter of writing, and it's been really fun. I have done so many things throughout the year, including teaching other students.
>
> To start the quarter, we wrote some biographical sketches. Biographical sketches are basically when someone else tells you a story of their life, and you try to make a story out of it. You have to have the person's consent before publishing the story that you are writing. We're responsible for writing it and asking to change things. Before actually publishing or sharing the story, you have to read the story to the person and he/she will possibly tell you things that are incorrect, so it was cool to see how everyone decided to write stories about people's lives. I had Ed interview me, and I shared my first funeral. I also interviewed Ed, and he told me about his first broken bone. The process was kind of hard, trying to figure out what some people had said, what it was like, and how you should put it all together.
>
> About a week afterward, we had a new thing that everyone was going to do: teach. We were all going to take a grammar topic assigned to us and put it into slides so we can present and teach the class all about it. In my case, I have to do conjunctive adverbs. My partner and I both worked on slides to share, but we won't share it until December. Having other students teach the class looked quite easy. It does make more sense when we teach each other. Through the teaching, we would put that technique into our Compose for 7 writing. I do try my best to put all we've learned into my writing, but sometimes, it doesn't work well. The first teaching we learned was dialogue. …

Here is an excerpt another student wrote about his reading experiences:

> Dear Mom and Dad,
>
> I am at the end of the quarter, and I am learning lots of new stuff. So far it's not been any difficult so far, and I got into a new book that I really like a lot. The things I have been working on so far is independent reading, blogging, poems, and book groups.
>
> First, let's talk about independent reading. The following is a list of books I have read so far (some in other classes like *Don Quixote* in Spanish:
>
> 1. *The Outsiders* by S. E. Hinton, realistic fiction, gangs/class
> 2. *Marcelo in the Real World* by Francisco X. Stork, realistic fiction, disability difference
> 3. *Don Quixote* by Miguel de Cervantes, fantasy, knights/adventures
> 4. *The Pearl* by John Steinbeck, parable, poverty
> 5. *The Real Boy* by Anne Ursu, fantasy, magic/adventures

6. *Following Fake Man* by Barbara Ware Holmes, fantasy, family
7. *Hack* by Tatsuya Hamazaki, manga, heroes/adventures
8. *Hack 2* by Tatsuya Hamazaki, manga, heroes/adventures

The books have been really fun to read a lot, and I really enjoyed reading them. Most of them have been like adventures and fantasies; the characters have been like heroes or normal people. some of the themes are friendship because in the book *Don Quixote*, Don Quixote was friends with his pal Sancho Panza, and both of them went on adventures. In *Hack*, Shugo and Rena, the main characters are having adventures with their new friends in a virtual video game. In book *The Real Boy*, Oscar is wishing to go on the same adventures as Caleb, but he has quite the trouble doing so. Out of all the books, my favorite one is *Hack* because the plot of the story is really good as well as funny; it has good characters and is enjoyable.

Next, the blogs. One claim that I made in blog 2.3 was about *The Outsiders*. The church where Johnny and Ponyboy were hiding from the police did not end up keeping them safe. What it means to make a claim is that you can back it up with evidence to make your point about what you are stating. How I support these claims are that I find evidence in the text. The feedback I am getting form my teacher is pretty good, but I need to improve on is explaining how the evidence supports the claim. I use that feedback to improve from the one before and try to fix mistakes, and when I am doing this, I always put my thoughts to what I think about the story, book, or claim.

Then, for poems, I read a poem called "Do Not Go Gentle." The poem is about how a teenager is talking to his father who was in the army or war about not dying. When I read this poem with my partner, at first we didn't agree on what we thought about it, but later on, we settled on the answer. It's useful to read with a partner because you can hear what they think about the poem. We'll see what the rest of the class thinks when we share our poem with the class ...

Here is one parent's feedback after having received her daughter's letter of learning:

I just wanted to take a moment to express how happy I am that K. has you as her reading and writing teacher this year. K. has enjoyed reading especially, and writing, from a very young age. I remember specific teachers in elementary school that did a nice job fostering this, however, as she got older, it was challenging to find material that interested her, was appropriate for her age, and was at her reading level. I feel as though you have rekindled that love of reading for her, and it could not be more refreshing to see her excited about this once again. It's always something that I've seen as special about K., and it was hard when I wasn't regularly seeing her get lost in a book as I had so many times before. She also likes to share her writing with us, and loves the feedback you give her.

I think this is an excellent approach! Letter grades don't always reflect what the student has learned or absorbed. The dialogue between the two of you is great! In fact, it was this exchange that made me think, "Wow! This is really challenging her to stretch her thinking!"

It's wonderful to see her challenged, inspired, and growing again! My sincerest thanks for all you do!

## End-of-Quarter Grade Conferences

The school district requires a letter grade at the end of the term. Thus, I had to contend with quarterly report cards even though my principal supported the no-grades pilot. Barnes (2015) suggests the final grade ought to be decided based on a "detailed assessment by both teacher and student of all that was or was not accomplished during a grading period" (p. 5).

To prepare for the final grade conferences, we had to develop language for arriving at a grade and practice the conversation because "deciding" on a grade—one that did not come from averaging numbers—was so unfamiliar to all of us. When a class is not using numbers or letters for assignments and projects, how do we arrive at a single letter? And what does that single letter communicate? And to whom?

Because we had been conferring about learning all quarter and because students had completed their letter of learning, students all had a pretty good sense of how they were developing as readers and writers. As Barnes explains, students who complete all the activities and rework skills or concepts will be in the A–B range, and students who don't earn something lower.

Students practiced final-grade conferences with partners:

- Did you complete all the activities? Where is your evidence?
- Did you rework skills or concepts? Tell me how?
- What are you learning about yourself as a reader, writer, thinker?
- What is your "best" work? What makes you say so?
- What do you still want to know and do better?
- Which letter grade best qualifies your evidence: A, B, C, D?

The partner discussions were quite revealing. First, no student failed because every student had evidence. There were no zeros to bring down percentage because we were not using points. Class time was for reading, writing, revising, sharing, and reflecting, so every student had evidence of this. Next, as a class, we agreed that what mattered was the evidence: how much evidence, how accurate the evidence, how well the student explains the process of creating and revising the evidence. Students who said they earned an A or B could articulate moves, risks, choices, and purpose. When I met one-on-one with each student to write a single letter on the grade report, I deferred to their self-assessment for the final grade.

## *Conclusions*

After spending the summer researching assessment and grading, after meeting with colleagues and my principal about facilitating a no-grades classroom that school year, after resisting numbers and letter grades on student work for nearly nine weeks, after countless hours of writing narrative feedback to students and teaching them to write narrative feedback to one another, at the end of each term, I wrote letters next to my students' names. Our beautiful conversations ended in, well, grades.

Between the face-to-face daily conferences and the online weekly conversations with students, I got to know what these human beings needed from me to stretch their learning. Still, I am concerned about the mixed message, the hypocrisy of it all considering the end-goal of a grade still looms. Students knew our class was different. Over time, students stopped asking *How many points is this worth?* and *What's my grade on this?* They adopted assessment language like "evidence," "feedback," "revision," and "re-assessment." We used these words all the time, and many grew to really appreciate the reframing of "learning" as a process rather than an outcome on a test. Students could point to evidence, talk through their revision process, explain the implications of their choices on meaning and message. They knew what they did, how they did it, what was meaningful and effective, and what was not. My role in the grading conferences was to pose questions, ask them to tell me the story of their learning. Many would say the feedback and revision process was less stressful than tests, points, and grades for every assignment, but knowing a "grade" would come out of our final conference stirred up stress and anxiety. Ultimately, I was the one who had the power and responsibility to put a letter next to their names on the report cards.

I don't teach with packets or worksheets anymore. I have reframed my whole approach to teaching ELA. There is no meeting of mandates or teaching about. Instead, we bear witness to lives lived in all that we read and write. It is a literacy which defies measurement. I teach students how to bear witness by engaging in a story exchange where we share narratives from our lives. I teach students to look for gaps in narratives through multigenre research projects. I teach students to share their emerging understanding of who they are becoming in the world beyond the classroom. To assess for emerging understanding of self and others, however humanizing, is not objective, concrete, or easily measured. Therefore, teaching in today's schools requires a conscious approach that honors our students' humanity while meeting the mandates of the system that makes public education possible.

Going gradeless may first be about minimizing grades, but it must lead to a reimagining of how we do school. English Language Arts is not about skills and knowledge accumulation; it's about learning how to, as Paulo Freire says, "read the word and the world." After a school year of being in a classroom that made explicit its mission to grade less and think about the *why* and *how* of English more, I think my students would say they have a greater respect for the "word"—specifically, who gets to write it, where it's published, who gets to read it, who has a say in whether or not the word is "good." And I would say they are more conscious of reading the "world" in the sense that they read and wrote widely, but even more so in the sense that we all tried to make visible the systems that decide their place in the world, specifically, the school systems that regulate their days, intervals of learning, and their place in the school (e.g., test scores, GPAs). With an approach to assessment that minimizes numbers, letters, sorting, and ranking and increases feedback, conversation, revision, and agency, students and teachers get a little closer to writing the world rather than having the world "write" them through a process like grading—one that will never capture the full humanity, potential, or intelligence of any student.

## References

Barnes, M. (2015). *Assessment 3.0: Throw out your grade book and inspire learning.* Thousand Oaks, CA: Corwin.

Donovan, S. (2017). *Genocide literature in middle and secondary classrooms: Rhetoric, witnessing, and social action in a time of standards and accountability.* New York, NY: Routledge.

Holocaust Museum Houston. (n. d.). *Genocide in Guatemala.* Retrieved from https://www.hmh.org/ed_genocide_guatemala.shtml

Kohn, A. (2011). The case against grades. *Educational Leadership.* Retrieved from https://www.alfiekohn.org/article/case-grades/

Loveless, J. (2006). Going gradeless: Evaluation over time helps students learn to write. *Language Arts Journal of Michigan, 22*(2).

Mikaelsen, B. (2005). *Tree girl.* New York, NY: HarperTempest.

Pink, D. (2011). *Drive: The surprising truth about what motivates us.* New York, NY: Riverhead Books.

Schwartz, K. (2014). The importance of low-stakes student feedback. *KQED.* Retrieved from https://www.kqed.org/mindshift/33230/the-importance-of-low-stakes-student-feedback

Tomlinson, C., & Moon, T. (2013). *Assessment and student success in a differentiated classroom.* Alexandria, VA: ASCD.

Vatterott, C. (2015). *Rethinking grading: Meaningful assessment for standards-based learning.* Alexandria, VA: ASCD.

Wiggins, G. (1994). Toward better report cards. *Educational Leadership, 52*(2), 28–37. Retrieved from http://www.ascd.org/publications/educational-leadership/oct94/vol52/num02/Toward-Better-Report-Cards.aspx

# 5. Pedagogies of Resistance: Reflecting on the Successes and Challenges of Humanizing Classrooms in a Time of Standardization and Accountability

Matthew Homrich-Knieling and Alex Corbitt

## Framing Our Teaching Contexts

Our experiences teaching in urban districts have taught us that school systems in the U.S., particularly in urban contexts, often mirror, reinforce, and maintain the systemic oppression that exists outside classroom walls. We've witnessed school discipline systems that reflect and funnel our students into the criminal justice system; we've experienced the disempowering impacts of education policy that pushes schools to prioritize standardization and test preparation over creativity and inquiry; we've taught in cities where an illusion of choice has left neighborhoods without schools and in competition for resources. As teachers committed to justice and equity, we have attempted to resist the historically oppressive institution of schooling and imagine new possibilities for our classrooms. Teaching for justice can be isolating, but we have found strength and direction by collaborating with each other, listening to our communities, and reflecting on the work of many esteemed educators, particularly educators of color. In this chapter, we will share our struggles and successes, and our new understandings, all with the intent of contributing to ongoing conversations about educational justice.

Matt teaches middle school English Language Arts in southwest Detroit, a neighborhood in the city that is mostly comprised of Latinx immigrants. Southwest Detroit is a close-knit, vibrant, and hardworking neighborhood, characteristics that are in many ways replicated among the students within the school community. Matt's first year of teaching in southwest Detroit, the 2016–2017 school year, was a particularly tumultuous time for immigrant communities, southwest Detroit included. With heightened attacks on their humanity and targeted ICE raids in their neighborhoods, there was an intensified state of fear in southwest Detroit. Simultaneously, Matt witnessed the ways in which his students' identities as Latinx immigrants were perceived as controversial and therefore silenced in school spaces. Because our national educational system pressures local districts to prioritize (through funding, evaluations, resource allocation, etc.) test scores over supporting students and families, many of Matt's students were left without necessary mental and emotional support amidst this traumatic crisis.

Alex teaches English Language Arts at MS331 in the Bronx, New York. MS331 is a public, neighborhood middle school located in New York's 16th Congressional District, the poorest congressional district in the United States (2010 Census). The ethnic makeup of MS331's student body is 76% Latinx, 21% African/African-American, and 2% Asian. In 2014, MS331 was placed on the Chancellor's Renewal List due to low testing performance. This designation was probationary. The students and faculty endured increased accountability over the ensuing years. This shift incentivized test preparation and standardized curricula, two forces inclined to ignore the identities and agency of his students.

## Possibilities of Schooling

There are many tensions between educating for justice and the priorities of education policymakers. Furthermore, because we are both White cis-men who are not from the communities of color in which we teach, we are constantly negotiating how to employ justice-oriented pedagogies that do not reproduce oppressive dynamics and unconscious biases. Recognizing the ethical and theoretical challenges to teaching for justice, we seek the perspectives of radical, justice-oriented scholars whose theories and pedagogies illuminate strategies for creating anti-racist, freedom-seeking classrooms. The pedagogies outlined in this chapter are inspired by Dr. Django Paris' *Culturally-Sustaining Pedagogy*, Dr. Lamar Johnson's *Critical Race English Education*, and Dr. Baker-Bell, Dr. Stanbrough, and Dr. Everett's *Pedagogy of Healing*. As we share our classroom stories, we will offer reflections that ground our classroom practices in these pedagogies.

The following sections highlight three enduring understandings that have emerged from our teaching experiences: (1). Radically centering students in our pedagogy requires the un-learning of teacher-centered approaches to teaching; (2). Sustaining and celebrating student identities can be a healing and community-building process; and (3). Targeting authentic audiences beyond the classroom allows students to reclaim agency. We will explore these themes through individual classroom vignettes and collaborative reflections.

## Un-Learning of Teacher-Centered Curriculum

Social justice education is subversive in that it strives to center students' humanity in a system that centers students' data. Teaching for justice requires shifting power to students in order to facilitate a classroom that allows us to practice the principles of freedom and justice for which we are fighting; we do this by making our classroom spaces democratic, participatory, restorative, and fair. This is no easy task; student-centered pedagogy often runs contrary to how educators are taught as K–12 students, undergraduates, and preservice teachers. As a result, we have learned that teachers and students must intentionally work together to unlearn teacher-centered pedagogies.

### Matt's Vignette

It was the third quarter of the 2016–2017 school year, and by this point in the year, after explicitly naming my support for my students amidst the increased discrimination against immigrants, inviting my students to reflect on and share their stories and their fears as they were comfortable, and opening up space for my students' experiences to drive our curriculum, my students and I had worked toward creating a safe space.

During this quarter, my eighth graders and I finished reading the play version of *The Diary of Anne Frank*. I vividly remember one of my students reading aloud stage directions from the scene where the SS officers arrive at the Franks' hiding place:

> *She breaks off as she hears the sound of a car outside, its brakes squealing as it comes to a sudden stop. [Sound Cue 31.] The people in the other rooms also become aware of the sound. They listen tensely. Another car outside roars up to a sudden stop. [Sound Cue 31 concluded.] Mr. Frank, book in hand, rises slowly. Everyone is listening, hardly breathing. Suddenly a heavy electric bell begins clanging savagely below. [Sound Cue 32.] Anne and Peter hurry from the Left room. She stops just outside the door. He remains on the first step. Mr. Dussel comes to u.c. Margot hurries into the room. Mrs. Frank puts down the potatoes and comes to above chair R. of C. table. Mrs. Van Daan comes down the stairs fearfully. Mr. Van Daan stays above at head of staircase. All eyes are fixed on Mr. Frank. He crosses slowly, calmly, toward the stairwell. He drops book on D. L. chair. The bell stops. [Sound Cue 32 ends.] Mr. Frank turns to the others, makes a reassuring gesture, then starts down the stairwell. The bell begins another long peal.* (Goodrich & Hackett, 1958, p. 98)

"This sounds like when ICE [Immigration and Customs Enforcement] comes to someone's house," one of my students gravely and angrily shared. This wasn't the first time one of my students made connections between scenes from the play and realities of their community of immigrants.

It was after this comment in particular, though, that I asked my students if they wanted to do a project around immigration. They enthusiastically and uniformly responded, "Yes!" I didn't, though, have any curricular plans for an immigration unit, so I explained to my students that they would play an integral role in shaping this project.

Once we finished the play, I started by asking my students questions that are typical in the unit design process: *What is our goal with this unit? What questions do we want to answer? What could a final project look like and who could be the audience of that project?* My students wrote reflections to these questions, discussed with their peers, and shared ideas with the class. One of the most salient moments came when we discussed the audience for this project. "I think the audience should be school staff," one of my students shared unabashedly, followed by several nods in agreement. Other students went on to explain the dissonance they experience as Latinx students living in southwest Detroit with mostly white teachers commuting from suburbs. "Teachers don't understand what it's like to be an immigrant," they shared. Though not every student in this class identified as Latinx or as an immigrant, every student found solidarity in the experience of feeling unrecognized through schooling; moreover, every student had relationships with students and ties to the community directly affected by immigration injustices.

As my students began to find deeper solidarity in their experiences as immigrant students and as students in an immigrant community, their goal for the project quickly emerged. The goal they collaboratively wrote read: "Our purpose is to educate school staff on the injustice that is happening to immigrant families and to build support for immigrants." Initially they hoped to achieve this goal by creating a video for the school staff to watch.

My students, then, developed critical questions about immigration, questions that they themselves wanted answers to (*Why is immigration such a touchy subject in school? Why do people choose to work for ICE? What is the percentage of ICE employees who are Hispanic? What is the process of becoming a legal citizen?*) and questions they thought teachers needed answers to (*Why do people take the risk of immigrating illegally? Do Mexicans really take Americans' jobs? What issues do immigrants face in the U.S.?*).

The process of developing these questions, goals, and visions for our project happened organically; however, now that we had this foundation, we were left with navigating *how* to engage in this work on a day-to-day level. First, we decided to split into research teams that would be responsible for answering specific research questions. Each day, my students engaged in research online with their respective team. After a few days, though, the project started to feel more and more like traditional schooling; every day, students would answer a warm-up question that I wrote, I would teach a brief lesson to address the content standards I was responsible for covering, my students would conduct their research before turning in their research notes and answering a debrief question, and then we would repeat the sequence the next day. My students seemed to become disengaged and felt less empowered. After all, this process of seeking answers solely through research did not recognize the knowledge that my students were already bringing to the classroom; it did not meaningfully center my students.

I realized, then, that both my students and I needed support and intentional, collaborative reflection on *how* we were going to disrupt traditional methods of schooling that are disengaging, disempowering, monotonous, and teacher-centered. Without that critical reflection and intentional shifting of our classroom dynamic, we found ourselves straying from our purpose.

When I tried to name this dynamic to my students, they emphatically agreed: "Yeah mister, this is kinda boring." Through our discussion of our classroom practices, it quickly became clear that our end goal of creating a video lacked energy among my students, which they, in part, attributed to the disengagement. As a result of this discussion, a new idea emerged: My students wanted, instead, to host an event for the teachers where they would present their research on immigration and share their own experiences on a student panel. This idea sparked a lot of energy and taught me an important lesson: when trying to facilitate a student-led classroom, it's important to collaborate on how you and your students will intentionally create a student-led classroom and to create spaces to regularly reflect on the process with students and make curricular adjustments accordingly. Simply ask your students: *Is this working? Do you have ideas of how we could do this work differently?*

## Alex's Vignette

My students and I co-facilitated a Teen Activism course during the 2016–2017 school year. The goal of the class was to create an academic space for us to explore social justice issues affecting our school community. This class was an elective and my administration allowed me the freedom to design the course from scratch. The lessons I learned, however, are transferable to any general education classroom.

My goal for the Teen Activism course was to inspire my students to own their learning. I had to unlearn traditional unit planning models to ensure the course authentically reflected the interests, needs, and identities of my students. Traditional unit planning models, such as backward design, typically center teachers, leaving the scope and sequence up to their discretion. I sought to invite students into the planning process, empowering them to generate unit themes and essential questions.

Student-led unit design can be unnerving because it requires a shift of power in the classroom. The teacher becomes a facilitator, equipped with elastic discussion starters rather than rigid lesson plans. Facilitators practice active listening and seek to accommodate the inquiries of students. I launched the Teen Activism class with a series of open-ended questions about social justice issues that piqued my students' interest. These conversations evolved into a list of unit topics that my students wanted to explore: racism, policing, substance abuse, mental health, bullying, animal rights, and LGBTQ identities. My students conducted a vote and decided the first unit would be *Racism in Society*.

Whole-group discussions helped determine the essential questions for our *Racism in Society* unit. Students shared their prior knowledge about racism and its various manifestations in society. I would occasionally ask targeted questions to complicate latent assumptions among the class. These conversations naturally led to large, open-ended lines of inquiry: *What causes racism? What forms of racism, obvious or hidden, happen in our daily lives? How might schools and other institutions be racist? How can we dismantle racism? Is it possible to be perfectly anti-racist; how do we identify our blind spots?* My role during these preliminary discussions was to help the group consolidate its thinking into concise, distinct essential questions. These discussions were valuable insofar as they gave me insight into potential texts to investigate throughout the ensuing weeks.

Choosing texts for the *Racism in Society* unit proved challenging. Creating a syllabus, like determining a unit, would have to be student-centered. Until now, I had unilaterally picked texts for my classes. Inspired by the structured choice of restaurants, I decided to compile "text menus" for my students. In the same way restaurant patrons use a food menu to select a meal that satisfies their hunger, my students used the text menus to select unit-related texts that informed their inquiry. The text menu for *Racism in Society* included a variety of news articles, book excerpts, and documentaries (all accompanied with descriptions to hook students' interest). In the future I hope to involve students more in the text curation process.

## Collaborative Reflection

We have learned that decentering ourselves in the classroom is essential. Critical Youth Studies scholars help us understand how teacher-centered classrooms reinforce the deficit understandings of youth and how "many dominant ways of understanding youth in education have negative consequences for students and teachers alike" (Sarigianides, Petrone, & Lewis, 2017, p. 3). The traditional paradigm of teacher-centered classrooms communicates that young people do not have the power, autonomy, or insight necessary to contribute to how and what they learn. Our students, however, showed us that they have a deep understanding of what they care about and how they learn best. Students can lead the way toward equitable schooling practices if educators give up control, make space for students' perspectives, and practice active listening. Matt learned to listen to his students' text-to-self connections as they compared scenes from *The Diary of Anne Frank* to the threatening reality of ICE raids. He created curricular space for his students by allowing them ways to express themselves and tell their stories through a class project. Alex learned to take an open-ended approach to unit planning and allow his students to generate unit topics, develop authentic inquiries, and self-select unit texts from menus. Though it can be an uncomfortable process for teachers, we have learned that we cannot engage in justice pedagogies without centering our students in our classrooms.

## The Sustaining and Celebrating of Student Identities as Healing and Community-Building

The majority of urban classroom teachers are White and not from the communities in which they teach. This poses an inherently problematic dynamic in which White teachers come into communities of color to teach young people what they "need" to know. This dynamic is glaringly colonial and the product of historical, structural racism. We are both part of this White demographic of teachers, and we recognize that teaching within this context requires critical, intentional, and collaborative reflection on identity, power, and schooling. One tool that has helped us navigate these tensions is Culturally-Sustaining Pedagogy.

Building upon Dr. Ladson-Billings's *Culturally-Relevant Pedagogy* (1995), Dr. Django Paris's concept of culturally-sustaining pedagogy (CSP) provides a framework for using pedagogy to sustain "linguistic, literate, and cultural pluralism as part of the democratic project of schooling" (p. 93). Dr. Paris explains that CSP is especially important as the increasing diversity of the nation's student population is contrasted by traditional pedagogical practices that erase the cultural and linguistic identities of students of color (2012). CSP, as our vignettes will highlight, offers a way to consider how our pedagogies can foster inclusion and sustain students' identities.

Given our positionality within our school communities, we cannot engage in culturally-sustaining pedagogies without meaningfully involving our students. Our experiences in the classroom have highlighted the recursive process of creating space for students to define their identities and co-creating curriculum around their moments of sharing and storytelling. This exchange reveals the potential for classrooms to become places of healing and community-building.

## Matt's Vignette

As the process of co-creating an immigration justice project unfolded, I was able to reflect differently on the shortcomings and problems of the previous justice-oriented units I had created. Earlier in the same school year, for example, I designed a unit for my seventh graders titled "Resistance and Change," where we read stories of activism and social movements by author-activists of color. Though my students were intrigued by the content and displayed moments of engagement, they didn't seem to experience a sense of ownership or community throughout the unit. I thought I was designing curriculum that was culturally-sustaining and anti-racist. However, through the process of co-creating this immigration justice project with my eighth graders, I discovered a major issue with the Resistance and Change unit: Because my students weren't involved in the creation of the unit, it was designed based on assumptions about my students' experiences, identities, and interests. My students couldn't begin to heal from experiences of systemic oppression (occurring in and out of schools) and build community through curriculum that did not directly involve them. I discovered, then, that I cannot create culturally-sustaining pedagogy on my own because I cannot be the one to define my students' identities and experiences, especially as a white teacher not from the community in which I am teaching. This realization led me to ask myself: *How can creating space for students to define their own identities, their own experiences and needs, both impact and become part of enacting culturally-sustaining pedagogy?* The immigration justice project with my eighth graders helped me to begin answering that question.

My students' initial idea for the final project of our immigration justice project, a research video, did not allow space for my students' personal and community stories; instead, it became a more removed project, where my students centered research over their own knowledge, lived experiences, and community stories. When my students redirected our project to work instead toward hosting an event for our school staff that involved a research presentation (including interviews from members of my students' community) and a student-led panel on immigration, they felt more free to validate their own knowledge and their own identities through our project. This shift toward storytelling allowed my students to sustain their own cultural and community identities. Moreover, the panel format allowed the shifting of power to my students to become more visible, as they were physically positioned at the front of the room, teaching their teachers about immigration injustices through their own stories. Following the panel, my students moderated a Q&A between the panelists and the school's staff. Most exciting was when teachers asked my students about ways in which they could be more supportive, because my students were able to articulate their own needs, validate their own knowledge, and demonstrate their understanding of teaching as a relational and community-driven process, much like what we created in our classroom through this project. The impact of the shift that resulted with the panel is evidenced through these two students' reflections:

> We were more serious and concentrated on this project because it was way more related to what is going on and is something closer to what some kids or people are actually dealing with in life.
> We started this project and it got pretty boring then we came up with a panel and everything changed and it all became real.

Our entire classroom dynamic also shifted when my students decided to host an event. Students shifted toward collaboration when they designed new working teams: **panelists**, who wrote personal narratives about their experiences as immigrant students; **event organizers**, who created advertisements, invitations, and agendas for our event; **researchers**, who continued to research immigration; translators, who supported other teams by translating information into Spanish; and **presentation-makers**, who synthesized the researchers' information into a presentation. Each of these teams regularly presented their progress to the class, asked each other questions, and collaborated with each other. Moreover, I was able to tailor small group instruction to the pacing guide of content standards I am required to follow. For example, with the panelists, we discussed narrative techniques, figurative language, etc.; with the researchers, we discussed evaluating sources, summarizing and synthesizing information, etc. I was then able to provide some whole group instruction around these standards that was rooted in the project (i.e., teaching connotation vs denotation and rhetorical appeals by discussing the impacts of saying "illegal alien" vs "undocumented").

The structure my students had designed, however, is in stark contrast to the traditional structure of schooling. Rather than community and co-dependence, our education system values individualism and competition through systems like high-stakes testing, where each student is both accountable for their individual data and measured against their peers. Such structures, though, are at odds with many of my students' cultural practices, which are largely defined through community and familial relationships. It was refreshing to see my students' desire for community manifested through this project, but it wasn't until I shifted more power to my students that that community dynamic could flourish and that we could create a classroom structure that sustained my students' cultural and community practices.

Moreover, because my students had constructed our classroom setup based on their needs and their vision of the event, they felt both ownership over it and community within it. As one of my students reflected, "I liked that the project was all on us and any teacher authority was only to make sure things remained on track." Another student, echoing their peers, shared, "I liked how much hard work we spread out to each other to help out in this big project."

These comments from my students helped me to understand the necessity of involving students in the creation of both curriculum and classroom structures/practices that are designed to center, sustain, and celebrate their identities and experiences.

## Alex's Vignette

Engagement waned as my students and I progressed through our *Racism in Society* unit. I asked students to select and analyze unit-related texts immediately after establishing the unit theme and essential questions. This transition was premature, prioritizing texts over my students' identities. My students voiced their interest in interrogating racism, but I didn't give them adequate opportunities to reflect on *why* they were interested in interrogating racism. What personal histories and experiences inspired their inquiries? What stories framed their interpretation of the content? Ignoring these questions stunted my students' ability to bring their entire selves to the unit texts. My students helped me realize that empathy is built on a foundation of self-knowledge.

Revising the trajectory of the unit, my students and I paused our analysis of articles, book excerpts, and documentaries. We turned our focus inward, to a previously ignored text: ourselves. I created a journaling exercise called "The Time Travel Interview" to help inspire unit-related introspection. The Time Travel Interview invited students to reflect on a time they witnessed, encountered, or endured racism. The students conducted self-interviews to process their experiences. They imagined traveling back in time and meeting their younger selves. They interviewed their past selves, asking questions about their experience and how they felt. The interviews concluded with students giving their former selves words of empowerment and guidance.

The Time Travel Interviews were intended to be a safe, private activity. I did not assess them, nor did I require students to share their reflections. Regardless, a few students were moved to share their personal interviews with the class. One girl shared her reflection on a moment she encountered racism in elementary school. She had recently emigrated from the Dominican Republic and was learning English. Her elementary teacher censored the books she could borrow from the library; the student was not permitted to read books above her English "reading level." The student felt that censorship and the rigidity of reading levels could be employed in racist ways. Her peers agreed and thanked her for sharing.

Beyond helping students personally contextualize the *Racism in Society* unit, The Time Travel Interview served as a method for healing and self-care. This self-care bridged an important gap between identity and content; it prepared students to empathize and immerse themselves in new texts. A student synthesized this revelation saying, "When we learn about ourselves, we can begin loving ourselves. When we love ourselves, we can begin loving others."

## Collaborative Reflection

At this juncture we see the interplay of our three grounding pedagogies: Culturally-Sustaining Pedagogy, Healing Pedagogy, and Critical Race English Education. Already we've discussed the transformative possibilities of shifting power to our students through CSP. When we create space for our students to share their experiences and identities, we can co-create curriculum around those stories in ways that validate and sustain our students' cultural and linguistic identities. We can also begin to understand how this process can heal and build community.

In order to engage in our respective projects, we had to use our pedagogy to address issues of race/racism and identity/power. We were pushed to reflect on the ways in which our subject area has historically been positioned as a space to maintain oppression and white supremacy. Prioritizing standard English and mandating English-only policies, condemning and delegitimizing the language and literacy practices of students of color (African-American English, Spanglish, etc.), drawing from a predominately White canon, and reading novels like *To Kill a Mockingbird* without critically discussing race and racism are all common ways in which the English classroom has and continues to be a site of racial violence and erasure. Recognizing this, we draw inspiration from Dr. Lamar Johnson's *Critical Race English Education* (CREE). Through CREE, Johnson maintains a pedagogical theory that explicitly "names and addresses issues of violence, race, whiteness, white supremacy, and anti-black racism within school and out-of-school spaces" (p. 17). With this critical lens, Johnson shares part of his vision for reimagining English classrooms:

> I envision English classrooms where the stories of the oppressed are storied through liberatory literacy practices such as movement, media, art, song, dance, and poetry. English classrooms or literacy classes where the educators love the multiple ways people from different racial and ethnic backgrounds express their pain and act of liberation through the means of legitimizing expression. I imagine English classrooms where Black children are being taught to love every ounce of their Blackness. (pp. 38–39)

We found that by shifting power to our students and allowing their experiences, identities, and stories to drive our pedagogy, we can begin to dismantle the historically oppressive impact of ELA classrooms. We can begin to manifest Dr. Johnson's vision.

Finally, when we create space for our students within the historically oppressive institution of schools, we also offer opportunities for collective healing through telling stories, building community, and creating opportunities for critical action. Dr. Baker-Bell, Dr. Stanbrough, and Dr. Everett's *Pedagogy of Healing* tells us that "The tools within a healing pedagogical framework are responsive to the needs of a given situation" (p. 139). Matt's immigration project was responsive to his students' experiences with immigration injustice. Alex's Teen Activism course was responsive to his students' experiences with racism. We could not have been responsive to the harm and pain our students experience without first allowing our students to bring their full selves into our classrooms and explicitly name the injustices they were experiencing.

### *Targeting Authentic Audiences Beyond the Classroom*

Listening plays an essential role in shifting power to students. We've explored how educators must listen to students and allow students' identities to shape pedagogy. As we continue to reflect on the power of listening, we must ask ourselves: Who else hears our students? How can we help students magnify their voices, enabling their reading, writing, and speaking to reach audiences beyond the classroom? When we work with students to strategically broaden their audience, we validate their capacity to shape the world around them.

## Matt's Vignette

The traditional structure of ELA classrooms and writing pedagogies is often-times disempowering, disengaging, and dehumanizing. In most cases, students are expected to write essays about topics they did not choose, to write with the teacher as the only audience, and to remove their own identity and their own personhood from their writing with commonplace rules like not using first-person pronouns. These practices communicate that students do not have capacity to write about that which interests or affects them, that students cannot contribute to conversations occurring outside the classroom walls, and that students cannot claim their own valuable ideas and perspectives.

As my students' immigration justice project continued to progress, and their research presentation/student panel event for our school's staff neared, I recognized the transformative potential in targeting authentic audiences beyond the classroom. Moreover, my students' process of choosing an audience for our project demonstrated the possibilities of borrowing practices from activism and community organizing within our classrooms and our pedagogy.

In community organizing and activist circles, organizers go through a process of issue identification by building community and sharing stories about issues that affect their lives. Once an issue is identified around which to build a campaign, it is common to engage in power-mapping, a process of intentionally mapping out individuals or groups of people along a spectrum of who has the most/least power to make the change for which you are fighting and who is most likely to agree/disagree with your organization's campaign. These strategic and community-driven decisions and processes allow organizers to build community and power and to fight for change.

Similarly, my students and I chose to engage in a project around immigration after my students had built solidarity and community around shared stories of immigration injustices. Specifically, my students identified how their or their classmates' identities and experiences as Latinx immigrants are silenced and unrecognized in school spaces. With that, my students strategically decided to target school staff as our audience, recognizing that teachers and staff have power to make changes that would affect their own experience in school. I came to believe that integrating community organizing practices into our classroom allows students to reclaim their own agency as leaders and as full humans within a system that undermines their autonomy and their freedom every day. Moreover, I realized that pedagogically using community organizing strategies (i.e., co-developing a project by first using storytelling as issue identification and power-mapping to select an audience) allowed me to develop simultaneously a pedagogy of healing, by "acknowledging that the wound exists and identifying its culprit" and "responding to the wound using a tool that works to transform the conditions that led to the wound" (Baker-Bell, Stanbrough, & Everett, 2017, p. 139).

When it finally came time for our event, my students were brave, powerful, and confident. The entire event—research presentation, student panel, and Q&A between staff and students—was led by my students. "This project was our project. We decided what to say and what to do. It made us feel even more empowered because we made this panel from scratch," one of my students reflected. My students resisted the dominant narrative that immigration injustice was too political or controversial to be discussed in school and, instead, candidly shared their personal stories of navigating school as Latinx immigrants and demanded that their teachers hear their stories so that they can meaningfully support them in the school and in the classroom.

And my students were heard. After the event, teachers answered an exit ticket that my students created, and their responses demonstrated the power of my students' stories:

> This was a great way for teachers to be able to understand and be able to be more aware about what else is worrying the students. Not just exams and grades, but the fear of discrimination.
> I realized or gained more perspective on the issue. I'm still analyzing myself about my perceived bias and reflecting on my societal privilege.

By the end of this project, I was left feeling so inspired and confident that, even amidst structures and policies that disempower and dehumanize students and teachers, K–12 classrooms and schools have the potential to become spaces for justice, healing, and community.

## Alex's Vignette

My students and I continued to develop our Teen Activism class against the backdrop of the 2016 United States presidential election. This was a time when hate speech and bigotry dominated the national discourse. My students sought to mobilize their voices as a counter-narrative, spreading messages of inclusion across the school community.

Inspired by the viral marketing campaigns of the hacktivist group Anonymous, my students created a mysterious underground newspaper. Each student assumed a pseudonym and wrote prose, poems, and aphorisms that celebrated inclusion. They compiled their writings into a collage-like paper, embodying the spirit of 1970's punk zines. After school hours, my students stuffed copies of the underground newspaper into every locker in the school. Everyone in the school encountered the newspaper upon opening their locker the following morning. Homerooms were ablaze with discussion about the newspaper and theories regarding the newspaper's origins. Some kids read the paper in groups, huddled around a single copy. Others read the paper by themselves, quietly smiling. My colleagues and I debriefed the text with our homerooms, and kids shared out their favorite excerpts. A compassionate, inclusive spirit permeated the school community.

The students' decision to omit their names from the newspaper was a contributing factor to the newspaper's mass appeal. Everyone wanted to know who wrote it. I had initially hoped my Teen Activism students would "own" their advocacy and attribute their writings to their real names. I grew to appreciate the project design insofar as it marked my students' gradual development into social justice advocates. The anonymity of the underground newspaper was a safe, edgy introduction into activism; they were allowed to negotiate the audience, scope, and shape of their voices.

## Collaborative Reflection

As referenced in Matt's vignette, our focus on authentic audiences is framed by Dr. Baker-Bell, Dr. Stanbrough, and Dr. Everett's notion of *Pedagogies of Healing*. These scholars contend that "it is important for educators to engage in revolutionary praxis by reimagining their classrooms as spaces for triage, self-care, healing, and social transformation" (p. 138). To that end, Drs. Baker-Bell, Stanbrough, and Everett explain how a pedagogy of healing has two tools: "(1) tools to heal: acknowledging that the wound exists and identifying its culprit, and (2) tools to transform: responding to the wound using a tool that works to transform the conditions that led to the wound" (p. 139). Pedagogies of Healing challenge us to consider the potential for healing in the exchanges between students and authentic audiences. Matt's students used the community forum to center their personal stories of immigration injustices. These stories, previously ignored in school contexts, were witnessed and acknowledged. Alex's students resisted racist ideology and hate speech by creating hype around an underground newspaper about inclusion. Our students used their voices to identify and dismantle oppressive ideologies in their communities. Our students spoke, their communities listened, progress was made, and the transformative power of our students' voices was recognized.

## Next Steps, Process, Lessons Learned, New Opportunities for Growth

It is important to emphasize that our respective classrooms do not epitomize Culturally-Sustaining Pedagogy, Critical Race English Education, or Pedagogies of Healing. Rather, we did our best to listen to the work of educators and scholars, particularly educators and scholars of color, who continue to shape conversations around educational justice. We look to their theories and pedagogies as roadmaps that orient our practice.

One of our biggest takeaways is that relationships and community make teaching for justice a sustainable endeavor. Learning from colleagues and students helps us develop our practice and foster a shared sense of belonging. Our co-author relationship, for example, began by connecting through the education community on Twitter (via hashtags like #EduColor and #NCTEChat), and since then, we have collaborated in a number of ways: reflecting together on our classrooms practices, sharing ideas for justice pedagogies, and writing this book chapter. Our reflective practice is always punctuated with moments of storytelling and laughter. This solidarity brings a renewed enthusiasm, conviction, and inspiration to our work.

Together, we've learned that our students, in particular, are our greatest asset. They will tell us what they need if we build trust and are open to their feedback. Centering students in the classroom is the best way to interrogate our blind spots, shift power to young people, and strive toward equitable and liberatory pedagogies. Teaching is a relational practice and process. When we intentionally invest in our relationships with our students, we begin to create classrooms that are community-driven.

We hope that our classroom stories have illuminated moments of social justice and resistance despite our nation's climate of accountability. Assessment is important, but we must be careful not to let the blaring din of data mute the voices and identities of our young people (especially youth of color and other marginalized persons). Sometimes grades distract us from making school an affirming and sustaining space to grow. During our projects we provided students with constant, personalized feedback without burdening them with the looming threat of grades. Our work was standards-aligned and even yielded increased test scores. Though we do not see standardized test scores as valid measures of learning, it's worth recognizing that teaching for justice and teaching content standards are not mutually exclusive endeavors. Because the pedagogies we highlighted engaged students authentically, our students learned more deeply than if we had taught prescriptive standards-aligned curricula that did not sustain our students' identities and experiences.

Finally, we acknowledge that we are lucky to have schools that, despite pressures to hyper-focus on testing and data, are receptive to these student-centered efforts. We are also fortunate to have been granted significant curricular freedom in our classrooms. Such open inquiry and personalized learning is not always permitted by administrators and school systems. We should all strive to integrate elements of Culturally-Sustaining Pedagogy, Critical Race English Education, and Pedagogies of Healing into our current structures and practices. Perhaps the transformational power of these methods will be proof enough to convince school leaders to be more pedagogically permissive. If not, then it might take organizing between teachers, students, families, and community members to reclaim educational justice. Indeed, the theories we've outlined call for a revision (and sometimes the dismantling) of current schooling practices and curricula. Change often requires radical movement. Again, teaching for social justice can be daunting. But we promise: you're in good company.

## References

Baker-Bell, A., Stanbrough, R. J., & Everett, S. (2017). "The stories they tell": Mainstream media, pedagogies of healing, and critical media literacy. *English Education, 49*(2), 130–152.

Goodrich, F., & Hackett, A. (1958). *The diary of Anne Frank.* New York, NY: Dramatists Play Service.

Johnson, L. L. (2018). Where do we go from here? Toward a critical race English education. *Research in the Teaching of English, 53*(2), 102–124.

Ladson-Billings, G. (1995). Toward a theory of culturally relevant pedagogy. *American Educational Research Journal, 32*(3), 465–491.

Paris, D. (2012). Culturally sustaining pedagogy: A needed change in stance, terminology, and practice. *Educational Researcher, 41*(3), 93–97.

Sarigianides, S. T., Petrone, R., & Lewis, M. A. (2017). *Rethinking the "adolescent" in adolescent literacy.* Urbana, IL: National Council of Teachers of English.

# 6. Compulsory Heterosexuality: Unsettling and Undoing the Hidden Curriculum of Heteronormativity in Schools

Mikela Bjork

What I have come to learn is that *everyone* has a schooling story. And that schooling story varies significantly in its content. Schooling stories are unique to the individual telling them and often include details that one wouldn't consider apropos of a schooling story. The purpose of this chapter is to highlight how queer women in AA come to understand themselves through their schooling stories of resistance, so that educators might glean from firsthand experiences how to educate and proactively support young women and girls of varying class, race and ethnic backgrounds. What's more, the purpose of this chapter is to create a counter conversation to the heteronormative, patriarchal structures that define past and present educational standards (Anandhi & Velayudhan, 2010; Freire, 1973; Horton & Freire, 1990; Moraga & Anzaldua, 1981; Solórzano & Yosso, 2001). My hope is that by reading firsthand accounts of how school was enacted, taken up and resisted, the reader will be inspired to take an honest appraisal of his/her own beliefs about what teaching/learning is, what spaces outside of the classroom impart teaching/learning, and how those outside pedagogies can inform what and how we teach inside the classroom.

Heteronormativity is a way of being in the world that assumes the superiority of heterosexuality and, therefore, the inferiority of homosexuality, bisexuality, and questioning sexualities. It assumes that heterosexuality is normal and that therefore anyone who does not identify as heterosexual is abnormal. When heterosexuality is understood as the norm, the act of being straight is immune to criticism, which allows it to be invisible yet dominant. This is a dangerous combination. As Atkinson and DePalma (2008) state, "heteronormativity is a tautology that explains things must be this way because that's the way they are" (p. 27). Organized religions have invisibly yet powerfully wielded heteronormativity to punish and proclaim deviant those who do not identify as straight. It is the same invisible, dangerous power that informs the GOP agenda to deny equal marriage rights to same-sex couples.

Heteronormativity as an institutionalized practice "legitimizes and privileges heterosexuality and heterosexual relationships as fundamental and 'natural' within society" (Cohen, 2005, p. 24). Adrienne Rich (1986) claims that "compulsory heterosexuality" naturalizes heterosexuality and pathologizes lesbianism, thus privileging heterosexual masculinity. Compulsory heterosexuality, Rich says,

> is a political institution which systematically works to the disadvantage of all women … the failure to examine heterosexuality as an institution is like failing to admit that the economic system called capitalism or the caste system of/or racism is maintained by a variety of forces, including both physical violence and false consciousness. (p. 313)

The institution of school is a site where heteronormative structures are typically unquestioned and reified. That is, "from the time they enter school, students are systemically calibrated with 'normal' characterizations of one of the two gender assignments, male or female" (Blackburn, Clark, Kenney, & Smith, 2010, p. 627). From strict gender roles (bathroom signs, boys and girls separated into single-sex lines and groups) to requiring core bodies of literature that favor heterosexuality (*Romeo and Juliet, The Great Gatsby*) to discourses that claim "boys will be boys" and "girls will be girls," the institution of heterosexuality is alive and thriving in schools that are populated with more and more students who do not relate or identify with the gendered boundaries within which they are positioned. Gendered roles for teachers and administrators mirror the patriarchal hierarchy, typically placing (white) male math and science teachers in classrooms, as well as advancing (white) male teachers to positions of authority such as school dean or assistant principal. Pinar (1994) posits that all schooling is a "gender ceremony that compels heterosexuality" (p. 176).

The gendered ceremonies of schooling do not occur in isolation, but rather within a specific figured world. A figured world can be understood as a socially and culturally constructed "realm of interpretation in which particular characters and actors are recognized, significance is assigned to certain acts, and particular outcomes are valued over others" (Holland, Lachicotte, Skinner, & Cain, 1998, p. 52). In the figured world of AA, for example, the particular characters who are recognized are the nondrinking alcoholic and the drinking nonalcoholic. These characters represent the present and past identities of the members of AA. In the figured world of school, the actors are teachers, administrators, and students. In this chapter, the voices of the students are women, reflecting back upon the hidden curriculum of heteronormativity, which fostered the belief system that straight, heteronormative identities were valued over their nonstraight, queer identities.

These worlds are "socio-historic, contrived interpretations or imaginations that mediate behavior and so, from the perspective of heuristic development, inform participants' outlooks" (Holland et al., 1998, p. 53). Thus, figured worlds contribute to the identity formation of those participating in such a world. In the figured world of AA, participants enter or are recruited into the program, unsure of the meeting format, the language used, including the humor, which can be off-putting to a newcomer. A recovering alcoholic in AA who tells her story might find humor in the insane behavior and choices made during drinking days; to a newcomer, this might not be humorous. Rather, the insanity of the disease of alcoholism might be too new and too relatable to be humorous to the newcomer. But over time, the newcomer learns by listening and observing that while the disease of alcoholism is deadly and destructive, within the figured world of AA, it is also important to laugh at oneself as a changed person. Similarly, within the figured world of school, the participants of this chapter formed their identities in response to and against the dominant discourse, which favored—via the hidden curriculum— heteronormativity. Just as alcoholics in the figured world of AA take up, bend and challenge their evolving identities via the narrative template of "experience strength and hope," so do the women in this chapter take up, bend and challenge their evolving identities within their schooling narratives.

The figured world of AA is peopled with alcoholics of varying sober time, from 24 hours to multiple years of sobriety. The AA discourse is one that is modeled and shared among the members of its community, with the intention to carry the message to other self-identifying alcoholics that they are not alone in their disease. In a similar way, the figured world of school is peopled with administrators, teachers, and students. These characters cocreate their world through daily activities, such as homework, class work, and recess. The discourses created and reproduced within the figured world of schooling include but are not limited to "the mean student," "the good student," "the bad student," "the nice teacher," "the mean teacher," and so forth.

According to AA pedagogy, it is by honestly sharing one's life experiences (i.e., self-authoring) with someone else that one is both liberated from self-obsession and able to be of service to another person, who in turn is liberated in knowing that she is not alone in her own self-centered obsession. The acts of narrating and bearing witness to personal experiences are courageous and, when done within the parameters of a mutually created safe space, offer qualities of healing, unpacking, (re)directing, (re)defining, and hope, for both the narrator *and* the audience. My hope is that by reading and engaging with the narratives in this chapter, the reader will be inspired to adopt and then share a pedagogy of self-reflexivity, modeling to their students/colleagues compassionate listening and speaking, which often translates into compassionate teaching and learning for teachers and students.

The narratives in this chapter highlight the self-authoring and self-healing discourses, which are in part inspired by the work the participants have done within the figured world of AA. I note throughout each of the narratives, how the pedagogy of AA intertwines with the schooling narrative, specifically in moments of clarity around self-acceptance in the face of extreme trauma. The discourse of AA informs the lens these queer, self-identifying alcoholic women use to make sense of trauma as it relates to their figured worlds of school. I encourage you to read these as counter-narratives—narratives that challenge a dominant discourse that defines "wrong" from "right"; "good" from "bad"; "worthy" from "unworthy."

As participants in figured worlds attempt to author their experiences, they engage in "social experimentation as well as social reproduction" (Holland et al., 1998, p. 238). In short, people come to know themselves in relation to their work with others. Within the figured world of school, there is inevitably a memorable story about a specific teacher who made an impact on a student in either a positive or negative way. Within the figured world of AA, there is the narrative template of the alcoholic story, which members learn and use to (re)create their own alcoholic narrative. "Agency lies in the improvisations that people create in response to particular situations" (Holland et al., 1998, p. 279). It is through this agentic practice of narrative and self-authoring that identities are (re)formed and a figured world is (re)imagined.

The discourse specific to the figured world of AA favors self-identification as an alcoholic. Members introduce themselves before saying, "Hello. My name is _____, and I am an alcoholic." Outside of the figured world of AA, this introduction of oneself would be frowned on, judged, or criticized. But within the figured world of AA the discourse around self-identifying with the disease of alcoholism is normalized. The dominant discourse in school is similar in that it assumes heteronormativity. Word problems revolve around heterosexual couples; required readings favor novels, rich with drama between heterosexual couples; teachers assume *upon* their students (as you will read) heterosexuality as the *norm*. The figured world of school is framed by a heteronormative discourse that shames girls and young women who do not look or act the part of what it means to be a "normal girl" in school.

In the figured world of schooling, "the absence of homosexuality reinforces the hegemony of heterosexuality as well as the constant re-inscription of heterosexuality," such as photographs of opposite-sex partners decorating a teacher's desk or (prior to the passage of the Marriage Equality Act, 2015) donning a wedding band on one's ring finger (Evans, 1992). The heterosexual matrix "designates the grid of cultural intelligibility through which bodies, genders, and desires are naturalized" (Butler, 1990 p. 151). Thus, the figured world of schooling is a space where heteronormative assumptions are both silently enacted and publicly performed (i.e., through the hidden curriculum), othering the bodies (and spirits and minds) that do not fit into that matrix while projecting gendered expectations on girls and young women at large.

How then do the women in this chapter—women who represent diversity in age, race, ethnicity and socioeconomic class—author themselves through the language and labels of their peers, their families, the media, and their teachers? How do they author themselves using words that have been used to narrate them in a world where they are not the primary author? As Rita Charon (2006) states, "narrative knowledge and practice are what human beings use to communicate to one another about events or states of affairs and are, as such, a major source of both identity and community" (p. 11). And, finally, how do these sober-identifying women find ways to (re)author themselves through the specific discourse and pedagogy of AA?

## *Anna*

> Um. I … I don't think I identified myself as a boy or a girl. I didn't have that distinction yet. In my house there was no boy or girl, man or woman. In my house … I guess that distinction wasn't really made for me. I mean, I thought I was going to marry my mother and live with my mother forever and just never really defined myself as man or woman, boy or girl. So it was just weird. Very strange.

Anna's languaging around not identifying as a boy or a girl, based on the fact that "that distinction wasn't really made for me," speaks to the lack of agency Anna experienced around her gender identity. As if something so intimate, so personal to one's identity formation, as identifying as a boy or a girl was not within her control at all, Anna highlighted that whether or not she was a girl or a boy was based on someone outside of her telling her who she was.

> I ended up living with a foster family, and my foster mother took me to the school, and they said, "Well, what do you want to do for extracurricular activities?" And I said I wanted to play football, but I don't know what else I want to do. It's what I've

*grown up doing, and I'm good at it. And they said, Well what about band, instead of football? And uh … [chuckling] I said, OK, I'll play the drums. That sounds amazing. Just the pop, pop, pop [she motions as if she has a drum set in front of her] you know, beatin' on … it's cool, and it's probably something I would enjoy because I don't like girl stuff. I wanna do boy stuff.*

*In sixth grade I wanted to play football. I grew up as a kid loving football, playing football with all the neighborhood boys. I was fast; I was tough; I wasn't afraid of getting hit [she says this while laughing]. I mean, I grew up getting my ass whupped, so it didn't bother me to get hit or knocked over, or like hit other people and knock them over. So I loved playing football, and when I got to sixth grade I wanted to play football. And they were like, "What do you want?"—you know, you had extracurricular activities: two electives. And I wanted to play football. And I—they did the talk with me that, you know, "You're a girl; boys play football." And I think the nice way they said it was that the boys' hands might be "too friendly." Something really weird like that; something I'm even uncomfortable saying now. Like, it's just bizarre to me that that's how you would … and so, uh, I couldn't play football.*

Within her figured world of school, Anna's teachers told her that she is a girl and therefore could not play instruments (drums) or sports (football) that boys play. A distinction was made *for* her rather than *by* her, regarding her gender identity. Anna didn't identify or feel the need to define herself as a boy or a girl within her figured world of home. Within her figured world of school, however, a distinction was made for her and imposed upon her, confining her to activities "for girls," nestled tightly into the hidden curriculum of heteronormativity and patriarchal values.

*You know, it was during recess, and all the girls would play … they would go off into this wooded area that was pine trees, and they would take straw and make beds and kitchens and make full houses out of it, and it was bizarre to me! And they would play house, and I would play football, and they would ask me to come and be their child for a moment or something. I don't remember; it was very strange, and I just wanted to play football.*

The hidden curriculum of heteronormativity, informed by patriarchal standards, influenced Anna's figured world of school and her sense of possibility within that space, creating a feeling of not belonging at an early age. The activities in school were divided between the sexes: boys played football; girls played house. Anna did not fit into the gendered niches that were carved out for her (by her peers and teachers). She was an outsider, who did not relate to the girls who played house and who was told by her teachers that football was not an option for her to play, due to the fact that she was a girl.

In Anna's figured world of school, she was denied, based on her sex, the right to choose her electives, and the reason she was offered to explain why she was prohibited from playing football was based on a heteronormative rape culture—one that is deeply situated in the education system. Anne was told that "Boys' hands might be too friendly," a pretext that punished *her* for being a girl rather than punishing the boys for sexually harassing her on the football field. At the expense of denying Anna her right to play football, the people in her figured world of school contributed to the normalizing of rape culture through this rationalization. The phrase used by school officials to justify Anne's exclusion from football was misleading at best, since, the boys' hands are, in fact, not friendly at all. The "too friendly" hands of the boys are invasive, terrifying, abusive, and a part of a much bigger problem informed by the often-uninterrogated patriarchal, heteronormative rape culture that exists within and beyond the school systems (Rich, 1979).

Anna admitted to wanting to play the drums because she did not like "girl stuff," something that came up a few times in our conversations together. I asked her to describe the "girl stuff" and what that meant to her. Her response was as follows:

> *I don't know. I think there was cheerleading or something? I just didn't even know what those options were. I had no idea cuz I was told that boys played football and boys played in the percussion. I didn't even know what my options were. I know I wanted to play football, and when I couldn't do that and they presented band to me, I was like, "I'll play the drums." The band instructor said, "Well, what about the trumpet?" And I was like, "That's crazy."*

Anna was denied access to playing football as well as access to playing the drums in the band because those activities were "for boys." The message that Anna received in these moments—which she remembered 15 years later—was that her interests and extracurricular passions did not correspond with the gendered figured world of school had been set up for her.

### Beth

> *I went to a school called Riverside Country Day School, and there was a junior kinder-garten up through the ninth grade. So when I was four I got to junior kindergarten. And I have a twin. And there was a kinda feeling—a truth, a something—which was that I was more developed than my twin brother, which I think is typical of girls and boys. But they had made a decision on some level that it would be bad for him, being a boy, seeing his sister move on ahead. So I had this feeling that I was supposed to always take care of him and protect him, and I didn't want to. But there was another part of me that felt like it was my job to make sure he was OK. So that was true for a lot of my school life. It was like there's me, but I also have to worry about him.*

This "truth" and "feeling" that Beth articulated, the knowledge that she was more developed than her brother, was a gift and a curse. As early as four years old, Beth was aware of her brother—his limitations, his differences, his abilities—and while she did not relate this *knowing* to her sex, I posit that her awareness of *other* is a skill that she learned because she was a girl (Belenky, Clinchy, Goldberger, & Tarule, 1986; Bunch & Pollack, 1983; Gilligan, Rogers, & Tolman, 1991). Highlighting the ecology of women's (and girls') work—both visible and invisible—Beth authored herself as a protector of her brother, while also navigating her own schooling experiences. She learned at a young age to juggle herself ("there's me") with her brother ("but I also have to worry about him"). While this is not limited to girls' experiences within their figured worlds of home and school, it is a much more pronounced burden to bear on girls than boys and is intertwined in the expectations of girls in their figured worlds of school. These expectations are additional manifestations of the hidden curriculum of heteronormativity.

The hidden curriculum of heteronormativity is present in Beth's recollection that "they had made a decision on some level that it would be bad for him, being a boy, seeing his sister move on ahead." The *they*s in this memory are not clear, but the people being referenced here were characters specific to her figured world of school—people who continued to make decisions about her progress as it related to her gender, as well as her identities as a sister, a caregiver, a troublemaker, and other roles that she took on over the course of her primary and secondary schooling.

> *I was also falling in love with girls and teachers and terrified about that because I thought, "Well not only am I fat, ugly, stupid, but god, am I gay?" So I just thought, "One more fucking thing." So I never did anything about it. And I tried to hide it, but I would be moaning and pining over these teachers.*
>
> *And my father said, "You're out of control. You have to go to the Bunch School in Connecticut," which is where his sisters had gone to school. And I did not want to go to Bunch. But I had to because they had complete control over everything, and so I went to Bunch. I remember at Bunch I did an experiment. I was so aware of pink, yellow, and green. All the girls—almost all of the girls came from Lake Forest, they came from Greenwich, they came from Grosse Pointe, they came from Darien. They all came from communities like that. And there was this uniform: it was pink, yellow, and green sweaters. And so you'd go into their rooms, and you'd see stacks of pink, yellow, and green, and Top-Siders, and we all looked the same. And I thought to myself, "OK. Maybe you just haven't tried hard enough. So just put on the pink, yellow, and green, and talk about the boys and just be like them." And I just couldn't do it. I couldn't do it. I tried so hard, and then I realized I cannot do this. I'm constitutionally incapable of being this way. That's when I went over to the dark side. That's when I'm going to be bad. It was after that experiment.*

The "pink, yellow, and green" sweaters were symbols of heterosexuality and heteronormativity in school. The "uniform" of heteronormativity was something that Beth attempted to wear but could not. Interestingly, Beth used AA discourse to explain her realization that she was "constitutionally incapable of being this way." In AA, the reference to being "constitutionally incapable" is in regard to the success rate for people who have entered Alcoholics Anonymous. "Rarely have we seen a person fail who has thoroughly followed our path. Those who do not recover are people who cannot or will not completely give themselves to this simple program, usually men and women who are constitutionally incapable of being honest with themselves" (Wilson, 1976, p. 58). Beth situated herself as being "constitutionally incapable of being this way." I consider "this way" to mean conforming to the heteronormative structures by which she was surrounded and that she attempted to adopt as her own.

Beth narrated this realization as a pivotal point wherein she "went over to the dark side." Once she decided that she was constitutionally incapable of being straight, of fitting in with the straight, good girls, she decided to be bad. Beth narrated her own agency, even through this challenging time; she was saying that she *made a decision* to adopt the identity of "bad." This was a powerful pivot in both her identity formation and her schooling experience, both of which inform the other. It also speaks to the internalization of "good girl" versus "bad girl" ideologies and gives great insight into the internal struggle of one "bad girl" who thought she had no other option than to *be bad* because, given her sexuality, she could not conform to the heteronormative expectations laid out by her figured world of school.

> *I had a very bad attitude because I was with the kind of girls I had grown up with: It was pink, yellow, and green. It was upper-middle class WASP. I mean, some of them were unbelievably wealthy. They were straight. They were thin. Most of them had mothers that were thin and attentive. Not all of them, but most of them. And they were straight and giggly and into boys. And it was, like, everything that I wasn't. So, I was like this hideous thing, back in with that group of girls.*

Beth referred to the "pink, yellow and green" types of girls quite a few times in her memories about attending Bunch, referring to the colors of popular cable knit sweaters, but they were symbolic of much more than a fashion statement. Beth began to describe the symbolism of the "pink, yellow and green" in this excerpt: they represented the upper-middle WASP socioeconomic class; they represented heterosexuality; they represented thinness; they represented young women whose mothers were also "thin and attentive." Beth was saying that the "pink, yellow, and green" represented everything that she was not. While she did identify as a WASP, she did not identify as straight or thin, nor did she have a mother who was attentive to her needs. Beth's coda in the above excerpt was her self-authoring as "this hideous thing, back in with that group of girls." She authored herself as an outsider; the type of girl that was symbolized by "pink, yellow and green" was the antithesis of what Beth was.

> *I started asking all these girls, "Have you lost your virginity? Have you lost your virginity? Have you?" I stirred the pot. Because I knew that I couldn't compete with being straight, cute, bubbly, perky, the boyfriend, the good student, so I guess I decided if I can't be good, then I'm going to be a fucking nightmare. So that's what I did. I stirred the pot.*

Beth described her acting out as "stirring the pot." What is most important in the above excerpt is her choice of characteristics with which she could not compete: "straight, cute, bubbly, perky, the boyfriend, the good student, good." A deep-seated system of beliefs that she learned through her figured worlds, evident in Beth's list of the qualities she did not possess, molded the qualities into a simplified, overarching concept of *good*. Beth did not identify as good; she did not identify as a good girl; she did not identify as a good student. And, according to the qualifiers listed above, most of her "bad" had to do with the fact that she was not straight.

> *I was very worried about people knowing that I was gay. I so didn't want to be gay. So I was a troubled child at Bunch. And the thing that really bothered me was that my friends got sent to the shrink, and I never got sent to the shrink. I was like, How could this be possible, that they're sending the people around me to the shrink, but not sending me? So I felt so invisible—again. Like, "Look what I'm doing; it's so awful! And yet you're sending other people who aren't obnoxious and hostile and defiant!" I felt so invisible. It was awful.*

This comment speaks to the double bind of what it means for girls and young women to be simultaneously hypervisible and invisible. Beth's actions screamed for attention; her acting out was intentional, as she made clear when she reflected on the lack of consequences and the disappointment she experienced not receiving the attention she was seeking through such extreme actions. "Look at what I'm doing; it's so awful!" was a plea to pay attention to her, to treat her with the same concern with which her peers were being treated, like getting sent to the shrink. Beth authored herself as a "troubled child," following her assertion that she did not want to be gay. Beth took up the identity of "troubled" and "bad" in direct relation to her sexual identity. Between the worry that other people knew she was gay and her internalized shame of not wanting to be gay in a heterosexual-hetero-dominant world of school, Beth's "trouble," although it was internalized, was enforced by external sources of homophobia, structured within the hidden curriculum of heteronormativity (Carlson & Roseboro, 2011; Evans, 1992; Rich, 1979; Robertson, 2017).

## *Anna*

> *There was this kid who always made fun of me because I was so tall. And I think he just had a crush on me, and he had a rattail, and I hated him because he was like me, you know? He was poor. He was angry. And he was looking for someone to take it out on. I took it out on the football kids. We would literally just nail each other, and I felt great about that, you know? Cuz we're doing it all to each other, so it's fine. But he would just lay into me, and he just would never shut up, and then one day I grabbed him in a headlock, and I—I just pounded his head until my hand was swollen and bleeding. [She holds up her hand and balls it into a fist and releases it, looking at her knuckles.]*

There is something very poignant about Anna using such strong self-hating language such as "I hated him because he was like me" because what she was saying is that she hated herself, and the reasons for her own self-hatred were that she was poor, angry, and looking to take it out on other people (which she did, by fighting—another activity, similar to football, that troubles the gendered expectations of boys and girls both in and outside of the figured world of school). She wanted to play football and found it therapeutic to "nail" the other football players. It was a way to get out her aggression; it was a way to be physical that did not feel like she was being violated, unlike the violence that she experienced in her figured world of home. It was a way that she could blend in and not be seen as a girl or a boy but as just another football player.

> *We moved to Keysville. I mean, it's the middle of nowhere, and sixth grade came around. And I guess up until that point I made really good grades. And um there was a huge shift in middle school, mostly because I got breasts. And I was devastated [laughs]. I was devastated, and I cried, and I had to wear a bra—and I can't play football, and I felt so betrayed by the world.*

Anna's figured world of (middle) school was deeply informed by puberty and, specifically, getting breasts. Educators and schooling in general need to be more mindful about the patriarchal values that inform the hidden curriculum of heteronormativity that denies girls the safe space to explore their (dis)comfort surrounding physical, sexual, and emotional changes related to puberty. There is still an overwhelming pattern of blaming the victim—that is, blaming adolescent girls for experiencing puberty in a public sphere such as school (Brantlinger, 1993; Finders, 1997; Gilligan, Lyons, & Hanmer, 1990; Gilligan, Ward, & Taylor, 1988).

## *Sara*

> *My gender was so strange as a kid. I was, like, wanting to be a boy. I wasn't; I was a girl. And then I was ADD and from a crazy, sexually violent and violent, alcoholic*

*home. Like I found no advantages of being a girl in school. I didn't have a lot of self-acceptance that I was a girl. So there was that. Everything was challenging.*

In addition to authoring her attention-deficit disorder into her identity—she *was*, rather than *had*, ADD—Sara also authored herself as wanting to be a boy, not able to have self-acceptance that she was a girl. Powerfully, in just a few sentences, Sara listed everything in her life that was challenging: her gender identity; the violence, including sexual violence, and alcoholism in her home; having ADD; and not having self-acceptance that she was a girl. While hearing Sara's description of navigating her figured world of school, an institution that embodies the hidden curriculum of heteronormativity, I was struck with the thought, "Of *course* everything was challenging."

*And just as an aside, I start getting crushes on girls. And all the pretty girls were super nice to me when they were alone, and then they would pretend like they didn't know me when other people were around. But they wanted to hang out with me. When nobody was around they were talking my head off. But also, they would ask me to walk them home from school.*

Sara acknowledged that by the second grade, she had started to have crushes on girls. This memory illustrates Sara's invisibility/hypervisibility in relation to the characters in her figured world of school. Her peers contributed to her feelings of invisibility through their mercurial behavior, pretending they did not know Sara when other people were around but asking her to walk them home when they were alone. Sara learned from these interactions that to perform "maleness" as a female was appreciated privately, but when performed publicly, it was a source of discomfort for others that led to further ostracization from her peers.

When asked how she identifies gender-wise, Sara responded,

*So, on my date last night, I can identify and feel more like a boy in a lot of ways. More male. More masculine. But my politics is that of women. And that's the most important thing to me, cuz I feel like I watch this gross imbalance in front of my eyes every single day, and I watched it my entire life. I mean, there was a time period where I did consider transitioning and living as a trans guy in San Francisco, and in the end that's not what I wanted. I wanted fashion. I wanted to look good in my shirts. But I didn't want to be a man. And even my gender expression, I don't want to be a man. Just talk about my dick* [she starts to laugh].*

*It's incredibly important to me to keep working for what I want to protect. Which is to say, little me. I wish somebody could've protected me. But they could not! I'm so glad I can smash my titties down.* [She says this while laughing.] *I believe it's incredibly important to continue to work to empower women and girls. Um. It's the most important thing to me—the protection of and the advancement of—we are still so incredibly imbalanced in this world with gender and discrimination that I'm not willing to take my power and move it to the other side. Nor will I ever be.*

Indeed, Sara has committed her adult life and multiple careers to highlighting the detrimental role that misogyny plays in women's lives via visual art, literature, music, politics, health care, and higher education. It is almost as if she has taken on the identity/role of The Protector as an adult that Beth and Anna also adopted during their childhood and adolescent years. Sara's decision to remain identified as a girl/woman was about power; her decision was a political stance that addressed the historical imbalance of power between men and women.

> *I think it was sixth grade when I got busted in the locker room from other girls wearing boy's underwear, and the whole locker room erupted. And I just remember people laughing and pointing at me. And it was really intense. I just remember it being really intense and then feeling like gym wasn't safe, either, which was just like—whoa.*
>
> *So sixth grade started, and I became really aware of my gender stuff. I wanted to be good. I really wanted to be good. I was afraid for my life. I was really afraid of what was going to happen. I played a shit ton of basketball. I played on the boys' basketball team. Like, I was really, really good at sports. And that felt super safe. Like, just put all your energy into that.*
>
> *I knew that I wanted to learn stuff. And I didn't want to be bad. And I wanted to be like the other kids. And I wanted to be—figure out how to be a girl. And it just felt fake in a lot of ways. I just faked it.*

Many of the participants (Anna and Beth included) talked about their engagement in sports and how, for so many of them, sports were their saving grace. In this passage, Sara narrated a range of emotions and wishes, from being afraid for her life to wanting to "be good," along with becoming aware of her "gender stuff" in the sixth grade. This "gender stuff" speaks to Sara's identification as a girl politically but as a boy physically. It is significant to note that Sara, who identified more with boys on a physical level, authored her experience within her figured world of school during this specific time period as one where she felt "super safe." Playing basketball with the boys provided for her a sense of safety as she began to become aware of her "gender stuff," similar to the way that playing football brought Anna a sense of joy and belonging in her figured world of school. It is also important to note that as Sara authored this memory of "becoming aware of [her] gender stuff," she immediately followed this with her desire to be "good." For Sara, as for many girls who do not fit into the heteronormative structures of school, to be "good" is to act like the archetypal "girl" even when one does not relate to the social constructs of what it means to do so (Butler, 1990).

I asked Sara what it looks like to be a "good girl" because her desire to be a good girl and a good student in the sixth grade was a crucial part of her identity formation in school. This was her reply:

*Compliant. Someone that people want to fuck. Someone that isn't too threatening, and isn't too loud, and doesn't have an opinion, and takes care of people and—a perfect girl. It's disgusting, what people say to women. But that was what I was trying to be during that time and was what people were talking about. That's when I started sleeping with boys. That did not help me, you know? It helped me feel worse about myself. Trying to be a "good girl." It was a setup, because it wasn't me.*

*But the message is so strong in society. It's like, if you can be this type of girl, you're going to be a good girl, you're going to be taken care of. I was not that girl. And then people made sure to tell me that I wasn't that girl, including the boys I was messing around with. So then I was slutty. It was used against me. It was used against me pretty quickly. And then I turned on myself. I also thought I was a piece of shit. I already had all these ideas about what my limitations were and where I came from, and then I failed being the good girl. The negative voices got louder. That's what I mean. Then there was another level of self-hatred that I couldn't be that—that I was a loser and I couldn't be that.*

The hidden curriculum that circulates in schools contributes to the belief systems of students—girls like Anna, Sara, and Beth—from a very young age. These systems of belief carry the message of compulsory heteronormativity to students and teaches them that they should "fake it" in order to fit in, to "be good." And for Sara, to fake it meant to be accepted, and to be accepted was a means of survival. This is not hyperbole: acceptance, or the lack of acceptance, of gender-nonconforming, trans, and queer kids within the figured world of school has been and continues to be a problem that is discussed openly in the media only after someone dies or is physically harmed due to bullying (Hutchinson, 2017; Payne & Smith, 2013; Wallace, 2011). The discourse that helps to unmask and reveal the violence of the hidden curriculum must be taken up and valued unequivocally.

In order to do this work, however, teachers will need to identify new ways of talking to and supporting students who do not conform to the mandates of compulsory heteronormativity. One such way is by adopting "the language of the heart" (Wilson, 1976)—a language of acceptance and self-reflection that is embraced in AA. Beyond the AA narrative template, which highlights an individual's experience, strength, and hope as she relates to the disease of alcoholism (experience with drinking and the strength it took to stop drinking and hope for the future of a nondrinking lifestyle), is a way of speaking that encourages people to listen to one another and learn from each other. Members of the AA community learn how to make sense of and talk about the past in an agentic and self-reflective manner; this practice can be viewed as a pedagogy unto itself. This manner of speaking and bearing-witness-to creates a community that specializes in honesty, safety, and growth—all attributes that schools employ in their mission statements but fall short of in practice.

The act of storytelling and bearing-witness-to is an act of healing for both narrator and listener. The power of this model is best signified by the growth of Alcoholics Anonymous, which started in 1935 with two men and has since expanded to an estimated 2 million people today (Living Sober, 2013).

AA's pedagogy provides us with a model for a more empathetic and holistic approach to schooling. Schooling and education cannot be addressed as a cut-and-dry problem of "good" teachers, or the mastery of content, or test taking skills. Reducing teaching and learning to such things is a disservice to everyone involved. This chapter highlights the unmet needs and wants of individual women as they reflect on their schooling experiences, in the hope of informing the ways in which other women's needs and wants can be met in schools now and in the future. The stories in this chapter serve as a collective counternarrative to the patriarchal, heteronormative discourses that pervade schools, politics, and everyday infrastructure.

Women are continually talked *about* but are not invited *in*—to have their voices heard. From the divisive topic of abortion rights to rape culture pandemic (but not limited) to school campuses, women's bodies, intellects, and experiences are discussed, criticized, and violently silenced.

The women in this chapter did not narrate their schooling experiences as if they were limited to the physical confines of school. What the women in this chapter contribute to education (and health) policy through their schooling narratives is that the two figured worlds cannot be detached from one another, if educators want to thoroughly address the needs of students while also teaching content. It shows that, in fact, in order to teach content, educators must first be willing to spend time looking at what students—and, more specifically, female-identifying students—are bringing with them from their figured worlds of home.

It is imperative that teachers and school culture are held accountable for the norming of (hetero)sexist and misogynist agendas. These regimes of truth must be actively challenged and replaced with language and actions that promote the voices and overall presence of girls and women. This includes (but is not limited to) carefully choosing literature written by and representative of women of diverse experiences (as opposed to literature written by historically glorified straight white men); the use of pronouns that represent girls and women when making generalized statements about *all* students; mindful noncorroboration of school rules that promote rape culture or shame girls for their appearance. For instance, instead of sending girls home or giving them detention for their choice of apparel, a school culture that fully supports its female students would send boys home or give them detention for making inappropriate (i.e., violent) comments.

When I teach about empathy, I am not teaching a concept but am instead modeling a way of being, a way of living that extends far beyond my classroom. Teaching empathy requires a willingness to be vulnerable. I unpack this with my students—the pros and cons of being vulnerable and the ways in which self-reflexivity inform educators' ability to see where to bring in components of their own social location that both help and hinder the pedagogy and, thus, the students. I refer back to the microscopic versus macroscopic solutions that I have to offer. I see, read, and hear the connections between the cultures of denial at home and at school, through not only the narratives of the women in this chapter but through the newly discovered social locations of my graduate students.

The beliefs that these students impart to their students are familial, historical beliefs that have been passed down to them from their own experiences of schooling and parenting. This means that the potential for sexism, racism, classism, ableism, and homophobia to seep into their own pedagogy is highly likely. By creating a discourse for and around these "-isms," we create a space to struggle, challenge, and reflect, in order to re-create a more expansive discourse. This is reflective of a pedagogy of hope that Paulo Freire (1994), bell hooks (2003), and Shawn Ginwright (2016) frame their work around and that has become most pertinent in my own teaching/learning practices. The pedagogy of hope is also embodied in the empathic listening and speaking skills that are modeled within the figured world of AA.

The pedagogy of AA, paralleling that of narrative medicine—a medical approach that uses people's narratives as a way to promote healing—includes both a speaking and a listening component. It entails active listening, without interruption, as one alcoholic shares her "experience, strength and hope" (Wilson, 1976) on a topic related to the disease of alcoholism. Because it is a self-referential program, participants are encouraged to keep the focus on themselves, even when they relate to another member's vocalized experience.

Alcoholics Anonymous is a fellowship of men and women who share their personal stories with each other to maintain their sobriety and help others get sober. The root of AA is sharing openly and honestly so that one person can be healed of his or her secrets or fears and another person may hear the honesty and feel comfortable to share her own secrets and fears. Using a redemptive narrative template, the community of Alcoholics Anonymous has grown exponentially in the years since its establishment in 1934. The power of the AA narrative is not limited to what is being narrated but how it is being received by the audience. Who is hearing one's own story through the voice of someone else? Layers of life experiences, grief, frustration, and shame are shared and absorbed in great detail by members of this program, the entire process a radical act of healing through sharing and relating. The pedagogy of AA has the potential to inform and implement a more empathetic and holistic approach to pedagogical structures within the institution of school.

*Women's Ways of Knowing* (Belenky et al., 1986) echoes the pedagogical practices of Alcoholics Anonymous, honoring "connection over separation; understanding and acceptance over assessment; collaboration over debate" (p. 34). Belenky et al. criticize the "banking method" of education (Freire, 1973) wherein teachers are authoritative figures who deposit knowledge into their students' passive brains. Instead, they praise the "teacher-as-midwife" model, drawing knowledge out of students, showing them, collaborating with them. The narrative community of AA, the collaborative community of Belenky et al. and narrative medicine are models of communities and communication that value human connection rather than human production or diagnosis. As Rita Charon (2006) states,

> In an age of specialization and fragmentation, how satisfying to discover the deep, nourishing bonds that hold us together—storytellers all bearing witness to one another's ordeals, celebrating our common heritage as listeners around the campfire, creating our identities in the stories we tell. (p. 11)

Telling stories—whether in a 12-step format or sitting in a room with close friends—is a radical act of intimacy. I integrate storytelling into every university class I teach, most of which are Common Core and assessment heavy, as a way of connecting to my students and modeling to them how they might also use storytelling to engage their students, thinking and acting beyond the tightly wound curricula with which they are working.

For instance, in a course that centers on writing appropriate lesson plans for inclusive classroom teaching, I ask my students to freewrite about a lesson or activity they enjoyed when they were their students' age. I ask them to write in depth about their experience and the feelings this activity conjured for them; I then ask them to read and share the memory with the entire class. What unfolds is a community of reengaged and reinspired teachers, having made a personal connection to the seemingly laborious activity that many of them resented at the beginning of the class. I observe students nodding, smiling, and making connections to one another's stories of intrigue, success, and creative or intellectual stimulation. This act of sharing narratives inspires my students to re-create lessons not as a burdensome job but as a means to engage their students in the same way that they were once engaged. The use of narrative sharing and listening reminds them of multiple fond memories that, once uncovered, can then be used to inspire a new generation of learners.

When I entered into the rooms of AA nearly 12 years ago, I was a nascent high school special education teacher and an inchoate member of Alcoholics Anonymous. I have come to realize just how influential both identities—as an educator and a nondrinking alcoholic—are to my pedagogy.

Informed by the figured worlds in which everyone lives and in which everyone has participated, personal narratives are a radical means to liberate each other and oneself from the oppressive self-defeating stories that people tell themselves and a proactive way to talk back to the positions, labels, categories, and identities that are given to individuals. Portelli (1990) states, "An inter/view is an exchange between two subjects: literally a mutual sighting. One party cannot really see the other unless the other can see him or her in return" (p. 31).

## *References*

Alcoholics Anonymous. (2013). *Living Sober: Some methods AA members have used for not drinking.* New York, NY: A. A. World Services.

Anandhi, S., & Velayudhan, M. (2010). Rethinking feminist methodologies. *Economic and Political Weekly, 45*(44), 39–41.

Atkinson, E., & DePalma, R. (Eds.). (2008). *Invisible boundaries: Addressing sexualities equality in children's worlds.* London: Trentham Books.

Belenky, M., Clinchy, B., Goldberger, N., & Tarule, J. (1986). *Women's ways of knowing: The development of self, voice and mind.* New York, NY: Basic Books.

Blackburn, M. V., Clark, C. T., Kenney, L. M., & Smith, J. M. (Eds.). (2010). *Acting out!: Combating homophobia through teacher activism.* New York, NY: Teachers College Press.

Brantlinger, E. (1993). *The politics of social class in secondary school.* New York, NY: Teachers College Press.

Bunch, C., & Pollack, S. (Eds.). (1983). *Learning our way: Essays in feminist education.* New York, NY: The Crossing Press.

Butler, J. (1990). *Gender trouble: Feminism and the subversion of identity.* New York, NY: Routledge.

Carlson, D., & Roseboro, D. (Eds.). (2011). *The sexuality curriculum and youth culture.* New York, NY: Peter Lang.

Charon, R. (2006). *Narrative medicine: Honoring the stories of illness.* Oxford, NY: Oxford University Press.

Cohen, C. J. (2005). Punks, bulldaggers, and welfare queens: The radical potential of queer politics. In E. P. Johnson & M. G. Henderson (Eds.), *Black queer studies: A critical anthology* (pp. 21–51). Durham, NC: Duke University Press.

Evans, M. O. (1992). An estimate of race and gender role-model effects in teaching high school. *Journal of Economic Education, 23*(3), 209–217.

Finders, M. (1997). *Just girls: Hidden literacies and life in junior high*. New York, NY: Teachers College Press.

Freire, P. (1973). *Pedagogy of the oppressed*. New York, NY: Seabury Press.

Freire, P. (1994). *A pedagogy of hope: Reliving pedagogy of the oppressed*. New York, NY: Continuum Press.

Gilligan, C., Rogers, A., & Tolman, D. (Eds.). (1991). *Women, girls, and psychotherapy: Reframing resistance*. New York, NY: Harrington Park Press.

Gilligan, C., Lyons, N., & Hanmer, T. (1990). *Making connections: The relational worlds of adolescent girls at Emma Willard School*. Cambridge, MA: Harvard University Press.

Gilligan, C., Ward, J., & Taylor, J. (Eds.). (1988). *Mapping the moral domain*. Cambridge, MA: Harvard University Press.

Ginwright, S. (2016). *Hope and healing in urban education: How urban activists and teachers are reclaiming matters of the heart*. New York, NY: Routledge.

Holland, D., Lachicotte, W., Skinner, D., & Cain, C. (1998). *Identity and agency in cultural worlds*. Cambridge, MA: Harvard University Press.

hooks, b. (2003). *Teaching community: A pedagogy of hope*. New York, NY: Routledge.

Horton, M., & Freire, P. (1990). *We make the road by walking: Conversations on educational and social change*. Philadelphia, PA: Temple University.

Hutchinson, S. (2017). Segregation now and forever: Betsy DeVos and the looting of public education. *The Humanist, 77*(1), 9–11.

Moraga, C., & Anzaldua, G. (1981). *This bridge called my back: Writings by radical women of color*. New York, NY: State University of New York Press.

Payne, E., & Smith, M. (2013). LGBTQ kids, school safety, and missing the big picture: How the dominant bullying discourse prevents school professionals from thinking about systemic marginalization or … why we need to rethink LGBTQ bullying. *QED: A Journal in GLBTQ Worldmaking, 10*(1), 1–36.

Pinar, W. F. (1994). *Autobiography, politics, and sexuality: Essays in curriculum theory 1972–1992*. New York, NY: Peter Lang.

Portelli, A. (1990). *The death of Luigi Trastulli and other stories: Form and meaning in oral history*. Albany, NY: State University of New York Press.

Rich, A. (1979). *On lies, secrets, and silence*. New York, NY: W. W. Norton.

Rich, A. (1986). Compulsory heterosexuality and lesbian existence. *Signs, 5*(4), 631–660.

Robertson, W. (2017). The irrelevance narrative: Queer (in)visibility in medical education and practice. *Medical Anthropology Quarterly, 10*(1), 22–49.

Solórzano, D. G., & Yosso, T. J. (2001). Critical race and LatCrit theory and method: Counter-storytelling Chicana and Chicano graduate school experiences. *International Journal of Qualitative Studies in Education, 14*(4), 471–495.

Wallace, S. (2011). Gold diggers, video vixens and jezebels: Stereotype images and substance use among urban African American girls. *Journal of Women's Health, 20*(9), 3–30.

Wilson, Bill. (1976). *Alcoholics Anonymous: The story of how many thousands of men and women have recovered from alcoholism*. (3rd ed.). New York, NY: A. A. World Services.

# Section III

# Unsettling Education Through Institutional Critiques

# *Introduction*

The authors in this section question why there is so very little discussion in schools and universities about how knowledge is constructed, packaged, and disseminated and for what purposes. They ask why teachers and students are being held responsible for doing more and more, while being given less and less of everything—less time, less compensation, less support. In turn, these authors show us that the way we understand what education is, as well as what it is for, has been fundamentally altered through the imposition of neoliberal mandates. Henry Giroux (2013) notes that the difference between the process of schooling and education as the practice of freedom is that an authentic liberatory education "draws attention to questions concerning who has control over the conditions for the production of knowledge, values, and skills, and it illuminates how knowledge, identities, and authority are constructed within particular social relations" (as cited in Tristan, 2013). In other words, education as the practice of freedom seeks to reveal that which goes unsaid about the very processes of schooling and about the way that institutions shape, challenge, or support these processes. This work requires that we unsettle that which appears fixed or uncontestable in our educational institutions. It means that we challenge and unsettle the ways of knowing and doing that so many people take for granted in these spaces. It means that we make the familiar strange and the strange familiar by exposing the contradictions that we negotiate in our daily work as educators (McLaren, 2017).

That daily work, however, is structured and organized by an institutional logic that appears "natural" and "normal" to those who do the work in schools and universities. That logic is so powerful that educators and students participate (sometimes unwittingly and sometimes by necessity) in schooling that not only works to prevent genuine student and community participation in the construction of knowledge, but also to limit the expression of alternative ways of knowing, doing, and being. Schooling—a process distinct from education—occurs when the participants act with little or no discussion about why or for what purpose they are doing the things they are being asked to do; the official pronouncements as well as the knowledge contained in the textbooks, mandated tests, evaluation systems, and syllabi appear "fixed" and uncontestable to those who enter our schools and universities. Thus, teachers and students, to use Maxine Greene's (1988) phrase, have a "tendency to accede to the given," as they become mired in particular ways of knowing, doing, and being. This process leads to a kind of disengagement and withdrawal from what the educators in this section have come to know as more authentic, or humanizing, approaches to teaching, learning, or being. So, instead of an active engagement with important questions about the health and sustainability of our communities, educational institutions become places where "messages and announcements fill the air; but there is, because of the withdrawal, a widespread speechlessness, a silence where there might be— where there ought to be—an impassioned and significant dialogue" (p. 2).

In most public school districts and universities, educators and students are not generally consulted (not in any meaningful way) when it comes to implementing or designing institutional reforms (Payne, 1998). Educators are not invited to participate in the impassioned dialogue that Greene imagines above. In fact, as Henry Giroux (1994) notes, "legislators and government officials are ignoring the most important people in the reform effort, the teachers" (p. 38). Rather than be encouraged to engage students and other educators in meaningful discussions about the purposes of education or the role of public schools and universities in a democratic society, educators are told to focus on creating harsher discipline policies, improving student character traits, and increasing student and teacher motivation. Where we should be discussing the value of the public good and the importance of democratic practice and participation in society, we find ourselves, instead, discussing things like test scores and student buy in on assignments. Where we should be discussing how to develop healthy and sustainable communities and identifying the resources to support teachers and students, we find ourselves discussing how to improve or "fix" individual teachers and students by improving study skills, importing new technologies, adopting best practices, or implementing new evaluation systems.

It is not hard to see how the education reforms of the past several decades, reforms that include a discourse of moral fitness and individual development, have shifted questions about changing our institutions and society toward questions about fixing individuals. Such rhetorical sleight of hand takes us away from discussions centered around resource redistribution, economic development, or equity in our educational institutions and communities, toward discussions about whether or not certain communities (filled with failing individuals according to state-mandated metrics) deserve additional resources. Dominant discourses that seek to describe and categorize individuals work in ways that alienate both individuals and their communities—discourses aided by data from standardized tests, crime reports, incarceration rates, poverty levels, etc.—shaping the way we understand our social and economic problems as problems of personal responsibility. Given, then, that within this framework certain individuals are perceived as unwilling to or incapable of conforming to seemingly neutral academic and social standards, the question of who deserves what has answered itself.

In the first chapter in this section, author James McCoyne examines the ways in which standardized teacher evaluations, evaluations that are ostensibly about improving instruction, often miss the most important work that teachers do to build positive relationships with colleagues, students, and families. His chapter illustrates how our educational institutions and the curriculum that we develop emerge from a set of predetermined norms and expectations. That is, the institution of school is organized around the expectation and assumption that every student that comes before the teacher is ready and eager to learn what is being taught.

McCoyne asks questions about what this means for teachers and students: "I wonder how many teachers are in that position of wanting to help, but not wanting to be vulnerable by deviating from expectations, or even hinting that the expectations are flawed." McCoyne notes that the data we harvest from these evaluations rarely present a fair or full portrait of the work of teaching. And, the same can be said for students. In our data obsessed culture McCoyne reminds us that "Perhaps the most troubling implication with the prioritization of data is that the only thing that matters about students, or at least what is most significant, is their ability to perform on assessments."

In "Motivation, Mental Health, and the Eclipse of the Social Imagination," author Kevin Carey explores the problems that arise for teachers and students as we attempt to do our work in a culture of hyper-individualism shaped by a neoliberal ideology. Carey observes that "we reduce 'public issues' to 'private troubles,' and in so doing, while we clamor more and more for individual accountability, we hold ourselves as a community and a society largely unaccountable." Working within such frameworks, teachers and students are taught to see their successes or failures as the result of individual effort and determination—as a problem of motivation. But, Carey reminds us that doing so may erase the complex humanity of our students and colleagues:

> [T]hey are, even already by pre-kindergarten, complex human beings with a host of needs, desires, interests, aptitudes, strengths, struggles, fears, quirks

and personalities, and they vary widely in terms of their histories, experiences, cultures, environments and resources, to name just a few of the salient factors that impact and play upon the desire to do a thing, which is basically what motivation is.

And, he offers us a warning about the overuse of evaluations that are often sold to teachers and students as mechanisms for increasing motivation. Carey notes that "the work of measurement, the power of evaluation, is a process of extracting certain values, energies, and actions while ignoring or excluding others." Carey suggests that we need to pay more attention to the way in which this evaluation process implicitly defines sites of knowing and determines both what knowledge is as well as what is worth knowing and doing.

Samantha Young and Deborah Bieler also look closely at the problems that evaluations and standardized examinations have posed for the work of teachers and on schools. In their shared story they explore the way that these evaluation systems function to reduce the complexity of the people most affected by them. They tell the story of Young's struggles to negotiate the competing demands of being a teacher in a high-needs school in an era of high-stakes testing, while also struggling to have a life outside the classroom. They look carefully at the role of the teacher and then ask the difficult questions about whether or not, given the demands of today's job, it's still possible (and worth it to try) to be both a successful teacher and still have time to reflect on, explore, and engage with the world outside of the schoolhouse.

Bieler, as Young's mentor, makes a series of attempts to support and encourage Young in her teaching life, but often feels defeated by what she sees and hears at Young's school. Bieler finds that the job of teaching has become so difficult and unappealing that she struggles to find the words that will help Young carry on and, possibly, make positive change in her school community. As Young makes clear, however, the idea of fighting the system, given the unmanageable workload that teachers shoulder, appears nearly impossible. Young notes that she does not "have time to fight or change this statewide initiative, so I might as well just do my best to make it as smooth and successful for my students as possible." The state mandates delimit and define what Young's teaching life is like, and she details the disruption and impact that "test-preparation mania had caused in her own and others' teaching." Young also makes the important point that in addition to the difficulty of the work of teaching, "she worked so many more hours and was being paid so, so much less than her peers in other professions." Young concludes by explaining that "teachers are being asked to participate in faulty, harmful teaching practices." This story is both a challenge to those making decisions about what happens in schools and a cautionary tale for those thinking of entering the profession in order to change it.

In the final chapter in this section, Russel Mayo presents us with another story of a teacher coming to see the work of teaching in new and unsettling ways. Like Young and Bieler, Mayo asks difficult questions about the purpose of our schools and role of teachers in them. Mayo tells the story of his evolution from student to teacher and the powerful effects that reading Ivan Illich had on him as a teacher. Mayo says reading Illich caused him to "forever think and speak differently about ideas and experiences that I have wrestled with since adolescence." In his story, Mayo picks up and advances Illich's claim that reforming school is the wrong approach to improving our schools, arguing that the way to improve education is not to reform schools, but to completely dismantle them. In other words, to make schools work, we need to get rid of schools altogether. While the paradox of dismantling public education to rescue it from itself may appear both counterintuitive and altogether unsettling, one of the points that Mayo makes is that such a process could result in a world where "students and communities might choose much more personally fulfilling and socially useful options without compulsory attendance." Mayo tells us that the problem with our education system is that "schools as such undermined non-schooled learning in that the 'schooled' came to view learning as something done *to* them by those who knew more than they."

The stories in this section encourage, unsettle, and challenge us to think in new and provocative ways about our visions for the future of education and society. This includes not simply thinking about how to redesign the curriculum we use for our courses, but also considering with students why and how we do what we do and for what purposes. And, finally, these stories push us to acknowledge difficult truths about what it means to work in solidarity with marginalized groups to create just and sustainable communities. This work involves the need to create opportunities to challenge those in power and then dismantle, redesign, and develop new educational spaces that reflect the knowledges, desires, and aspirations of communities.

## *References*

Giroux, H. A. (1994). Teachers, public life, and curriculum reform. *Peabody Journal of Education, 69*(3), 35–47. doi: 10.1080/01619569409538776

Greene, M. (1988). *The dialectic of freedom*. New York, NY: Teachers College Press.

McLaren, P. (2017). *Life in schools: An introduction to critical pedagogy in the foundations of education*. New York, NY: Routledge.

Payne, C. (1998). *So much reform, so little change: Building-level obstacles to urban school reform*. Institute for Policy Research, Northwestern University.

Tristan, J. M. (2013, February 6). Henry Giroux: The necessity of critical pedagogy in dark times. Retrieved from https://truthout.org/articles/a-critical-interview-with-henry-giroux/

# 7. *Managing Teachers: Efficiency and Human Relations in Education*

JAMES MCCOYNE

### *Gotcha*

The school I work at is small; this year my department includes one other teacher. As a single-sex high school, we currently have under 200 young women enrolled. The size of the school was a comfort when I started a year ago, fresh out of college. Small schools can provide a wonderful intimacy to the work environment, but close proximity without the buffer that more people provide can also lead to escalated conflicts over minor issues that would go ignored at a school even double its size.

I'm running the creative writing club when an announcement comes over the intercom, static and broken sounds, but distinct enough to understand: I am needed in the main office if available. It is a small school, and my administrators know I have a club after school on Tuesdays from 3:20 to 4:00. The routines of the staff are not private, but administration wants to see me. So, I make myself available. The three students in the room understand.

Even as a teacher, being called to the office creates knots in my stomach. Perhaps even more so as a teacher than when I was a student, considering the fact that I never got called to see the dean, principal, or really anyone when I was in high school myself. I walk to the office and see two administrators, both standing, one near the entrance and the other by the window. Outside is not a particularly nice view, but she isn't looking out; both eyes are on me.

"You're not in trouble." Always great first words to hear, especially if you're prone to anxiety as I am. "We've received some concerning complaints from some of your colleagues—"

"Not me," says a social science teacher, who I only now notice is standing in the office.

"No, not her," says the administrator, in a voice I'm pretty sure is meant to be reassuring. She continues, "Some teachers have been complaining that there is a 'gotcha' culture at this school. We wanted to speak to some teachers who we feel have no reason to be dishonest to us, so please feel free to give your honest feedback."

"What exactly do you mean by 'gotcha' culture?" I inquire, unsure what I'm supposed to be giving feedback about.

The other administrator steps in to explain. "One of the things we've been receiving complaints about is my pop-in observations." Indeed she had begun to come into our classrooms to check in on how well we are hitting the Targeted Instructional Areas. This year there are several: differentiation, rigor, data-driven instruction, and academic vocabulary. When an administrator began to enter classrooms with a clipboard and checklist, word spread fast amongst teachers. Although the claim was that these visits were non-punitive, teachers still felt disgruntled by the unannounced observations.

"I'd say that the problem isn't a 'gotcha' culture here." My people-pleasing tendencies kick in. (Once when I asked what she thought I added to the school, my principal told me that she appreciates that I'm not a complainer.) Plus, I don't always excel when put on the spot, so any complaints I have don't immediately come. I am also still recovering from the fright of being asked to speak with the principal in the first place. I opt for diplomatic honesty. "I'd say that the problem isn't a 'gotcha' culture here. I think that it's kind of just the state of education right now."

## Teacher Assessment and Management

Observations are purportedly about instructional coaching to provide teachers with the tools they need to be better instructors. Most teachers I've spoken to do not like being observed. To be completely honest, the sense of isolation I feel in the classroom is one of the perks of the job, so a career where I'm more or less given control over my own setting and then left to my own devices is ideal. I believe in the work I'm doing, and I appreciate the privacy I'm given. Although unit plans are collected and gradebooks are audited, what happens day to day is in my hands; there's not even another person who teaches the same courses to co-plan with. The dozen or so observations that teachers receive throughout the academic school year are an interruption of this arrangement.

In *The Principles of Scientific Management*, Frederick Winslow Taylor analyzed the role of the laborer in the manufacturing industry and theorized that a worker needed management to perform labor more efficiently. In his

perspective, the time a worker spent performing labor yielded no expertise. Rather than respecting laborers as individuals striving to do their best
work, Taylor instead felt that their actual goal was in fact to do "as little as
[they] safely can" (1913, p. 13). In other words, left alone workers are inef-
fective at best, and lazy at worst.

In contemporary education, administration serves as a form of management for teachers. Its aims are framed as benevolent, using terminology like
"instructional coaching," but the conceptual framework is the same as Taylorism: the "development of" teachers to the "state of maximum efficiency so
that [they] may be able to do, generally speaking, the highest grade of work
for which [their] abilities fit [them]" (Taylor, p. 11). The sentiment then
remains that teachers cannot be trusted to do their jobs without receiving
clear, detailed instructions about what to do and how to do it.

Observations are when teacher errors are identified, and the correctional
work begins. Through observations, administrators get snapshots of what a
classroom looks like, taking single lessons to be indicative of the work being
done in the over-170 attendance days in a school year. At my school, teachers
are formally observed once during first semester. That observation is used
to rate teacher performance using Charlotte Danielson's (2013) *Framework
for Teaching*. There are four domains in the Danielson Framework: Planning
and Preparation, The Classroom Environment, Instruction, and Professional
Responsibilities. Each domain includes four to six categories that are graded
on a rubric ranging from one to four. Classroom Environment (Domain 2)
and Instruction (Domain 3) are evaluated during the formal observations,
while the first and fourth domains are judged more cumulatively based on
the work the teacher has done throughout the year both in and out of the
classroom.

It is not uncommon during full staff meetings for my administrators to
reference which domain one of the tasks we are being asked to do falls under
on the Danielson Framework; recently when the staff was emailed about submitting corrections to our unit plans we were reminded that these corrections
would impact our scores in both Domains 1 and 2. The evaluations teachers
receive become part of our records, and in some cases are made available to
other schools we apply to work at. In other words, they're a pretty big deal,
and two out of four domains are essentially determined by a single, fifty-min-
ute observation.

Of course, administrators try to frame formal observations as delicately as
they can, explaining that the purpose of the observations, especially the one
in the fall, is to help them identify areas in which they can help us grow. They
want us to do the best work we can for the students we teach, and they view

observations as essential in determining what we're doing well and where we can improve.

Still, these observations are clearly punitive. Poor rankings can lead to probations, firings, or even just a diminished opinion from administration. I have a friend who teaches second grade at an elementary school that offers tenure. We were talking about an observation she had that didn't go well: some students were rolling around on the ground, others were outright fighting each other in front of the observer. She was near tears, fearful that she would be taken off her fast track to tenure. The very real consequences to poor scores on the Danielson ranking encourages teachers to put on some sort of dog and pony show during the window that these observations might take place, and it also means that when we receive negative feedback, our professional growth is unlikely to be the first thing we think of.

### *Pushback*

The difficulty with things like standardized tests and formal observations is that as critical as a person might be of these systems' fairness, most teachers still view them as reflections of whether we're doing a good job. I concurrently hold a skepticism for these rankings and a not-so-secret pride that I have consistently earned an average score of 3.5 out of 4 or higher. Perhaps if I didn't like my scores so much I would be even more dismissive of how teacher evaluations are implemented.

When planning for the most recent lesson I was to be observed teaching, I had been mindful of the various rubrics on Danielson, and I had reviewed my scores from my previous lesson to see where I wanted to improve. While my careful planning might seem like the positive consequences of these evaluations, I have to admit that I hadn't spent much time looking at my previous score after I had my post-conference meeting, and I had forgotten most of the areas I was supposed to be working on. Oftentimes, I've been given shortcuts or loopholes by more senior colleagues for how to increase scores on different rubrics: asking students to pass out papers instead of doing it myself means the students are involved in management of the classroom, or sending home a monthly newsletter means I regularly communicate with parents. These suggestions aren't explicitly bad, but they also don't meaningfully grow one as a teacher either. What they do show, though, is how evaluations often are viewed more as a numbers game than as a means to effectively help teachers better serve their students.

When developing the instruction that I would be observed on, I structured activities that would activate prior knowledge and interest, provide opportunities for the students to serve as leaders in classroom management and instruction, and incorporate assessments to provide data on student performance. In class, we began by discussing the novel we had read in the previous unit before watching a clip from Disney's film *Aladdin* to introduce Edward Said's concept of Orientalism. Students worked in small groups and, using a jigsaw instructional strategy, reviewed and shared their evaluations of elements of Orientalism. I thought that it had gone well, and when my administrator left the room I felt relieved. A few days later I got her initial ranking for my observation and a Google invite to meet for my post-conference. During that meeting, I would have the opportunity to offer my own insight into how the observation went and to discuss areas where I and my administrator didn't see eye to eye. It was also when we would determine my rankings for Domain 4, Professional Responsibilities, which she had not yet submitted.

"Have a seat, McCoyne."

The office is always a little smaller than I think it will be, though perhaps it's more an optical illusion brought on by the large table that dominates the space. I sit at one of the six chairs, only two of which will be filled.

"Do you have any questions about Domain 1?" my administrator asks.

I shake my head no. I had received a 4 in all portions of Domain 1, Planning and Preparation, on my Danielson Rating. No need to discuss anything there. We both know the area that I have the greatest concern for.

In Domain 3C, Engaging Students in Learning, I had received a score of 2: Needs Improvement. The lesson had certainly seemed engaging to me. While planning I had thought that my use of pop culture, small group work, and student-led presentations of content would encourage student engagement throughout the lesson. The explanation given on my rubric for the 2 was that a student had her head down for five minutes.

"Give me pushback," my administrator commands.

"Well, I don't think that a student having her head down for a few minutes means that she didn't engage with the lesson."

"But for 'Proficient' it says that there is all-student engagement."

"And I think she was engaged, just not for the entirety of the lesson."

"But you never addressed her when she had her head down."

"I wanted to give her the opportunity to self-assess before I said something. To give her the opportunity to adjust." Now to be completely honest, I had not initially noticed that the student had her head down. During that five minutes I was likely working with another group and had my back to her. Still, that's not exactly a good defense, so I bend the truth a bit.

"But she shouldn't have had her head down in the first place. If protocol was made clear, she should have known not to put her head down."

I tend to be an expressive person, and I unintentionally make a face that shows my displeasure because my administrator repeats her new catchphrase. "Give me pushback."

"For 'Proficient,' it says that 'all students are engaged in work of a high level of rigor.' Over the duration of the lesson, all students were engaged in rigorous work. She had her head down but was able to correct her own behavior, and later participate fully in the lesson."

We go on like this for a few minutes. It's a bit of a dance, and it seems like my administrator enjoys the mental sparring. I return to points I had made before with a new angle, or I refer to a different category on Danielson's Framework to justify the student's head being down, and my reaction—or lack thereof—to it. I reference Domain 2, and the student's ability to self-monitor, since she did pick her head back up without my intervention. I even bring up assessment, Domain 3D, since when giving herself her participation points for the day she only gave herself 3 out of 5 points. After I exhaust myself of potential justifications, my administrator gives me a resolute look.

"I don't think I'm going to give you this one, McCoyne," she eventually says.

"I understand. Thank you for hearing me out, at least."

"Of course. I'll always give you that respect. Now don't go thinking about working somewhere else because of this disagreement," she says in a tone of voice somewhere between joking and warning. I smile back and nod.

Over the course of the rest of the discussion I'm able to move a few "Proficient" rankings up to "Excellent" in Domains 2 and 3. Walking away my average score from all 4 Domains for this year is 3.65, up from the previous year's 3.5. An increased score would suggest growth, and certainly I do feel like a better teacher. But the year before I hadn't received any 2s. I don't like the feeling of being a "Level 2" teacher, even in only one category, and especially the category of student engagement.

After the observation I thought about the student who had her head down. Admittedly, my initial reaction was one of frustration. It seemed like she had screwed me over. After all, didn't she see that I was being observed? Of all days, why did she need to put her head down then? It seemed selfish to me, and I was sure that when I was her age if I had been in her position I would have been more considerate to my teachers. Although looking back now, I cannot think of a single time when my teachers had been observed.

But, of course, my student didn't intentionally jeopardize me. She put her head down because she hadn't slept well the night before, or she had a headache, or her stomach hurt, or a myriad of other reasons that had nothing to do with me. It would be the height of hubris to believe that students make all their decisions with me in mind, even during my class. The evaluation system for teachers simultaneously views teachers as omniscient beings in total control and students as malleable beings who just need the perfectly engaging, differentiated lesson to be able to focus for 51-minute increments throughout the entire day. All we need to do is use the tools at our disposal effectively, and learning will always take place.

## *The Role of the Student*

In contemporary education, data-driven instruction is the tool teachers are being told we must use. While data has always been a fixture in education (teachers have always used student performance to guide instruction), data-driven instruction tells teachers that we should use each assessment as a data point. At the school where I teach, we then use this data to categorize students into groups of homogenous skill levels, providing tiered, differentiated work to ensure that all students have appropriately challenging work to help them grow. The guiding assumption behind data-driven instruction is that without data we would not know which students are at which level. As one of my colleagues put it, we're using data as evidence to support what we've always done.

Perhaps the most troubling implication with the prioritization of data is that the only thing that matters about students, or at least what is most significant, is their ability to perform on assessments. If I were to do strictly score-based grouping, I would have to ignore student personality types that might clash. I would also ignore my own judgement that a student's poor performance on an assessment was a fluke, or that a student's unusually high performance does not necessarily indicate mastery of a concept or standard. There would also be little room for collaboration across skill levels among students. As an automated laborer working under the conditions set forth by my managers, I would seem to have no professional expertise to rely on.

There are limitations to using traditional discourse regarding labor and production in discussions of educational policy. A central difference is that the product of labor by teachers is not a material good, but rather some form of lasting intellectual, social, and emotional impact on an actual living human being. The students with whom teachers work can interact with the means of production (the educational process) in ways that could perhaps best be compared to a manufacturing machine in the context of Taylorism. If teachers are workers, students are the machinery that only passively engages in the creation of the product of education. That being said, the machine is still necessary. Taylor states that "the greatest prosperity can exist only as a result of the greatest possible productivity of the men and machines of the establishment"

(1913. 12). While lacking agency and autonomy, the mechanized student is still clearly a requirement for education to take place.

While managerial administration is a patronizing system for teachers, data-driven instruction is outright dehumanizing for students. An emphasis on efficiency strips interactions between humans of humanity itself. By viewing students as data points, we reduce them to their ability to perform on an assessment. It is perhaps unsurprising that one of the data points my school requires we use is student performance on PSATs. After all, the implicit, and at times explicit, objective given to teachers during this process of data-driven instruction is the improvement of standardized test scores. Student learning that is not reflected on standardized tests becomes unimportant, or at least less important. Learning for both teacher and student becomes less about the process and more about the end result that can be clearly articulated in a test score.

Students feel the limitations of depersonalized production. They have social and emotional needs, and the reduction of students to pieces of data actively discourages teachers from addressing those needs. In some ways, experiences like my own formal observation, when a student's off day was perceived as a shortcoming on my part, leave teachers with the idea that once a student enters the classroom, their outside needs become irrelevant. With the student as a machine, compliance to what the teacher demands should not even be a question. A teacher I previously worked with had a poster in her classroom with a Bill Gates quote: "If you think your teacher is tough, wait until you get a boss." Gates, and that teacher, explicitly linked education to capitalism, and learning to an occupation. Also reinforced is a system that leaves the student—the machine of educational labor—as powerless.

The concept of the powerless student is not new. Paolo Freire critiqued the tendency to view students as "depositories and the teacher [as] the depositor" (2000, p. 72). His argument suggests that students are often too passive in the process of education, though arguably Freire's conception of a banking model of education is slightly outdated itself, giving too much autonomy to the teacher. The banking model posits that "the teacher knows everything and the student knows nothing," and most critically, "the teacher chooses the program content, and the students (who were not consulted) adapt to it" (p. 73). In the current climate of Common Core State Standards, as well as the push for standardized tests, it is clear that teachers have far less control over curriculum than Freire articulates. Indeed, teachers often get about as much influence over what is taught as the students do.

Neither student nor teacher is meant to feel powerless. The instructional coaching teachers receive is meant to help encourage student growth, and language of student empowerment is often used at my school. Still, students are not part of the conversation about instructional strategies. Even opportunities for student choice come in strictly defined terms, with clear instructions that can be graded on a rubric. At my school, student choice is most frequently referenced in the context of differentiation, and it is less about empowering students to feel control over their education and more about offering structured freedoms for accessing the set curriculum so that students can develop focal skills and thus perform better on standardized tests.

Differentiation *is* critical, and as a teacher I try to be open to the new instructional strategies recommended by my administration. Because my administration suggests that teachers divide students into data-determined homogeneous small groups, I do so. Each group works on analyzing a different poem or answers different questions about the same text, differentiated for depth of interpretation required. I recognize that using a single lesson to reach all students will seldom work, and I think homogeneous small grouping can be a useful way to give each student the support she needs to grow. While the use of this style of differentiated instruction came from administrative mandates, that does not mean that it is without value.

One of the benefits of being a small school is having frequent communication with administrators. As we went through a semester of administration-led professional development, every few weeks we were given anonymous surveys to share our thoughts and feelings on the work we had been doing. Many teachers didn't like homogeneous small grouping, and my administrators were open to feedback. In the following weeks of professional development trainings on differentiation, administrators exposed us to a wider variety of instructional strategies, strategies ranging from Socratic seminars and carousel dialogues to student choice tic-tac-toe boards. The professional developments also became more teacher-driven, with forums to share our experiences with differentiation, talk about activities that went well, or share the ways we were still struggling to meet the needs of all our students. A more open dialogue that allows teachers to have input, using their expertise and personal knowledge of their students to shape their instruction while still implementing the well-reasoned directives of administration in the ways they see fit, feels like a compromise—a tentative, fragile compromise, but one that does hint at another way schools can operate.

## Another Way

"It's not a great lesson. I'm just introducing the play to the students, so it's mostly just lecture."

"That's OK, it's just a pop-in visit."

This is how many text or email exchanges with my Golden Apple mentor go.

In college, I was in the Golden Apple scholarship program, which involved month-long summer institutes for future teachers, and upon graduation each scholar was assigned a mentor. Our mentors observe us for several hours of instruction three times a year for our first two years teaching, offering us guidance and support as we begin our careers.

I feel self-conscious when she visits. Really, I feel self-conscious whenever anybody is in the class. While I stand behind the teaching I do, it is never easy to let someone else in to see what my instruction looks like. I'm always afraid I'm going to glance at the observer and be met with an expression of shock, horror, or disgust. It's not a reasonable fear, and it might be one that only I have, but I have a feeling that this insecurity is common enough amongst newer teachers.

After about twenty minutes into the period, I begin to think that my mentor is not coming after all. My A.P. Literature and Composition class has been discussing nature in the context of Henry David Thoreau's "How I Lived and What I Lived For" to prepare to read *Life of Pi* by Yann Martel. After I took the A.P. exam while in high school and faced an essay question about setting and the environment, I resolved to add ecocriticism as a lens of study in my own classroom. I first read *Life of Pi* while I was applying and interviewing for jobs out of college. During a tempestuous time in my life that book gave me some buoyancy. I was reminded that books can be powerful sources of comfort, and I was eager to share my experience with my students.

The discussion is not going according to plan. Open-ended conversations where everyone has an equal voice can hardly be mapped out, but this discussion seems to be going on a web of tangents, connected by only the most tentative of silky threads. I am in the middle of explaining that, actually, asexuality means something different for humans than it does for plants when my mentor walks into the room. Over the winding course of the conversation we also veer into the role of technology and social media in contemporary society, gender norms, and a psychological analysis of serial killers. It feels like performing a gymnastics routine to return to the activity planned: a free-write about the last page of Thoreau's essay. Tomorrow, the students will share their free-writes, which we will then use to interpret Thoreau's views of nature, putting them in conversation with our own. It will be a clearly structured analytical activity, which is not what my mentor teacher is getting to see now.

It is then with trepidation that I approach her while the students write their responses, but she has a wide grin on her face. "You relate to these girls so well," she says in that hoarse, quiet voice of hers.

"Thank you so much," I respond, flustered.

"They're so comfortable with you, and they're so eager to share. You're doing a wonderful job."

My initial concerns melt away, and there isn't any room for even a hint of resentment towards my students for leading the lesson astray. What my mentor teacher liked about the lesson was that it was spontaneous, with students interjecting often with amusing anecdotes and interesting connections. I would never teach such a lesson during a formal observation, yet this kind of learning is the space where the students, and I, feel the most relaxed and enthusiastic to engage.

If my mentor teacher didn't like how my lesson went there would be no career-altering consequences. It was a low-risk setting, which made it easier for me to accept her feedback, which she went on to provide more in depth later during a planning period when we had more time to sit down and discuss the lesson. In turn, I did not feel inclined to put on such a performance, allowing her to see my class in a more authentic setting, making the whole experience more sincere and realistic.

In a climate of teacher management, teachers need liberation as much as students do. It is important to create a solidarity between the two, both facing mutual oppression from an education system that fails to fully acknowledge the humanity of either. This requires honesty and vulnerability on both parts, but especially from the teacher. As bell hooks describes in *Teaching to Transgress*, "Any classroom that employs a holistic model of learning will be a place where teachers grow, and are empowered by the process" (1994, p. 21). I have sought my own empowerment in the classroom by writing alongside my students, particularly with creative or narrative prompts. We often share writings with one another, creating a community of writers that I am as much a part of as are the students. In fact, I even shared an excerpt from an early draft of this very chapter with my senior class that was at the time writing about their wishes for the world. Operating under a progressive definition of literature, I find common interests in music and popular culture to analyze song lyrics or award show speeches that the students have spoken about. Ultimately, for education to be beneficial for student and teacher, we need to acknowledge the dehumanizing nature of the system and work together through partnership to carve out a space that lets us all learn and grow.

## *Advocating*

We want to become a Level One School. We spend meetings talking about various categories and rankings, and the different possible routes to get us to this goal. We use words like "synergy." All the decisions we make, and all the instructions teachers are being given, are to help us go from Two-Plus to One. With a Level One rating, we will receive more positive media and online attention, which will help us with our recruiting efforts. We will always be a small school, but we want to be a little bit less small than we are now. There's more money in being less small, and with more money comes more resources, which will help us to do even better work for our students.

When I later discussed the "gotcha" culture my administrators asked me about with my sister, I thought about an incident that had happened in the first semester. It was late fall and our dean had sent out an email explaining that students weren't to wear jackets, sweaters, or anything other than the uniform polo shirt with khaki pants or skirt in class. My classroom had problems both with the heat as well as with a constant flow of cold air coming from my adjoining office. I made it clear to my students that they would be allowed to wear whatever they needed to stay warm in my class. Upon speaking to an administrator during a meeting later on in the day I was told that my arrangement would be fine.

What I did not expect was for the dean to then enter my class the next day, interrupting my lesson for Advisory, a sort of homeroom class during the first fifteen minutes of the day, to reprimand the students for wearing jackets, and by default me for letting them. I ignored the interaction for the time being, telling my students to still feel free to wear jackets when they had my class later in the day, since I also taught all the students English.

I dropped the issue until I went to the main office to check my mailbox during my planning period. The administrator I spoke to the day before was there and I said hello.

"Mr. McCoyne, are you one of the people on my bad list?"

"I'm not sure. Why would I be?"

"Did you have students wearing jackets in your classroom this morning?"

Now I was annoyed, but I maintained a respectful, if slightly defensive tone. "The heat in my classroom doesn't work and it's been cold. You said during the meeting that it was up to teacher discretion whether students could wear jackets. I didn't have the opportunity to contact the dean about my room's temperature."

She seemed understanding enough, responding, "I get it. Just make sure that you email her."

"I'll do it right now," I said. And I did, returning to my room to craft an email that I hoped would express my frustrations while maintaining an undeniably professional tone—an important defense to have when you know you're going to ruffle some feathers. At the end of the email I mentioned that I will continue to do my part through teaching to help us become a Level One school.

At the time my administrator had been ending her emails with "#race-tolevel1." The ranking wasn't what was in my mind when I initially allowed students to wear their jackets in my class. My greater concern was their physical wellbeing and the inability to learn when essential needs aren't met—basic Maslow's hierarchy.

Still, I felt inclined to include a reference to the "race to Level One" for two reasons. One, it is something important to administration, and thus seemed like a good angle to persuade them into letting me get what I wanted. I also wanted to remind the administrators of their own goal when considering the initiatives they enforce. After all, how will forcing students to endure uncomfortable temperatures in polo shirts help us reach a higher ranking?

Following that email I never had any trouble with the administration, especially as heat began to fail throughout the building and the uniform policy collapsed on itself. More importantly, though, I wanted my students to know that I would defend them. Conditions at my school are imperfect, as they are at most schools. In a system of teacher management, it is critical that we remember the humanity of the students.

I had a conversation with a different teacher about situations where we want to defend students regarding some small policy or indignity. "I don't like to rock the boat," she told me. I wonder how many teachers are in that position of wanting to help but not wanting to be vulnerable by deviating from expectations, or even hinting that the expectations are flawed. Perhaps a new, more lax grading policy seems to fly in the face of our school's target for increased rigor, but nobody wants to defy what an administrator is saying during a faculty meeting. A colleague once said to me in passing that she would do something different if she saw another teacher doing it. I understand what she meant. It is easier to keep your head down and go along with the crowd; keeping your head down doesn't jeopardize your relationship with administration, nor does it jeopardize your Danielson ranking. Although this is all anecdotal, I get the impression that while many of us see issues in the educational system, nobody wants to be the one to take a stand. I certainly remember last year being a first-year teacher who just wanted to keep my head down. It took a year of proving myself through strong performances on evaluations, founding a now award-winning literary arts magazine, and frequently attending and participating in out-of-school events to feel I had the right to stand up for myself and my students.

Months after the initial disagreement over jackets, we reach the end of the school year. The May sun is warm and windows are open to let breezes cool the classrooms, rather than closed tight to keep out the cold. Small groups of teachers are meeting with administration to discuss how the year has gone, and what can be done better in the future.

In this more intimate setting that my administrator has carved out, I feel safe to speak. "I think that we need to recognize that in Chicago winter is not a two-month thing. When discussing the uniform policy we need to have a more consistent plan for when it gets cold."

"That's so true," another teacher immediately follows. "Policies change day by day and we're the ones who need to explain them to the students. Having to spend so much time dealing with what the students are wearing distracts from the teaching we're trying to do."

If the others in the room don't speak they at least murmur in agreement.

"You're right," my administrator concedes, "especially with the problems we've been having with heat, which I think we'll still have next year. I'll talk to my team, but I think we'll need to let them wear hoodies or sweaters over their uniforms."

Someone suggests that the disciplinary team may be more willing to support a change in policy if the students need to at least stick to uniform colors. It is a dialogue meant to offer different ideas to reach a compromise.

It is not easy to rock the boat. I think that I'm a particularly sensitive person when it comes to feeling like someone is unhappy with me. I tend to be overly apologetic, even if I'm not certain what I'm apologizing for. At the same time, my sensitivity makes me empathetic to the needs of others, which makes it hard for me to sit by as other people struggle with discomfort. It is important to stand up for yourself and others if you want to be taken seriously, and to take yourself seriously. A willingness to stand up for your students is also necessary to teach for social justice. Opportunities for justice don't just exist in the often decontextualized "outside world." Students need to feel a sense of justice even in, or especially in, school and the classroom. As with all types of teaching, it is necessary to set an example, and thoughtfully working towards solutions for schoolwide issues shows students that change is possible. For me it required earning enough clout in the eyes of those in charge to feel like I had the right to speak up. Certainly, I know my administrators respect my opinion in part because I don't complain about everything. But I'm glad that I didn't buckle about students wearing jackets. If I had, I'm sure I would have lost the respect of some of them. As much as it's important to have clout with administration, it's students with whom I work every day, which makes my relationship with them the central relationship in my mind as a teacher.

## *The Managers*

But just as teachers and students struggle under the system of scientific management, so too do administrators. While studying Sophocles' *Antigone* in my tenth-grade world literature class, we discussed the importance of leaders following through with what they say they'll do. Although the initial focus was on King Creon from the play, when justifying their perspectives students brought in their personal experiences.

"I think sometimes someone says they'll do something but then something else comes up. Like there's an emergency in the family and they just can't do it. And people need to understand that."

A student responded to her, "But that doesn't really have to do with leaders. Like that doesn't have to do with the president."

A third student interjected, "Why not? Leaders have lives too. And even if it's not the president, there are more local leaders."

At that point, I asked for an example.

"Like a teacher. They might say they'll grade something, but if they need to go to a funeral or they get sick, it might take an extra week. And we'd understand."

This line of thinking interested me. "But you know teachers well. You see us every day. That's a very local type of leader. What about if it was someone you didn't see so often or didn't feel as close to?"

"Like the principal?" a student asked.

"Sure," I said.

"It might be harder for me to sympathize with the principal like that," a student admitted. "I just don't see them like that."

"Like what?" I asked.

None of the students responded with a concrete answer, but I have a feeling what they were thinking was "like a human." Despite systems of teacher management and lists of instructional mandates, teachers do have opportunities to reveal their humanity to their students. Naturally, relationships are formed which allow students to understand their teachers, and vice versa. Administrators, by nature, are tucked away. They might greet students at the entryway or invite students to come to their offices to talk. But ultimately administrators are separated from the act of teaching and learning, which creates a disconnect between them and both students and teachers. This disconnect does not mean that relationships and mentorship are not possible, but it does create an added pressure on administrators to compensate for the preexisting distance between them and students. While teachers might feel burdened by reform measures enacted by their administrators (similar to reforms enforced by modern managers), more often than not these reforms are either mandated by someone higher up the ladder or else a response to demands for higher performance. It is unlikely, for example, that my administrator decided unilaterally that my school was on the #racetolevelone.

Though a case can be made to equate administrators with the managers of Taylorism, to frame administrators as the enemies of the teacher and student is reductionist and simplistic. As I told my administrators, there is a "gotcha culture" in education, and it doesn't just come from administrators. Often administrators deal with "gotcha" moments just as much as teachers, with random state audits, legislation, unexpected budget issues, mandates from the school board, and probably more things that I as a teacher simply don't know about.

As with any systemic issue, there is no easy fix. This is not a young adult dystopian novel with a clear villain with a scary name who just needs to be defeated for peace to be restored. The problems with education are much more entrenched. The problems are cultural, and it takes cultural change for substantive change to occur. In the meantime, the smaller cultures of each school must individually determine how to deal with these problems, and to figure out what the purpose of education is and what it means to teach.

## *Culture*

Schools are small places. They are microcosms of the world, with societies and conflicts that play out on a day-to-day basis. Mandates are sent out, meetings take place, and conversations between two people can become something large. Habits develop into a culture that is difficult to shake, but there is an underlying sense of urgency in my school, as there is in many schools, that something needs to change, and soon.

Few people at a school disagree with that assertion, but the question is always what needs to change. With legislation being written by those out of the classroom, teachers only have so much institutional power to enact significant change. What we do have control over is our own attitudes and behavior.

When I am at my liveliest and most optimistic, I feel like everything that happens in my class is connected and the work I am doing matters. I feel like I am successfully engaging the students in a thoughtful, culturally relevant curriculum that will help them grow as thinkers ready to interact critically with the world around them, while also preparing them for any standardized tests they may face. Other days I feel a sense of dread, as if the work I'm doing is futile and only perpetuating the systems I'm seeking to dismantle, that the instruction I give is based on antiquated ideas of what knowledge is valuable and that the students don't really care and aren't really learning anything— and definitely not in any way that is measurable.

The struggles in education are not tidy, and in many ways teachers are left to pick up the mess made by broader cultural problems. Taylorism as a concept demonstrates that it is not just schools that fail to value the individual (since at least the manufacturing industry doesn't afford full humanity to workers), and certainly the inequity of education—a topic I don't have room to discuss in detail in this chapter—stems from institutionalized bigotries based on categorizations like gender, class, and race. In the face of such massive problems, we may feel powerless.

Solidarity and an acknowledgement of mutual humanity are necessary for education to become empowering for teachers, students, and administrators. While the legislative focus on standards and tests may remain a fixture in the foreseeable future, by demonstrating empathy and allowing for vulnerability, teachers may begin to fulfill the promise education makes to young people: the promise of a transformative opportunity to learn and grow, and to become something more. In the classroom, teachers need to be willing to make space for students to have a voice, just as administrators need to give teachers a voice in the school. At different levels, those involved in education seem to feel like they simply need to do what they are told. Administrators need to comply with district mandates, teachers need to instruct the way administration demands, and then students need to perform the tasks they are assigned. All may find themselves acting more out of fear of punishment than a belief in the work they're being asked to do.

Instead, students, teachers, and administrators must act out of a true motivation that only comes from choices made from personal agency. Empowering education occurs through dialogue that validates the needs and perspectives of all participants, letting them feel heard and respected as equals working towards a valid, worthwhile goal. This dialogue requires patience, understanding, and tact to be successful. As the world around us continues to reward cruelty and meanness, we cannot forget that compassion becomes radical.

## References

Danielson, C. (2013). *The framework for teaching: Evaluation instrument, 2013 instructionally focused edition*. Princeton, NJ: Danielson Group.

Freire, P. (2000). *Pedagogy of the oppressed*. New York, NY: Continuum.

hooks, b. (1994). *Teaching to transgress: Education as the practice of freedom*. New York, NY: Routledge.

Taylor, F. W. (1913). *The principles of scientific management*. New York, NY: Harper & Brothers.

# 8. *Motivation, Mental Health, and the Eclipse of Social Imagination*

Kevin Christopher Carey

Education in the era of neoliberal reform is troubling, as can be witnessed by key changes in the educational framework over the past 50 years: the skyrocketing of college tuition and the shifting of financial aid from schools to students; the rising role and prevalence of standardized testing; and the co-optation of public education policy and teacher training by private companies (e.g., Pearson) and philanthropic organizations (e.g., Bill and Melinda Gates Foundation), to name a few. In this essay, I address what I see as the crucial role played by the logic of individualism as it informs neoliberal thinking and as it structures neoliberal interventions in educational and social policy. What I hope to provide is a sketch of some of the ways in which seeing the world through the lens of neoliberal individualism shapes and limits how we educators understand ourselves, our students, and education, and to show how these understandings lead to and support some material practices while at the same time devaluing or erasing others. One of the major consequences of this worldview, I argue, is what I am provisionally calling a "psychologicalization of the social." By this I mean a shrinking of what C. Wright Mills (1959, 2000) called "the sociological imagination," such that we reduce "public issues" to "private troubles," and in so doing, while we clamor more and more for individual accountability, we hold ourselves as a community and a society largely unaccountable.

In order to depict this logic at work, I look at how those in education as well as in the wider public talk about students and learning in two separate but related discourses: (1) discourses of motivation, which are oriented toward promoting the individual efficacy of teachers and learners; and (2) discourses of mental health, which are oriented toward identifying "troubled" students and getting them access to appropriate resources. That these discourses share a psychologizing bias—by which I mean, a tendency to view issues with wider social dimensions almost exclusively in terms of the individual—is not surprising given that they spring mainly from psychological research. What is concerning to me are the ways in which many social issues today—here, specifically, educational ones—are coming more and more to be framed solely in terms of psychology, and thus in terms of individual actors, with a consequent lessening of the visibility of (and ability to make recourse to) larger social, ethical, and systemic analyses and solutions. In what follows I aim to show how current discussions of student motivation and mental health exemplify the assumptions of neoliberal individualism, and I reflect upon some of the troubling implications and practices that such an outlook enables.

## Key Terms

At the outset I want to define a little more clearly what I mean by *neoliberalism* and *individualism*. By *neoliberalism* I refer to:

> a theory of political economic practices that proposes human well-being can best be advanced by liberating individual entrepreneurial freedoms and skills within an institutional framework characterized by strong private property rights, free markets and free trade … [with t]he role of the state [being] to create and preserve an institutional framework appropriate to such practices. (Harvey, 2007, p. 2)

Two points should be noted here. First, as counterintuitive as it may seem, this radical free market ideology is anything but *laissez-faire*; rather, it requires a tremendous amount of public and private coordination to pull off. Second, such coordination necessarily exceeds the boundaries of the marketplace and is not limited to economic issues and practices. I find communication scholar Jennifer Simpson's (2014) account to be especially helpful here:

> Central to the implementation of neoliberal economic theory across the social landscape has been the general acceptance of the idea that neoliberalism, as an economic set of principles, ought to be applied to all forms of organization and public life. Thus, going well beyond the bounds of the economy, neoliberalism and market competition have become a desirable and appropriate framework for any and all arenas of social interaction, including government, public policy, the family, education, and the individual. (p. 188)

Within a neoliberal framework, institutions of higher learning function to develop human capital according to the needs of innovation-driven knowledge and technology economies. In doing so, they instill values, inform ideologies, and constitute identities conducive to a neoliberal orientation and logic, which at the same time is inattentive and resistant to other value systems and ways of knowing. As Simpson notes,

> Neoliberalism asserts a set of values that prioritizes efficiency, sameness, and private gain. ... Working at ideological and social levels, neoliberalism supports the logic of an "I," reduces the space for a "we," and appears to many a desirable logic even as it destroys possibilities for the public good. (p. 188)

To be clear, it's not that neoliberal ideology makes impossible other values and logics outside of the market, yet it does measure them all in terms of it. The work of measurement, the power of evaluation, is a process of extracting certain values, energies, and actions while ignoring or excluding others. One of the key components of neoliberal ideology is the way in which it takes the individual as the basic unit of reality from which greater socioeconomic theories are to be drawn.

Raymond Williams (1976) calls *individualism* "the main movement of liberal political and economic thought ... a theory not only of abstract individuals but of the primacy of individual states and interests" (p. 136). As Williams tells the story, at the end of the 17th Century and continuing through the 18th, "a new mode of analysis, in logic and mathematics, postulated the individual as the substantial entity ... from which other categories and *especially collective categories* were derived" (p. 135, italics mine). This logic, Williams writes, largely informed Enlightenment political theory, wherein

> argument began from individuals, who had an initial and primary existence, and laws and forms of society were derived from them: by submission, as in Hobbes; by contract or consent, or by the new version of natural law, in liberal thought. (p. 136)

Two models of such thinking include classical economics, "which postulated separate individuals who decided, at some starting point, to enter into economic or commercial relations"; as well as utilitarian ethics, wherein it was theorized that "separate individuals calculated the consequences of this or that action which they might undertake." Individualism, then, is one of the pillars in the "epistemological architecture" of neoliberalism.[1] In accepting the worldview of individualism, we explain the world—people, cultures, societies—in its terms. A central function of worldviewing, then, is explaining causal relations, or how events and situations came and come to be. Individualism as a worldview takes the isolated (but assumedly fully formed) person as the starting point for thinking larger categories of reality and relationships. The problem with this worldview is not the ascription of freedom or agency to human beings, but the essentialist and totalizing ways in which this freedom and agency are construed, undermining and diminishing our ability to imagine the larger social and systemic forces at work. As Stuart Hall (1988) says of ideology, the problem is not that it is false, but rather "it offers a partial explanation as if it were a comprehensive and adequate one—it takes the part for the whole (fetishism)" (p. 82).

In the following analyses, then, I draw attention to how individualism functions in framing educational and social issues within a neoliberal epistemological architecture: it refers to the given, unexamined background of causal relations that posit the individual as the privileged source of knowledge, action, and agency in a way that is conducive to the larger set of socioeconomic presuppositions, values, and practices currently in vogue. What follows is my attempt to make sense of some current trends in education that might be partially illuminated by this theoretical framework.

## Is Motivation a Problem, and If So, What Kind of Problem Is It?

In 2017, during my second semester teaching Communication Studies at a large public university in Ontario, the Center for Teaching Excellence (CTE) sent out a Call for Proposals (CFP) for the university's annual Teaching and Learning Conference.[2] This year's theme: *Motivating Our Students and Ourselves*.[3] Reading it, I experienced a series of familiar and conflicting emotions: a desire to meet with fellow teachers to discuss students and pedagogy; tentative excitement that the conference was addressing the affective dimensions of teaching and learning, rather than the current frenzy over knowledge and skills transmission; pressure to propose a panel and simultaneously a resistance to taking on any more work; guilt at not contributing to a conversation I care about; anxiety that I might take it on anyway despite my already considerable work load; vulnerable and defensive in advance for what I might say there and how it might be received; and wary that the whole thing, like many professional development events I had attended before, was less about creating a space for teachers to openly reflect on their working conditions, their students, and their pedagogy, and more about something else. It's that something else that I want to address here.

The conference topic was motivation. As the CFP explained:

> A student's motivation plays an important role in learning, from providing a sense of purpose to developing a genuine love of learning. The desire to spark or sustain student motivation shapes how instructors design their courses and informs our instructional and assessment methods. Our own motivation as instructors is also important, from staying motivated to sustaining and continuing to grow our teaching. ... [W]e invite you to ... share your practices and research related

to motivating deep learning in students and motivating ourselves as instructors.
(University of Waterloo, 2018)

The blurb above is certainly not remarkable in any way, and I imagine that most people, especially, perhaps, new teachers, would see nothing but the potential good that might come from concerned teachers and scholars coming together to discuss student motivation. While I neither question the individual motives of the conveners and participants, nor condemn outright a concern for motivation, I do have questions regarding how motivation is being framed and the implications this framing has on our understanding of and our practices regarding students and teachers.

The first thing to strike me about this framing of the issue of motivation is that it focuses exclusively on the individual. It asks: *what can students do to become more motivated about their learning; what can teachers do to help students become more motivated about their learning;* and *what can teachers do to motivate themselves to do more to motivate their students about their learning.* It does not ask, for example: *what conditions are conducive to student motivation; what kinds of work environments help motivate teachers;* nor *what can institutions of higher learning do to create conditions conducive to motivating teachers to motivate students.* While the CFP's summary blurb may not in itself be indicative of a rhetorical motivation to frame the topic in a particular way, I believe the "Questions and Ideas to Consider" section leaves little room for doubt in this regard, and thus I cite it in full:

- What beliefs and mindsets do students hold that can hinder or benefit their learning?
- How can instructors help students feel that they are able to succeed in their courses?
- How can we encourage students to take charge of their own learning and persist to reach their goals?
- How can we encourage students to see the "why" and real-life applications of what they learn in the classroom?
- How can we address the diversity in students' identities, perspectives, and experiences in our teaching to promote motivation?
- How can we challenge ourselves to make changes to our teaching and to envision what is possible?
- What assumptions, obstacles, incentives, and contextual factors hinder or motivate instructors to try new things in the classroom?
- What does motivation look like for instructors near the start of their careers versus those mid-career or further along?

- How does motivation differ between students and instructors? How might they be the same? (University of Waterloo, 2018)

With the exception of the seventh bullet point, we are not asked to consider any questions or ideas regarding student and teacher motivation outside the bounds of the individual actors. And while point seven does explicitly reference "contextual factors," it does so only in reference to teachers' motivation to "trying new things in the classroom," once again conflating student motivation with teacher performance, as well as imagining motivation to be linked to innovation—"trying new things." While I don't deny the role individuals may play in motivating themselves or others, I refuse to accept that they have the exclusive or even most important roles to play in this scenario. As most teachers know (and perhaps, sadly, more so at the primary and secondary tiers of education than at post-secondary institutions) students are not learning machines whose only requirement is that their pumps be primed or ignitions sparked by motivation in order to succeed. Rather, they are, even already by pre-kindergarten, complex human beings with a host of needs, desires, interests, aptitudes, strengths, struggles, fears, quirks and personalities, and they vary widely in terms of their histories, experiences, cultures, environments and resources, to name just a few of the salient factors that impact and play upon the desire to do a thing, which is basically what motivation is. What does it say about us that we should choose to understand motivation simply as the possession or responsibility of an individual student or teacher, rather than the complex matrix of factors that give rise to and support it? What does such a simple understanding portend for our students, ourselves, and for education? What or whose interests does it serve? What other understandings are possible?

For one, I believe that framing motivation as a purely individual phenomenon to the exclusion of social factors prompts us so see motivation more in terms of quantity than in terms of quality. By this I mean that problems of motivation as articulated in contemporary discourses of education center overwhelmingly on questions of just how or how much students are motivated and how teachers can motivate them more. The complexity of human motivation is reduced to a simple problem of supply and demand wherein teachers are understood to be motivation providers until such time as students develop into self-starting, self-regulating producers of their own learning. But what if we don't accept the starting assumption that students (or teachers for that matter) lack motivation? What if we pose the question of motivation not in terms of quantity but in terms of quality? In my years of teaching across four different institutions of higher education—public and private, community college and research university, American and Canadian—I have not found issue with the amount of motivation students and teachers possessed, but rather with what students and teachers are being motivated by. An email I received yesterday from a student after the second class of the term may be instructive here. This student wrote to inform me that s/he was enjoying the class, but that because s/he was taking 5 courses and working a part-time job of 30 hours a week, s/he wondered if I could make the first paper prompt available as soon as possible so s/he could get a jump on it.

This was an exceptional email in many ways: the student's frank confession of enjoying the material; the level of maturity and responsibility in addressing her/his time constraints directly; the polite and well-written quality of the missive. Unfortunately, what were not exceptional were the course load and work schedule described. At both of the public research universities where I have worked, as well as at the private liberal arts school and the community college I taught at, students taking five or more courses while also working 30 or more hours a week (here, laughably referred to as a "part-time" job) is the new normal. What this suggests to me is that this student, and many others, are not suffering from a lack of motivation; rather, they are over-motivated by the exigencies of work and study (and likely future debt) to pursue their education in the manner of meeting extrinsic benchmarks and qualifications rather than by the "genuine love of learning" that the conference would like to cultivate.[4] The same could be said, by the way, for many (if not most) university teachers.[5] Posing the question of student motivation in terms that take seriously the constitutive role that social factors play in its development allows us to see beyond the simple binary of "is/is not motivated" (or motivated enough), to consider how a person's interest, willingness, and ability to learn a particular content, at a particular time and place, and in a particular way is highly contingent upon a palimpsest of factors irreducible to individual character traits such as "grit," "perseverance," or "resilience," to name a few.[6] Alternately, it allows us to question whether or not there really is a motivation problem at all.

In my ten years of teaching in higher education—as well as five years, in a previous life, teaching reading enrichment skills to students of all ages across the U.S.—I have never come across a student whose struggles I framed as "lacking motivation." On the other hand, I have worked with hundreds, perhaps thousands, of students who didn't understand the point of or value in what they were doing or being asked (or forced!) to do. Their questions were more specific, more capacious, and more profound than those posed by the CFP. They were and are asking questions such as: *Why am I here? What are you asking me to do? What is this good for?* These are questions not of motivation, but of purpose. Why aren't we talking about the purpose of education? Why/how has motivation come to replace purpose as the primary question of education? The CFP touches on this issue when it states as a matter of course that "motivation plays an important role in … providing a sense of purpose." Yet it puts the cart before the horse: while purpose is indeed a strong motivator, how is "motivating deep learning" to happen without a sense of purpose?

To recapitulate my critique, I take issue with three assumptions in this CFP, and by extension, current trends in educational discourse more broadly: (1) that individual students and teachers are the most import factors in questions of educational motivation; (2) that the problems of student and teacher motivation are quantitative—that students and teachers are lacking in/don't have enough motivation—rather than qualitative—that they are largely motivated by exigencies extrinsic to education; and (3) that there is a problem of motivation at all. The problem as I see it has to do both with the phenomena prompting discussions of student motivation in the first place—phenomena including poverty, inequality, social and economic injustice, to name a few—and the inadequacy of posing education as the sole or most important remedy to these social issues. The logic that reduces complex human motivation to the simplicity of individual effort is a facet of the same epistemological architecture that transforms dynamic social issues into technical educational problems. It is a form of cultural, ideological scapegoating that in misrepresenting the problem (consciously or unconsciously) makes individuals responsible for social issues the causes of which (and the interests served) are rendered largely unaccountable.

One of the most destructive effects such a logic and worldview entails is the corrosion of people's identification with the community and the reciprocal bonds of caretaking between people and communities that such identifications engender. According to Wendy Brown (qtd. in Simpson, 2014), "the model neoliberal citizen is one who strategizes for her- or himself among various social, political, and economic options, not one who strives with others to alter or organize these options" (p. 189). Attempts to consider one's wider social and ethical relationships are, as Simpson puts it, citing Iris Marion Young, "countered by a logic of 'others do not have any obligatory responsibilities for helping us, and we have none toward them,'" (p. 189).[7] In the CFP for the conference held to address issues of student motivation, there is no sense of a wider social or ethical responsibility toward students on behalf of teachers, much less the university as a community, beyond a technical optimizing of one's teaching efficacy. One is called to master the subject of student motivation, rather than to care for the human subjects in one's charge. So long as "instructors help students feel that they are able to succeed in their courses," these instructors are acquitted from actually having to consider the wider social and community factors constitutive of student success. There is no hint in the CFP of mutually striving even to consider other options for thinking about student success outside of the narrow framework of motivation described, much less of altering the options given. Rather than a community taking responsibility for its members, we have a plurality of individual actors seeking a kind of self-improvement or upgrade. Whether or not such an improvement actually helps promote conditions conducive to equity, social justice, and student success, are considerations outside one's responsibilities: "That's not my job!"

If neoliberal logic assumes that academic success is largely the result of individual effort on the part of students and/or teachers, it similarly views student failure through the same individualist framework. By way of exemplifying this final point, I'd like to turn now to a few contemporary examples of mental health discourse as they intersect with schools and school communities. In examining discussions surrounding recent acts of school violence (shootings and suicide), I argue that the framing of these incidents as caused by mentally ill individuals (and the corresponding call for more mental health resources) is of the same logic that posits student success in terms of motivation (with corresponding calls for greater innovation on the part of teachers).

## Lone Wolves/Lonely Worlds

On February 14th, 2018, 19-year old Nikolas Cruz entered the Marjory Stoneman Douglas High School in Parkland, Florida and proceeded to shoot and kill 17 people and wound 17 others. It was one of the world's deadliest school massacres, surpassing the Columbine, Colorado massacre of 1999 (Laughland, Luscombe, & Yuhas, 2018). Nikolas was a former student of Stoneman Douglas. He was adopted at birth. His adoptive father died in 2004, when Nikolas was still a child. His adoptive mother died in 2017, just three months before the shooting (Wallman, McMahon, O'Matz, & Bryan, 2018). According to reports, Nikolas started having "behavioral issues" in middle school, resulting in him being transferred in and out of six schools over the course of three years. In 2014 he attended a school for students with emotional and learning disabilities, but returned to Stoneman Douglas in 2016, from which he was reportedly "banished" the following year for "disciplinary reasons"[8] (Miller & Gurney, 2018). Psychological assessments of Nikolas over the years found him to be suffering from depression, autism, attention deficit hyperactivity disorder (ADHD), and developmental disability (Wallman et al.). Reports from fellow students and others in contact with him have described him as angry, "super stressed out all the time," "trying to hide his face," (Darrah, 2018) "fearful of other people … threatened by bullies," and "consumed by sadness" (Sanchez & Flores, 2018). In February 2017, Nikolas walked into a gun store in Coral Springs, Florida and legally purchased an AR-15 semi-automatic rifle, a military grade assault weapon euphemistically termed a "modern sporting rifle" in 2009 by the National Shooting Sports Foundation, and dubbed "America's rifle" by the National Rifle Association (Herrera, 2018). One year later, Nikolas assaulted Stoneman Douglas's students and teachers, leaving 17 dead and 17 wounded before he was apprehended.

No single answer will provide an adequate explanation for Nikolas's actions, and certainly nothing so simple as an identifiable "motive." Many factors, however, seem collusive in this event. Nikolas's childhood seems troubled and sorrowful. His multiple school transfers depict an unstable environment, to say the least. His various diagnoses indicate genetic, psychological, and social disorders. At different stages throughout his life it seems clear that Nikolas did not receive the type of care and treatment he needed. But that's only part of the story. The ease with which an 18-year old boy with a long history of emotional and behavioral issues was allowed to walk into a store and purchase a military grade weapon is also a salient factor here, as is the fact that such weapons are available at all to civilian customers in a country that aspires to greatness. No less relevant is the ready availability of violent hate speech and virulent xenophobia so prevalent in our culture. Nikolas's "political" views and affiliations comprise a melting pot of usual suspects: racist, homophobic, islamophobic, antisemitic, and anti-immigrant. Nikolas's experiences are, unfortunately, not unique (Murphy, 2018). Many have undergone such traumas, and worse, and not gone on to commit massacres. Many, however, have, though more so in the United States than in any other country. So many, in fact, that mass school shootings are known internationally to be a uniquely American tragedy.[9]

The following day U.S. President Donald Trump addressed the massacre by assuring his audience that Parkland "is a great and safe community," and calling for increased attention to "the difficult issue of mental health," while asking students and teachers to "treat cruelty with kindness" and "turn classmates and colleagues into friends and neighbors" (Sorkin, 2018). And yet, research has shown for some time now that mental health, far from being the most significant factor in gun violence, is hardly a factor at all. Two days after the shooting, the *New York Times* published an article with the following figures: "mass shootings committed by people with serious mental illness represented

1 percent of all gun homicides each year"; "Americans do not appear to have more mental health problems than other developed nations of comparable size which experience far fewer mass shootings"; and that "less than 5 percent of gun-related killings in the United States between 2001 and 2010 were committed by people diagnosed with mental illness" (Qiu & Bank, 2018). With available research such as this, why do President Trump and nearly 50 percent of Americans yet believe either "failing to identify people with mental health problems is the primary cause of gun violence or that addressing mental health issues would be a major deterrent" (Qiu & Bank, 2018)?

Despite the mentally ill being an easy target for scapegoating, more seems to be at work here. The mentally ill are not the only ones blamed for these occurrences. Trump's call to students and teachers to treat each other more kindly is a subtle shifting of the responsibility to them. His tweets earlier in the day before his address were not so subtle: "So many signs that the Florida shooter was mentally disturbed, even expelled from school for bad and erratic behavior. Neighbors and classmates knew he was a big problem. Must always report such instances to authorities, again and again!" (Qiu & Bank). The FBI, as well, expressed frustration that with so many warning signs, they had not been able to prevent this. Others have expressed similar frustration with the FBI. I argue that rather than a cynical attempt to avoid responsibility, or even simply ignorance, a neoliberal logic of individualism accounts for these ways of making meaning of the Parkland shooting, and mass shootings in general. Whether constructed as "pure evil," as Florida Governor, Rick Scott called it (Weber, 2018), mentally ill, or irresponsible, the dominant causal explanations given for such phenomena single out individual agents: the perpetrator, parents, teachers, students, neighbors, counselors, law enforcement, etc. Even when blame is put on a group, like a school or the FBI, the critique does not frame the group in systemic terms, but as a collection of individuals: students and teachers need to be trained to better notice the signs, and thus be better prepared to (individually) act on them; law enforcement needs better protocols so that individuals more proactively address warning signs, etc. Not to mention the fact that even if such groups evolve their practices, it is only in order to better anticipate and confront the dangerous individual that is imagined to be the root of the problem.

Such a logic sheds light on Trump's baffling non sequitur in light of Stoneman Douglas's 17 dead and 17 wounded that Parkland "is a great and safe community." The logic of neoliberal individualism not only explains causal relationships, but protects one from the knowledge of alternate causal explanations even more threatening. To quote Jennifer Simpson again, "neoliberalism supports the logic of an 'I,' reduces the space for a 'we,' and appears to many a desirable logic even as it destroys possibilities for the public good" (188). If the reduction of the space for a "we" destroys possibilities for working collaboratively for a public good, it also erodes possibilities for imagining and assigning collective and/or systemic guilt. Trump's claim of the safety and greatness of Parkland is more than consoling words for a frightened, grieving community (the same community he had earlier chastened for not being vigilant enough in preventing the shooting). It is a form of epistemological prophylactics warding off the dangerous notion that what happened in Parkland was not the result of a lone mentally ill individual, but symptomatic of a larger set of socioeconomic and political circumstances, not least of which is the ready availability of guns in this country. According to this logic, which takes the safety and greatness of the Parkland community as a given, violence can only ever be the result of individual actors, the mentally ill or some "bad dudes." However, if it is the case that such violence has larger social and systemic origins, then Parkland is neither so safe nor so great as Trump imagines. And by way of metonymy, neither is America, whose renewed greatness Trump's election was meant to signal, which is the real threat here.

I take time to analyze the logic of the rhetorical response to the Parkland shooting not only because it is another example of what I've been calling the logic of neoliberal individualism as it applies to a crisis befalling American schools, but also because it is so similar to the response to another incident of school violence that took place at my own institution around the same time. On March 5th, 2018 a fourth-year student committed suicide by jumping from a 12-story student residence (Monteiro, 2018). This was not the first student suicide here. Just last year two students committed suicide within two months of each other.[10] Commenting on this most recent suicide, the university president confessed that, "Like many of you I am asking what was going on in this young man's world where taking his life seemed the only way out," and asserted that "We need to turn talk into action to make sure we are doing everything in our power to remove stigma and connect people with the help they need." The help that the president refers to here is mental health care. And it is true that our school's mental health care resources are woefully inadequate, boasting only two campus locations with a total staff of 25 employees to service 36,000 students. Many students report having gone to the counseling center for emotional distress, only to be asked whether they were planning to harm themselves or someone else, and, replying they were not, being scheduled for an initial intake session 3–5 weeks later.

Despite these troubling indicators, what is even more troubling is that the president's response to the incident, and the institutional *sensus communis* it reflects, is almost identical to Donald Trump's addressing of the Parkland shooting. "Like many of you I am asking what was going on in this young man's world where taking his life seemed the only way out." The reference to "world" here is not the world at large or even the campus community—no environmental or systemic issues are called into question. It is the young man's world that is called into question, his inner world and his reasoning faculties such that "taking his life seemed the only way out." Not only does this framing of the young man's suicide pin the responsibility for the action upon an individual whose personal inner world (and not the social outer one) is inscrutable, it also imagines the suicide took place as the result of a faulty exercise of reason, as if the student sat down and considered his options, and as a result "taking his life seemed the only way out." This phantasmal construction of suicide as a kind of faulty deliberation, rather than a succumbing to despair or being "consumed by sadness" is a common trope of neoliberal individualism, where individuals are imagined to be rational agents, even if their reason is faulty. If only they were more reasonable, they would make better choices, so the thinking goes.

There were and are, however, multiple indicators that this issue is larger than the individual actors concerned. On March 8th, three days after the suicide, students staged a Walk Out for Mental Health (Monteiro). Getting up and leaving their classes at an agreed upon time, they gathered from all over campus to protest the mental health climate of the university. The dearth of available resources was just one of the concerns articulated by students.[11] Just as compelling were the multiple accounts of students about the stressful, lonely, and hypercompetitive study/work conditions they endured. Anecdotes about disciplines where student ID numbers represented their ranking in the program or professors who began class by telling students how many of them would fail by the end of the term were some of the most egregious stories, as were multiple accounts of faculty who required death certificates as proof of absence for attending a funeral. In addition, while my school boasts an extremely comprehensive and successful co-op program wherein students can earn up to two years of paid working experience while completing their degrees (70% of incoming students report choosing us precisely because of this co-op offering),[12] this also means that in addition to facing the usual pressures of college (being away from family and friends, more time-consuming and difficult course work, building a whole new social community, and, for most, working a part-time job, to name a few), these students are constantly applying for and competing with each other for co-op positions. Many of us in academia would readily admit that the most stressful period of our lives came near the end of graduate school when we were simultaneously teaching courses, finishing our dissertations, and entering the job market.

Indeed, most academics I know describe the application process as a full-time job in itself. Students at my school exist in this overextended state for years before even completing their bachelor's degree. At a public airing of a report commissioned by the president to discuss the mental health issues confronting students and how the university intended to handle them, one student claimed the campus "is dead," by which he meant, not that there were no students on campus, but that they were ground down by work stress and competition. While the president committed to increasing the amount of mental health resources on campus, as to the issue of an overworked and overstressed campus culture, the president reportedly answered that "intellectual rigor would not be sacrificed."

As a sad addendum to the this troubling story, during the writing of this essay I received another email from the student I mentioned earlier who had written me to ask I make the paper prompt available early so that s/he could get a jump on it. S/he was taking five courses and working a 30-hour a week job. This student was bright, and regularly turned in quality work for most of the term. I noticed, however, that s/he was often absent, and I assumed must be getting lecture notes from a colleague. This second email came about three-quarters through the term. The student apologized for their absences, sharing that s/he had recently undergone a traumatic family event, and that in conjunction with their stressful workload, they had suffered a breakdown and had stopped attending classes. The student wanted to know if they had earned strong enough a mark already to be able to miss the final and still pass the course. S/he missed the final but passed with a low C. There was no question of this student not being motivated. What s/he was motivated by, and choices and consequences it entailed, is another matter.

## The "Stigma" of Mental Health

The claim that students' and teachers' mental health has a direct relation on the education they receive and provide is uncontroversial. Even conservative critics don't deny the importance of mental health; they simply see it as more a matter of grit and individual responsibility, than a matter of social or institutional concern. The real questions here are: What kind of a thing is mental health? What are the roles played by, and the impacts of, cultures, institutions, communities, and others in relations to a person's mental health? And who do we want to be in light of these circumstances?

That a person's mental health is something not entirely (or even mostly) dependent upon their own actions is also a relatively unprovocative claim. Indeed, not too long ago, mental illness was seen as a sane reaction to unstable and disturbing social conditions, and the antipsychiatry movement of the 60s and 70s launched successful critiques of the ways in which psychology colluded with dominant political ideologies to scapegoat "deranged" individuals for societal ills (Staub, 2011). Since that time we've seen a conservative backlash against those theories, and the individual is once again emerging as the hero of his own narrative: if you're not making it, you're not trying hard enough. (Conversely, if you are making it, it's not because of any advantages you were born into and continue to benefit from, but because you earned it.)

The great danger we face as our social imagination continues to deteriorate is not so much that people more and more find neoliberal individualism convincing, but that they less and less see it at all. As it becomes a part of our epistemological architecture, it ceases to be a theory or a position that we can question or resist, as it becomes the lens through which we view the world as such. Part of what this means is that even individuals or institutions characteristically concerned with issues of social justice, approach those issues having already accepted the assumptions of a neoliberal individualist worldview. Take, for example, the National Communication Association's (NCA) recent Special Journal Forum on "mental health stigma" in education (National Communication Association, 2018). As their website claims,

> Educators are hired to teach, research, and focus on other academic issues, not to be counselors. And yet ... a 2017 American College Health Association survey found that 55 percent of students stated they had been diagnosed or treated by a professional for some form of mental illness while in college—and teachers often serve as the front-line responders.

To address this issue, here are a few of the contributors' recommendations:

- C. Kyle Rudick and Deanna P. Dannels "suggest better instructional practices and advanced disciplinary knowledge among faculty about identifying and addressing mental health stigma on college and university campuses" (National Communication Association).
- Rachel A. Smith and Amanda Applegate (2018) define mental health stigma as "profoundly negative stereotypes about people living with mental disorders" and suggest that "students, instructors, and administrators ... can avoid creating new stigmas through word choice ... [and] ... embrace neurodiversity in our instructional design and institutional policies."
- Cheri J. Simonds and John F. Hooker (2018) offer a trifecta of: better training for teachers and administrators in identifying students with mental health issues; better directing of students to campus resources,

such as the counseling center, where students will learn that "many of these [mental health] issues can be effectively addressed with a little help ... cop[ing] with difficult emotions and life stressors"; and better accommodating of students with mental health issues, wherein "instructors can work with their respective university services to develop a plan of action unique to a ... course and within the parameters and processes of a specific institution."

- Finally, Zachary W. Goldman (National Communication Association) identifies "three areas for development: changing the narrative around mental health, encouraging students' self-regulation and awareness, and investigating further ways to address students' mental health."

While I don't for a minute doubt the sincerity of these scholars' attempts to grapple with issues surrounding students' mental health, I do have grave reservations about their ability to effect substantive change or good for students so long as the problem is posed almost exclusively in terms of better identifying individuals with mental health issues in order that they get access to better coping strategies. The above call to "embrace neurodiversity" is telling in this regard. Like many calls for inclusion today, the substance of material equity (as might be addressed by policies of reparation or socialized health care or free education, for example), is sidestepped for the veneer of social visibility (diversity statements, Black History month, the Pride parade).[13]

Which brings me to my final point. While the CFP I analyzed in the first part of this essay as well as the recent special issue published by the NCA do illustrate a real concern for student learning, not only is their theorization of the problem insufficient (as well as serving to uphold a host of dominant social inequities surrounding education and mental health), so too is their formulation of the solution. In each case, both the problem and the solution are localized in individuals, in students and/or teachers. Making teachers ground zero for addressing student motivation or mental health is of the same faulty logic as seeing motivation and mental health as matters of personal integrity, individual worldview or reasoning, and self-regulation. This is in part why so many college and university teachers are pushing back against such measures. While elementary and secondary school educators are well familiar with the cliché—*I'm not just a teacher but a friend, a parent, a counselor, a coach,* etc.— (and by calling it a cliché, I don't mean to diminish its truth), teachers in higher education are not so used to assuming this multiplicity of roles (which is not to say that they don't.)

While even as recently as 50 years ago colleges and universities were still assumed to act towards students in their care *in loco parentis*, being attentive to needs and concerns not strictly limited to what happens in the classroom, in the neoliberal unsettling of education that has taken place since that time, institutions are largely seen as access providers to learning content with no greater social responsibilities or ethical obligations toward students or society at large than Jamba Juice has to serving up a quality smoothie. Witness some of the backlash to a recent *New York Times* article on another case of campus suicide that took place at Hamilton College in upstate New York in 2016 (Hartocollis, 2018). The article largely focuses on the role that the Family Educational Rights and Privacy Act, or FERPA, played in preventing the school from communicating with the student's parents regarding "warning signs" of his impending action.

While the article is problematic to the extent that its horizon of responsibility extends no further than individual teachers or campus employees identifying "troubled students" and communicating their knowledge to relevant parties, it yet does see schools as sharing the responsibility for the physical and mental wellbeing of students. This suggestion, however, has created an outcry among both the public at large as well as university teachers. In the comments section in response to the article, we see on one hand those who refuse to acknowledge anything other than personal responsibility as the relevant factor in the case: "If not at 18 when does a person become responsible for their choices? Will we invent a society where employers of 25 year olds are responsible for calling Mommy when an employee is missing work and deadlines?" "This is an incredible [sic.] irresponsible article that treats adults as if they were minors. Parents need to back off. College is not about you. If your child commits suicide, it's their decision, and their fault. Back off." "If you have raised your child to be so incapable that by the age of 18 you don't feel comfortable having them handle their now affairs, then don't send them away to college. They can spend the rest of their lives living in your basement." On the other hand, there are also criticisms raised here by teachers that deserve more serious attention: "I see students a few times a week for 3–4 hours in a classroom with at least 23 other students, sometimes 99 other students. Are you that clairvoyant that you can divine which students are suicidal, and when, given this limited contact?" "Suicide intervention skills? How much of a burden are instructors supposed to shoulder? You do know that most teaching faculty are adjuncts making almost no money and balancing enormous teaching responsibilities. And you want to make them also responsible for assessing and determining someone's mental state? Increasingly those in the classroom are being asked to take on the responsibilities of a broken system."

It is this last comment that I want to close with. The problem is at least twofold. On one hand, in the epistemological architecture in vogue with the arrival of neoliberal capitalism, colleges and universities no longer see themselves acting *in loco parentis* on behalf of their students, which, to whatever extent they were successful in this role in the past, and to whatever extent their performance of it was problematic, at the very least allowed for the possibility of thinking higher education's social and ethical responsibilities beyond merely providing access to knowledge and skills. On the other hand, without the institutional support of schools and universities, not to mention the socioeconomic support of the culture at large, taxing individual teachers with being accountable for the motivation and mental health of their students is just another way of passing the inequality buck. In reducing social issues to personal problems we see vividly how "the logic of an 'I' … reduces the space for a 'we,' and … destroys possibilities for the public good" Indeed, as Simpson further asserts, such ideologies "render a sense of the public unimaginable" (189). In such a bleak and dreary context, is it any wonder that institutions of higher education are experiencing problems of motivation?

## Notes

1. I borrow this term from Jennifer Simpson (2014), who describes epistemological architectures as "structures of believability" (a term she in turn borrows from a conversation with R. Walcott). Such structures, Simpson writes, "construct or close off spaces for what we can know … inform[ing] our responses to knowledge that is, at least for the knower, 'not yet'" (p. 165). "Not yet knowledge" for Simpson is that which resides outside what is familiar to us, perhaps challenging what we already know or believe. Not yet knowledge is "a way of making meaning that is at once beyond what one knows and within reach of what one might come to know." (We might see Lev Vygotsky's "zone of proximal development"—the space between what a student can do on her own and what she can do with help—as a corollary concept.) Such structures largely shape the ways we "engage or refuse what we find challenging, new, or upsetting." Thus, epistemological architectures play a formative role in constituting human subjects who take a certain set of values and logics as "natural" or at face value, while not seeing or dismissing others.
2. For an eye-opening analysis of the rhetoric of excellence in higher education, see Patricia Harkin's (2006) "Excellence is the Name of the (Ideological) Game."
3. This year's conference (CTE's tenth) drew 263 faculty, staff, and student attendees from across campus and Ontario. It ran all day, offering 23 panels and 15 poster presentations. Guests were treated to light breakfast refreshments, lunch, and a wine and cheese reception. I include these details by way of illustrating the event's institutional support and visibility. Teaching is not taken lightly by the university.
4. In the spirit of full disclosure, I am deeply suspicious of pieties like "the genuine love of learning," as I believe they function more as a way of gatekeeping and scapegoating students than express an actual concern for the socioeconomic conditions in which learning takes place.

5. While the increasingly casualized workforce (adjuncts, sessionals, lecturers, etc.) have the worst of it here, tenure track and tenured professors are also being assailed by growing amounts of service work, production protocols, and evaluative procedures.

6. For more on the current craze over developing successful character traits in students, see Nicola Rivers and Dave Webster's (2017) blog piece, "What is 'motivation porn,' and why does Higher Education seem addicted to it?"

7. For a clear example of how this plays out in academe, see Stanley Fish's (2008) *Save the World on Your Own Time*, which is nothing short of a paean to neoliberal individualism as it applies to teachers and scholars in post-secondary education.

8. There is debate about whether or not Nikolas was officially expelled from school, as such a move is against federal law.

9. In 2014, in response to the mass shooting at UC Santa Barbara that killed seven people and wounded over a dozen others, Jason Roeder, a writer for the satirical newspaper *The Onion*, aired the now (in)famous headline, "'No Way To Prevent This,' Says Only Nation Where This Regularly Happens." Since then, the headline and accompanying story has been recycled six times, changing only the relevant locations and number of victims: June 2015, Charleston, SC; October 2015, Roseburg, OR; December 2015, San Bernardino, CA; October 2017, Las Vegas, NV (Rosenberg, E., 2017); and November 2017, Sutherland Springs, TX ("No way," 2017); and the latest installment featuring Parkland, FL.

10. There have been at least ten reported suicides here since 2012. However, the statistics on campus suicides are surprisingly (or perhaps not so) hard to find. Universities in general do not keep good records of such information, and they are even less forthcoming about sharing such data with the public. My university is no exception here. In addition, my university only records those suicides that take place on campus (another practice common to universities and not particular here), and so trying to determine how many of our students commit suicide yearly is difficult to estimate since those that take place off campus are not recorded by the institution. (I find this practice similar to how graduate programs typically tout how many students they placed in jobs, but not how many are still looking or gave up trying, or those who, even finding employment, only secured part-time, exploitative teaching labor rather than tenure-track positions.)

11. Details of the walkout are from my own experience, having attended the event.

12. "Co-Operative Education," University of Waterloo website.

13. To be clear, I do not in any way mean to diminish the importance of these policies and events in themselves, nor the hard won battles that were fought to achieve them. I do, however, take issue with those who would see these achievements of greater social equality as indicative of an established material or political equity.

## *References*

Co-Operative Education. (n.d.). Welcome Waterloo co-op students. Retrieved from https://uwaterloo.ca/co-operative-education/

Darrah, N. (2018, February 14). Nikolas Cruz was living with Florida high school student in months leading up to shooting, attorney says. *Fox News*. Retrieved from http://www.foxnews.com/us/2018/02/15/nikolas-cruz-was-living-with-florida-high-school-student-in-months-leading-up-to-shooting-attorney-says.html

Fish, S. (2008). *Save the world on your own time*. New York, NY: Oxford University Press.

Hall, S. (1988). The rediscovery of "ideology"; return of the repressed in media studies. In T. Bennett, J. Curran, M. Gurevitch, & J. Wollacott (Eds.), *Culture, Society, and the Media* (pp. 52–86). London: Routledge.

Harkin, P. (2006). Excellence is the name of the (ideological) game. In B. T. Williams (Ed.), *Identity papers: Literacy and power in higher education* (pp. 29–41). Logan, UT: Utah State University Press.

Hartocollis, A. (2018, May 12). His college knew of his despair. His parents didn't, until it was too late. *The New York Times*. Retrieved from https://www.nytimes.com/2018/05/12/us/college-student-suicide-hamilton.html

Harvey, D. (2007). *A brief history of neoliberalism*. Oxford, NY: Oxford University Press.

Herrera, C. (2018, February 15). Gun shop owners distraught over firearm sold to teen now held in school massacre. *Miami Herald*. Retrieved from https://www.miamiheraldcom/news/local/community/broward/article200434884.html

Laughland, O., Luscombe, R., & Yuhas, A. (2018, February 15). Florida school shooting: At least 17 people dead on "horrific, horrific day." *The Guardian*. Retrieved from https://www.theguardian.com/us-news/2018/feb/14/florida-shooting-school-latest-news-stoneman-douglas

Miller, C. M., & Gurney, K. (2018, February 20). Parkland shooter always in trouble, never expelled. Could school system have done more? *Miami Herald*. Retrieved from http://www.miamiherald.com/news/local/article201216104.html

Mills, C. W. (1959, 2000). *The sociological imagination*. New York, NY: Oxford University Press.

Monteiro, L. (2018, March 6). UW students plan to protest lack of mental health services on campus. *The Record*. Retrieved from https://www.therecord.com/news-story/8312538-uw-students-plan-to-protest-lack-of-mental-health-services-on-campus/

Murphy, P. (2018, February 17). Exclusive: Group chat messages show school shooter obsessed with race, violence and guns. *CNN*. Retrieved from https://edition.cnn.com/2018/02/16/us/exclusive-school-shooter-instagram-group/index.html

National Communication Association. (2018, May 22). Communication scholars discuss mental health stigma in higher education in a special journal forum. Retrieved from https://www.natcom.org/press-room/communication-scholars-discuss-mental-health-stigma-higher-education-special-journal

"No way to prevent this," says only nation where this regularly happens. (2017, November 5). *The Onion*. Retrieved from https://www.theonion.com/no-way-to-prevent-this-says-only-nation-where-this-r-1820163660

Qiu, L., & Bank, J. (2018, February 16). Checking facts and falsehoods about gun violence and mental illness after Parkland shooting. *The New York Times*. Retrieved from https://www.nytimes.com/2018/02/16/us/politics/fact-check-parkland-gun-violence-mental-illness.html

Rivers, N., & Webster, D. (2017, December 3). *Fruits of the pedagogic life*. What is "motivation porn," and why does Higher Education seem addicted to it? [Blog post]. Retrieved from https://davewebster.org/2017/12/03/what-is-motivation-porn-and-why-does-higher-education-seem-addicted-to-it/

Rosenberg, E. (2017, October 3). Why this Onion article goes viral after every mass shooting. *The Washington Post*. Retrieved from https://www.washingtonpost.com/news/the-intersect/wp/2017/10/03/why-this-onion-article-goes-viral-after-every-mass-shooting/?noredirect=on&utm_term=.0dc1f191473b

Sanchez, R., & Flores, R. (2018, April 12). Letter asks judge to show mercy on Parkland shooter. *CNN*. Retrieved from https://www.cnn.com/2018/04/12/us/nikolas-cruz-supporter-letter/index.html

Simonds, C. J., & Hooker, J. F. (2018). Creating a culture of accommodation in the public-speaking course. *Communication Education, 67*(3), 393–399.

Simpson, J. S. (2014). *Longing for justice: Higher education and democracy's agenda*. Toronto, Ontario: University of Toronto Press.

Smith, R. A., & Applegate, A. (2018). Mental health stigma and communication and their intersections with education. *Communication Education, 67*(3), 382–393. Retrieved from https://nca.tandfonline.com/doi/full/10.1080/03634523.2018.1465988#.Ww6YiRMvxE

Sorkin, A. D. (2018, February 15). President Trump's victim-blaming response to the mass shooting in Florida. *The New Yorker*. Retrieved from https://www.newyorker.com/news/our-columnists/president-trumps-victim-blaming-response-to-the-mass-shooting-in-florida

Staub, M. E. (2011). *Madness is civilization: When the diagnosis was social, 1948–1980*. Chicago, IL: University of Chicago Press.

University of Waterloo Teaching and Learning Conference 2018. (2018, April 26). Call for proposals: Motivating our students and ourselves. Retrieved from https://uwaterloo.ca/uw-teaching-and-learning-conference/call-proposals

Vygotsky, L. S. (1978). *Mind in society: The development of higher psychological processes*. Cambridge, MA: Harvard University Press.

Wallman, B., McMahon, P., O'Matz, M., & Bryan, S. (2018, February 24). School shooter Nikolas Cruz: A lost and lonely killer. *Sun Sentinel*. Retrieved from https://www.sun-sentinel.com/local/broward/parkland/florida-school-shooting/fl-florida-school-shooting-nikolas-cruz-life-20180220-story.html

Weber, P. (2018, February 15). Florida Gov. Rick Scott calls Parkland school shooting "pure evil," says now's not the time to talk gun law. *The Week*. Retrieved from http://theweek.com/speedreads/755388/florida-gov-rick-scott-calls-parkland-school-shooting-pure-evil-says-nows-not-time-talk-gun-law

Williams, R. (1976). *Keywords: A vocabulary of culture and society*. New York, NY: Oxford University Press.

# 9. A Look Into Leaving: Learning From One Equity-Oriented Teacher's Resignation

Samantha Young and Deborah Bieler

### Sam, September 1, 2015, 1:05 p.m.

"Hey Sam," I hear my principal say, cheerfully. "Do you have a minute?"

For him, I do. He stops by my classroom often, always making the walk down to my room, rather than emailing or asking that I come down to his office. Since I am now the English Department chair, he defers to me on every decision that affects the department.

"Sure," I say, as I hop off the student's desk I'm standing on to staple a bulletin board. It reads: "Attitude—Step One: 'I can.' Step Two: 'I will.'"

His eyes glance out my window, then back to me. "Ms. T has officially accepted a learning support coach position. Her last day will be this Friday."

This news comes as no surprise. Ms. T was my partner last year. The two of us were the only eleventh-grade English teachers; we spent all year navigating a new curriculum, grading thousands of essays, and being dragged through a month-long round of state testing. We all knew that she was making the switch to her new position and supported her. So even though the district couldn't officially offer her the position until after the school year started, we made the decision for her to move out of the tested year—eleventh grade—so as not to jeopardize a smooth start to the school year for those students. She wasn't the first to make a move like this. Many English and Math teachers had decided to switch to other positions, schools, and even professions.

"Oh. Okay. So do you want me to call Ms. M this week and touch base with her? Or invite her in to start observing Ms. T's classes?" Ms. M had been hired as our new English teacher.

"Actually," he looks down at his shoes, then back to me, "I was wondering if you think there might be a position with a smoother transition for her. Instead of her replacing Ms. T, maybe someone else?"

"Hmmm," my gaze shifts to the bulletin board I just finished, one of four I've re-created for this year, then to the numbers I've taped to each desk, the seating charts I've posted around the room. "Yeah, sure. Maybe one of the ninth-grade teachers? They teach one prep and have the fewest students … and that team is really solid. They would be good role models for our newbie."

"Yeah. That's what I was thinking, too. So maybe she could take on Ms. K's schedule, and Ms. K could take on Ms. T's schedule? Ms. K could probably handle that, right? And she'd be a good fit with the tenth and twelfth-grade team?"

"Definitely," I hear myself saying, "Ms. K would be a good fit with any team. She's amazing and works so hard."

We nod our heads with a shared understanding of how hard everyone works in our school. My principal and I have talked about this at length. It's one of the reasons he's so supportive of us; he knows it's only a matter of time before the work suffers, the teacher suffers, or the teacher decides to leave. He talks as if he expects it—as though it's a given. As though all these demands from the higher ups have created a culture of burnout and he's accepted it.

"Okay, good, then we'll go ahead with that. Would you mind swinging by Ms. K's room before you leave today and let her know what's happening? She can't start moving her room until Friday, but let her know now. That way, she can meet with her new team and start to look over the curriculum."

"Yeah. Sure. I'll swing by."

### Sam, September 1, 2015, 3:45 p.m.

I walk through our front door. The cats and dog run to greet me. I give them each a quick pat on the head, and then head for the piano bench, where my husband is getting ready for his next lesson. I slouch onto the bench, my elbows plop on the keys, my head falls into my palms, and I finally let go of the tears I've been fighting back all afternoon.

I tell him about the changes going on at school. He knows Ms. K. We meet for book club meetings each month, and she's come out to see his band play, too. He listens with his arm around my shoulder.

He brings me in for a hug as I begin to despair. I explain that this particularly ambitious teacher spent all summer rewriting curriculum, set up her classroom a month and a half ago, and finally has a great team to work with this year. She's met all of her students (the ninth-grade students start earlier than the rest of the school), printed all of their names and medical concerns in her binder, laminated each of their birthdays onto cute little owls and pasted them onto a giant tree she made herself and hung on her classroom wall.

Now, a week after school has started, she will be moved to a new classroom on the other side of the building, to work with new students and a new team, teaching two courses she's never taught, in two new grade levels.

I feel like we're pulling the rug out from under her just as she is feeling comfortable and confident about the course she is teaching.

My husband reassures me that everyone will quickly adjust. That people change jobs all the time. I smile and try to feel good about making a nervous new teacher's job a little easier and express gratitude for a slightly more experienced teacher's willingness to change assignments after working so hard.

I remind myself that I am also happy for my former teaching partner for being brave enough to make this change in her career. Now, Ms. T doesn't have to choose between grading papers and training for a marathon, or planning lessons and spending time with her boyfriend. I hope that instead of inspiring students to find what they love, but ignoring her own passions because of her workload, she will have a manageable schedule and be able to impact students in a different way.

I take a deep breath, play a quick *Heart and Soul* on the keys, then shuffle off to the kitchen to make my sixth cup of coffee for the day. When I return, my husband gives me a squeeze and says, "Cheer up. It's Tuesday. Deb's coming over!"

"Good," I mumble, "Maybe she can help me. I hate that I get so emotional about all this."

My husband knows that Deb, the mother of his next two students, was my college advisor and one of my favorite professors. She taught my classmates and me that teaching is the most important job in the world. That teaching for social justice is possible. That teaching for positive change begins in the classroom, if teachers are willing to be their authentic selves, engage with their community of students, and challenge the status quo.

Deb was, and is, one of the warmest women I'd ever met. She made every one of her students feel heard, accepted, and valued. The values she taught me to embody and discover in my teaching permeated every aspect of my life. Her classes went beyond teaching us what it means to be a good teacher; there was something more soulful about our meetings than simply following the syllabus.

Since then, Deb and I have kept in touch. She's in my school often— knows my students, my principal, and has a clear view of the various initiatives going on. She's developed a partnership in which she brings her pre-service English teachers to teach an after school SAT prep course to our juniors every spring. I know I can be honest with her, but I'm afraid if I start, I won't be able to stop. It's just impossible to hide it from her when I feel like the wind has been taken out of my sails so completely.

"I feel like this department chair position forces me to do all the dirty work," I mumble to my husband, "And usually that makes me angry, but today I just feel sad."

"Yeah. I mean, I didn't want to say anything, but it's only the first day of September and you're already crying," he says as he tries to make me smile.

"I know," I say as I reach into my bag and pull out my laptop. "I need to forget about how bad I feel for Ms. K and remember how bad *I* have it," I attempt to joke.

He flashes me a concerned smile that says, "Why are you still doing this again?"

### *Deb, September 22, 2015, 4:05 p.m.*

"I think I need a break from teaching," Sam says, curling up on her living room sofa and petting her dog Taylor, who has hopped up into her lap. "Maybe a year off. And then maybe try to teach at a school where there's a little more support, where it's not quite as challenging."

She is a sixth-year teacher at an urban public school, and seven years ago, she was a student of mine as she was studying to become a teacher. I have visited her classroom, been inspired by the beautiful relationship she develops with every single one of her students, and observed her infuse her loving spirit and sense of hopefulness into all aspects of her teaching. I think about how she runs an aromatherapy diffuser in her classroom that creates such a lovely, calming (and unexpected!) environment for her and her students, and I think about how that diffuser, in this space, is such a great metaphor for her as a teacher. She infuses, she diffuses, she de-fuses …

I don't know what to say. I nod, to try to show her I am listening intently, that I support her, that I care about her well-being. But inside, my heart is breaking and pounding "No!" I hear one of the girls start "Sunday Bloody Sunday" on the drums, and in my mind, Bono sings the introductory lyric about not being able to believe today's news and not being able to make it go away.

She continues. "I don't want to neglect my first priority, which is my family, my marriage. I can't keep trying to grade 600 papers at home every week."

"I know. You've been working really hard to keep your priorities straight, to protect some time for yourself, to re-fill your bucket. A lot of teachers are really good at filling their students' buckets but don't take time to fill their own. I know that *you* know that that leads to burnout."

"It's just that it's exhausting. Like—get this: Saturday, I spent 5 hours creating lesson plans for the American Dream unit, and that felt really good; I was really excited about what I had prepared for the kids. I did it because the [required curriculum] was so awful. All of the readings the textbook includes about the American Dream are so negative." She names them, and I agree. I feel sick.

"So I found and included more positive texts instead. But because the kids at our school have knowledge that doesn't match the knowledge [the curriculum] assumes they have, the unit assessments are still going to be a nightmare for them. How can I teach them about parallel sentence structure if many of them can't tell me which words in the sentence are nouns? Redesigning the curriculum to be not only more positive but more connected to the kids' needs was really exhausting and frustrating. There's no time. Also, last year, I knew so many of the students because I'd had them before; this year is so much harder because I'm building all of these new relationships, and assessing all of their gaps and needs, you know?"

I ask many questions.

"Do you think you would still feel this way if you weren't Department Chair?"

"Maybe ... maybe not. ... I'm not sure."

"Do you even get a course release for all of the work you're doing as Chair?"

"Yes, but I also have to take on an additional Department-wide prep."

"Do you get paid for it?"

"No, well yes, but I chose not to because I didn't want to be required to stay after school to work on that prep a certain number of days a week in order to get paid."

"So you're doing more work but not getting paid to do it?"

"Something like that."

"Do you remember that class a couple of years ago that was just notorious, from grade level to grade level?"

"Yep, it was the Class of 2015!"

"Is it possible that the students you have right now are unusual like that class was? That it's possible you just have an unusually tough group right now?"

"Maybe. It's possible."

I try moving into fixing mode. "Does the principal know that you are feeling this way?"

"No."

"What do you think about telling him?"

"Hmm. I'm not so sure about that."

"I think he would want to know. Maybe there is something he could be doing to help you. And I think principals are really sensitive to teacher burnout, so that is a term that he would definitely hear."

I talk a little bit about Sonia Nieto's book *What Keeps Teachers Going?* and then Sam tells me about how one of her colleagues is trying to form a book group. I ask what kinds of books they might be reading together and then suggest that they consider books that would help them keep going, help them stay and thrive in the classroom.

But I am remembering all of the conversations we've had over the past year, when Sam often lamented the ever-changing policies that are always harmful to students and teachers, critiqued the poor substitute for teaching and learning that test-preparation mania had caused in her own and others' teaching, and expressed anger that she worked so many more hours and was being paid so, so much less than her peers in other professions. "Is this really how I want to spend my 20s?" I remember her asking.

Two days later, I re-read Nieto's book entirely with Sam on my mind. I have not been able to stop thinking about the possibility of her leaving. I cannot imagine a world in which Sam Young would not be teaching. Or (worse?) a world in which she was earning thousands more by teaching more privileged kids in the suburbs.

### Sam, October 13, 2015, 4:03 p.m.

"So how was your day?" Deb asks with a warm smile as my husband and both of her daughters begin playing "Happy Birthday" on the piano, each in their own octave.

"Actually, it was really good. Today in class we listened to a really inspiring podcast about Thomas Edison. The kids seemed to really like it."

"Awesome," Deb says, "It wasn't as dry as some of those texts in [the required curriculum]?"

"No, thank God. This one, of course, wasn't in the book ... something we added in on our own. I thought it would be a good example for their upcoming definition essay on 'What is an American?'"

"Hmm, that's a weird question," Deb smiles. "I'm guessing you didn't choose that?"

"No," I roll my eyes. "The writing assignments in this unit are terrible. But I'm just trying to give the kids the best resources possible. They're not allowed to use texts they find on their own."

"Wait, so they're being asked what it means to be an American, but they have to base their ideas on texts chosen for them?" Deb looks away. "Wow."

"I know," I sigh, "It's ridiculous. But I'm trying to make the most of it because I'm tired of being depressed." I'm reminded how much last year's students fought me on this assignment.

"It's hard enough when they struggle so much with the actual essay-writing," I continue. "The inaccessible texts we're supposed to use would just push students away from writing even more. So Thomas Edison it is, and let's be honest, that certainly would not have been their first pick, either, but it was the right Lexile level, and I think in the end they liked it. It led to some really great conversations about failure, perspective, and persistence."

Did I choose this text for them or me? I wonder to myself.

"Well that definitely sounds more inspiring than the texts you told me about last week," Deb adds.

"Yeah, well, I'm gonna *need* some inspiration if I'm gonna make it through this unit. Last year, the kids were so confused and frustrated by this assignment. This year, I had to supplement the unit with more interesting texts or I knew I would lose this group, too."

"Good idea," Deb reassures. "How did it turn out last year?"

"Not well," I recall. "About 25% of the students just didn't turn the paper in. We did organizers, outlines, drafts and discussed the readings as a class, but something just didn't click for them. They could understand the readings when we talked about them together, but when it came time for them to explain the values demonstrated in each text, they struggled. And you know me, I walked them through every step of the process, stayed after school for several hours to help, and still nothing from some of them. And there's no way they can pass for the marking period without completing a summative essay, so I spent countless hours after school talking to parents, trying to get these essays."

Deb shakes her head. "That sounds so stressful—for you and for your students."

It really was such a terrible way to start off the year. Many students felt an immediate blow to their confidence about the course and their writing because they struggled to understand the assignment and the texts. That's not how I want students to come into my class and approach writing. The students for whom I called home, for the most part, felt betrayed and put on the defensive, not realizing that I was required by the district to call for any student with a D or F.

"I'm really hoping this year is better," I muster.

"They liked Thomas Edison, right?" Deb asks hopefully.

"Yeah, they liked Thomas Edison," I smile.

### Sam, October 27, 2015, 4:25 p.m.

"So that's a formative *and* summative performance task—four days;" I count on my fingers, "A DOE pre- and post-test—two days; a unit pre- and post-test for each of five units—ten days; Smarter Balanced—two days; PSAT—one day; SAT—one day; and eight Embedded Assessments which will take a minimum of eight days *if* we made every one a timed essay."

I throw my hands up in the air. "When are we supposed to teach? Forget bonding with students. God forbid we do *anything* relevant to their lives or something that they want to do. I mean, we don't even have enough class time to get them ready for all these damn assessments!"

My glance darts to Deb's nine-year-old daughter doing her homework on my ottoman, patiently waiting for her turn with her piano teacher. "Sorry."

"No! Don't be sorry," Deb reassures. "The amount of assessing is ridiculous. The girls have to take *pre-tests* now every week before their spelling tests. In third grade! Anyway, do you think you could bring this to someone's attention at the district level? Is it possible that they just don't realize it?"

"I mean, I guess," I say with a sense of hopelessness. "They have to know that all these new data protocols, curriculum changes, and state mandates add up. They clearly don't know what it's like to stand in front of a room full of 30 teenagers and explain to them why all of these assessments are necessary. Forget necessary. Most of them aren't even relevant. They don't assess skills that we're required to teach in the curriculum. When I've asked about them in the past, the answer is always, 'it's just an exposure benchmark … to see what they know.' Like spelling questions, for instance. Are you kidding me? Every single time we review the assessments beforehand, we already know the questions and concepts they'll struggle with—which is most of them, unfortunately. These mandated tests are terrible."

Deb lowers her gaze and shakes her head, as if in mourning.

"I have kids who are actually excited to be in class and I feel like all I do is test them," I say ruefully. I switch to sarcasm: "'Oh, cool, kids. We're taking *another* assessment today! Oh? You didn't know about this one? Don't worry, your teacher didn't either. Don't sweat it. There's nothing you could have done to prepare for this one anyway. Well, sorry! Here ya go!'" Deb and I trade wistful looks, then turn to listen for a moment to one of the girls playing Bach's "Prelude I" on piano.

I continue, "Maybe I *will* say something to the district. I have to submit a monthly report for the English department and there is a 'Concerns' section. Maybe I'll break down all the testing days compared to the total number of days in school."

"I think that's an awesome idea," Deb says supportively.

That evening, I calculate the amount of class time devoted to assessment. We see students every other day in eleventh grade, so there are 87 total class days. Out of 87, at least 28 of those days (not including any review or additional writing days) are to be spent assessing. That's 32% of our time together. I explain in my report that these assessments oftentimes are not good measures for assessing skills and concepts, and so additional assessment may even be required. I ask if there is a district philosophy around the amount of time spent assessing.

For good measure, I throw in a section about how much out of school time these assessments force teachers to spend grading. For instance, each eleventh-grade teacher spent over 20 hours grading just the first embedded assessment.

And I add that I have serious concerns about keeping teachers motivated and feeling supported.

## Sam, November 10, 2015, 4:08 p.m.

"So we met with the History department today," I say to Deb after handing her daughter a pencil to borrow for her homework.

One of my responsibilities as English department chair is to facilitate writing professional development with non-English teachers who teach writing.

"It went … okay," I smirk as I lower myself onto the sofa.

"Yeah?" Deb says, reaching into her bag to pull out her laptop. "Tell me about it!" One of the girls has started a drum lesson, so we are shouting to each other even though we are sitting right next to each other.

"Well, we all clearly learned to write differently," I say loudly. "And certainly learned to teach writing differently. It's going to take a lot of work to get us on the same page for sure."

"The History teachers realize you're just trying to help students by being consistent, right?"

"Yeah, I think they do. And now we can finally have conversations around concrete examples because Smarter Balanced just released eleventh-grade writing exemplars—that was nice of them, right? After a year of already taking the test, they finally release examples of what they're looking for?"

Deb scowls and shakes her head in solidarity. She is experiencing the same difficulty as she prepares her pre-service teachers to teach our juniors to take the newly redesigned SAT this spring. In a hurry to roll out new required assessments, like Smarter Balanced and the SAT, companies often seem to forge ahead without regard for the realities of teaching and learning.

"*Anyway*. We start looking at the exemplars, breaking them apart and unpacking them. Immediately one of the History teachers gets defensive and says, 'Well, that's just *not* how we write in History.' Realizing we only have 15 more minutes to get through looking at the exemplars and rubrics together, I say 'Look. We all have our priorities for teaching our content, but this meeting is about preparing students to be assessed on this specific test. If this is the way the state says students should be assessed in writing, then this is the way we're teaching it. I don't want our students to feel blindsided on these assessments.'"

I feel myself flinch a little when I say that out loud, but that's just what it comes down to. I don't have time to fight or change this statewide initiative, so I might as well just do my best to make it as smooth and successful for my students as possible.

"And how did the History teachers respond to that?" Deb asks.

"Well, not so well," I laugh. "They weren't very excited about changing the way they teach to conform to a test. I guess they haven't been beaten into submission yet like the English teachers have." I reach down and grab my *Star Wars* mug, take a sip of coffee, and pause during a particularly loud drum part. "I decided to move away from the exemplars. They were super long, and I told them that they could look at them later and find similarities and contrasts to what they are already teaching. In the last 10–15 minutes, I wanted to highlight the differences and similarities between the state's required rubric and the Smarter Balanced rubric."

"Oh, well, that seems helpful," Deb shouts, rubbing my dog's belly.

"Well it *might* have been if the History teachers had ever seen those state rubrics before. At all of our district department meetings, we were assured that these were the rubrics all content areas were using for writing. That was the whole reason we were being required to meet—to begin the transition from state rubrics to Smarter Balanced rubrics and practice rubric scoring together. Instead, we just left our meeting more confused and very angry about all of the testing and all of the miscommunications. We left agreeing that we obviously needed to schedule another meeting to continue the conversation, with approximately one minute to clear our minds before our first period class."

We shake our heads. I wonder, as the drum lesson on "Seven Nation Army" comes to an end: Did I really just say that I don't have time to fight or change this state test?

### *Sam, November 17, 2015, 4:04 p.m.*

"You'll never guess what I was doing until 7 p.m. last night." I say to Deb as soon as she sits down on my sofa. "I was at school feeding a machine Scantrons for unit tests. Now the district requires each school to complete unit pre- and post-tests with these old-school Scantrons. They say it works better with their system." I roll my eyes. "It's such a pain. First, the students fill out each answer—on a test that is nearly impossible for them mind you; it's so pointless to collect this data in the first place. We already know they aren't going to do well."

I shake my head. "Then the teacher grades the short answer questions and bubbles in a corresponding letter on each one. If the student knocked it out of the park, the teacher bubbles an 'A.' If they include textual evidence, but don't elaborate, the teacher bubbles a 'B'; otherwise, it's an 'E,' which basically means 0. Ridiculous." I roll my eyes. "Once I have them from every teacher in that grade level, I send them through the machine individually."

"Yikes," Deb winces.

"We review the scores as a team, and for the valid portions of the test, that's helpful. But much of the test is unfair, and in my opinion, unethical. There are questions about topics not covered in the required texts for the units; concepts that really are taught in elementary school and students are penalized for here if they don't remember. Not so much an assessment of the texts and ideas covered in the unit, but a fragmented pairing of recycled SAT questions. The majority of our time spent analyzing the data is about whether or not we should throw out a question, not what the data may signify about student learning. More than half the time, the teachers can't even agree on an answer because the questions have multiple right answers and are highly subjective."

"What do you mean, 'throw out a question'? Like no one gets credit for it?" Deb asks.

"Right," I nod, "we are allowed to throw out any question more than 75% of students answer incorrectly, but they make it pretty difficult. The teachers have to submit a justification to me, and then I have to add it to a document that all the department chairs share. From there, the district reviews and either confirms or denies the request. Then they contact me, and I relay the approved removals to our teachers."

"Wow, sounds like a really time-consuming and tedious process," Deb says, sounding worried.

"Yep," I agree, "the whole process takes about a month just for this one assessment. At least a week for me to get the graded Scantrons from the teachers, a few days for me to scan the forms, then a few more days for teachers to discuss the data. Once they discuss and formulate their justifications for why a question is unfair, they email it to me, I add it to the district document, and it usually takes two weeks before they are approved or rejected. Once all that finally happens, teachers can redistribute tests to the students and review the results and allow students to start making corrections. It's so time consuming. The last test we gave took so long that the students didn't even remember the questions when we went over it! And forget if a teacher has a lot of absentees. That complicates everything."

Deb stares at me in silence, looking sickened by these new details.

"Ugh," I sigh, "sorry to vent so much. I just can't believe that I'm stuck at school after hours with all this to do." I rub my temples. "And all for a test that we didn't even get to create and we all agree is terrible!"

"Wait, what? So why are you still giving it?" Deb asks.

"They say they need data to back up the decision to change the tests," I say, annoyed. "It's so ridiculous."

"Wow," Deb says, horrified. "It's like they don't trust you to create your own assessments at all. What's the point of being so-called highly qualified or getting a degree at all if they just want someone who does what they're told?"

"Exactly," I say, frustrated. "All those student loans for an undergraduate *and* graduate degree in education and I can't write my own assessment."

"Have you expressed this to anyone?" Deb asks, concerned.

"Yeah, it seems like all we talk about at our English department meetings and our district department chair meetings. We were told that not all teachers have the skill set to write rigorous assessments that align to Common Core standards and prepare students for state testing."

"As if we know which test will actually be used to measure schools this year, right?" Deb adds sarcastically.

"Right," I roll my eyes. "The sad part is that in some cases, they're right. Some teachers haven't been taught how to create rigorous assessments— whether they don't have a degree in education or assessment writing wasn't a major focus of their program, some just struggle with it. It's definitely not easy. But rather than support them and teach them—God forbid we host a beneficial professional development with real learning—the district would rather just purchase assessments for every teacher." This is one of the hardest parts of my job. We're an extremely high needs school, so positions are hard to fill sometimes. And often, teachers who are highly trained in assessment writing, unit planning, and instruction design choose to teach in an affluent district where they can make more money teaching what they love. It has become abundantly clear to me that teachers are taught how to teach very differently—or some not at all, through programs that push people into hard-to-staff schools and let them sort of learn as they go. The district doesn't feel comfortable trusting each teacher to design an assessment that would meet the state's standards for funding.

"Maybe you could suggest that for the next PD?" Deb offers.

"Yeah, definitely," I say with optimism. "The district has already announced they'll be putting together curriculum writing teams to revise the unit planning materials, suggested text lists and assessments. Teachers can sign up to meet for three hours every other week for the rest of the year to revise these materials with other teachers throughout the district. Department chairs are required to go," I say, annoyed again. "Of course I want to have input on these materials, but I just already feel so burnt out. I don't know how many after-school meetings I can take before I go crazy."

"I totally hear you" says Deb. "That sounds really draining. You've taken on so much this year. Please, can you make some time for yourself? You have to take care of you."

"Thanks, Deb," I smile.

### Deb, November 24, 2015, 4:04 p.m.

Today, Sam shows me the amazingly nonsensical and extensively time-wasting activities that are currently taking all of her time, time that she wants and needs to spend on the real work of supporting her students (through curriculum for an upcoming unit on *The Crucible*, which she wants to make much more theme-based and relevant to students' lives) or her teachers as their department chair. She shows me seemingly countless rows and columns of student data on their Unit 1 [required curriculum] test that we talked about last week. As Sam scrolls through pages and pages of the teachers' polite but pointed concerns about particular questions, I focus in on one in which the teachers wrote, "We believe that many students were unfamiliar with the word *camaraderie* in this question and therefore did not fully understand what the question was asking."

I am furious after hearing Sam's frustrated description of this process last week and then seeing the actual document this week. Teachers like Sam and her colleagues are being asked to pull the knives out from their backs, conduct reparative surgery on themselves, then clean the knives, dry them, and give them back apologetically to their assailants: "I'm sorry, were you missing this?" First, they are being required to use district-level-sponsored curriculum that they know is far inferior to what they would have designed themselves. Second, they are being required to use pre- and post- district-level-sponsored tests that demonstrate a failure to understand even the most basic principles of assessment, including that assessments and curriculum should align and that assessments should be reliable and measure what they profess to measure. Third, to add further insult to injury, they are being required to take time away from teaching and learning to write out how exactly each of the test questions was poorly designed—likely by someone much less knowledgeable and skillful than they are and with much less experience than they have. Teachers are being asked to participate in faulty, harmful teaching practices and to do the work of district-level administrators (such as curriculum and instruction directors) in addition to their full-time work as teachers, and they are not compensated for this work. In fact, many teachers are being forced to serve as pro bono consultants, while many at the district level enjoy their status as only-one-job-performing, highly-paid but less-skilled administrators. When teachers are actually the ones with more knowledge, skills, and experience, why are district-level administrators who are less knowledgeable, skilled, and experienced enabled to have authority over them?

### *Deb, December 1, 2015, 3:59 p.m.*

It is December, and Sam has stopped smiling.

It is two days after Thanksgiving break, and in spite of the few days of vacation, she looks as if someone has turned her internal lighting from vivid to sepia. She is fighting back tears as she tells me the latest atrocity at her school: Suddenly, today, she heard from another teacher that the district administration might have decided that there will not be Smarter Balanced testing this year. This is in spite of all of the urgent! district! mandates! requiring teachers to change all of their curriculum so far this year and use the test-aligned materials and pre-tests—and in spite of the fact that it is, yes, December. She also heard that, suddenly, they want all of the seminars to be redone, all the students to be re-assigned to classes based on some new measure. Again, this in December.

My eyes tear up with hers. What is happening to the profession I love? To students and teachers I love?

Letting her stories sink in, I am suddenly struck by the thought that what she's been experiencing is like a kind of abuse. There are so many similarities: being asked to obey stringent rules and then having the rules suddenly and capriciously changed; constantly being demeaned and threatened; and experiencing an ever-diminishing sense of agency in a culture of fear and punishment.

I wonder what laws are in place to protect teachers from this sort of environment, which seems to have been growing every year in recent memory.

What about "hostile work environment" laws? In 2007, the US Department of the Interior defined a hostile work environment as "a form of harassment [that …] is demonstrated by such severe and pervasive conduct that permeates the work environment and interferes with an employee's ability to perform his or her job."

As so many people with business training but little teaching experience have infiltrated district-, state-, and federal-level educational leadership positions, those with the most power have the least expertise, and there seems to be no way to stop them from telling those with the most expertise—teachers—how and what they should be teaching and, even worse, forwarding the ideology that education is really about data and measurement, not about teaching and learning. This is an untenable situation, one manifesting in a highly-funded propaganda war that has hijacked the rhetoric around equity in education by positioning teachers and teacher educators as *personae non grata* of all that ails our schools rather than the everyday heroes that they are. I suspect that particularly in our least-resourced urban and rural areas, this dismissal of teacher expertise contributes heavily to the current—and massive—teacher exodus.

### *Sam, December 8, 2015, 4:01 p.m.*

"So how's it going this week?" Deb asks as she pets my sweet dog, who has now come to expect her undivided attention for the duration of each visit.

"Good, I guess," I shrug. "No Smarter Balanced. Kind of infuriating for them to change it on us like that, but it's nice to know that we won't have to miss almost a month of class like we did last year. You remember me complaining to you about it during SAT prep."

Deb and I had worked together the past couple of years on a free SAT prep program at my school. Our students get a free SAT prep course, and her students get classroom and lesson planning experience. It is a great program and a time Deb and I always get to catch up briefly.

"Last year, we decided it would be best if students tested with their content teachers in the room," I remind her.

This is what we had done in the past with the former state test. But since there are only two eleventh-grade teachers for each English and Math, and because the new test took at least two five-hour sessions to complete, it took about a month for us to test all of our students.

"Right," Deb nods, "I do remember that. And they had different people covering your class each day, right?"

"Each *period*!" I blurt out, remembering how exhausting it was. "Some class periods went really well—we were reading a novel and students had consistent tasks to do each day. But so many times the kids didn't do their work. The whole experience left me so on edge. In the testing room, I was anxious hoping our students would do well, not to mention anxious about all of the rules and formalities."

It was a new test with an instruction component involved. This required very specific preparation and scripting on the part of the teacher, and made everything more complicated. "And I was anxious about what was going on in my classroom at the time of testing. Students not doing their work meant more out of class calls I had to make to parents. Don't they know I don't want to call home? It's so much more work."

Deb shakes her head. "It's really degrading. Is your instruction and your time with students thought to be so insignificant that you are expected just to be out of your classroom for a month?"

"And of course the testing happens during my favorite unit," I sigh. "The only time we got to read a whole novel the entire year, and I'm out of the room for the majority of it."

"To be fair," I admit, "they did ask for our opinion about the testing logistics. Lots of other schools had the tests done in just one week. But in the past, with our students, if they didn't test with their classroom teacher, they didn't take the test seriously. Some would just blow through all of the questions and didn't care about doing well. So we didn't feel like we had much of a choice with all the pressure we felt from the district to perform well."

"I'm glad that they asked you about this, but teachers should really be the ones making the bigger decisions, like how and what to test in the first place!" Deb protests.

"Well, anyway," I look down at my hands, "we tried it last year, and it was a giant headache. So now we'll just test the SAT like we've always done, with students' first period teacher, all on the same day and then be done with it."

"And will students take it seriously?" Deb asks.

"The ones who know they want to go to college will," I say. "But I worry many might get frustrated and give up."

### Sam, February 23, 2016, 6:03 p.m.

It's February. It's dark and gloomy and cold. And I'm exhausted.

I've been waking up every day at 4:30 so that I can meditate and write for an hour before school. Otherwise, I think I would snap on someone.

I found out last week that one of the other department chairs only teaches two class periods. The rest of the day she has free for her department chair duties. No wonder she's always advocating for the district's policies at our meetings. If I had all the time in the world to get these tasks done, maybe I'd be a little more open to them, too.

She obnoxiously supports everything they say in our meetings and acts like it's always the best idea. Meanwhile, the rest of us are drowning in work. I have 120 students, countless essays to grade, only a 45 minute period to allocate to department work which is never enough time to type reports, conduct observations, scan unit tests, and countless other department chair tasks.

Not to mention the additional remedial course that I'm required to plan for all of our juniors. No other school in the district has one of these, and I totally support it. Hell, it was my idea. But I get stuck planning it, and there isn't enough time for me to do it all.

And then I find out that another department chair has less than half the students and one third the class load? I'm furious.

I don't even know why I took this position anymore. I love my principal, fellow teachers, and students and wanted to improve our curriculum and delivery as much as possible. As a sixth-year teacher, I somehow have the most experience in our department, so I thought I needed to step up and contribute what I could, but all it's doing is taking away from my students and me.

My students are exhausted, too. They're fighting with each other, not submitting their work, and overwhelmed with the number of assessments in all their classes, not just mine. I think I'm going to change the topic of our upcoming Socratic seminar to the failures of the American public education system. Is that too cynical? They all bring it up every time we complete a mandated assessment, and they certainly know where their teachers stand on the issue. I'd be lying if I said I hadn't been honest with them about my feelings about education.

I try to be honest with them so that I don't lose their trust, but unfortunately, right now, the honest truth about public education is grim.

## Reference

U.S. Department of the Interior, Equal Employment Opportunity Program. (2007, April). *Hostile Work Environment.* Just in Time Series #5. Retrieved from https://www. pdffiller.com/jsfiller-desk7/?projectId=230965288&expId=4026&expBranch=3#f-46d15283e794cf18bccfb6fb71432a9

# 10. "all schooled up": One Teacher's Path Toward Deschooling

RUSSELL MAYO

> If people are seriously to think about deschooling their lives, and not just escape from the corrosive effects of compulsory schooling, they could do no better than to develop the habit of setting a mental question mark beside all discourse on young people's "educational needs" or "learning needs," or about their need for a "preparation for life." I would like them to reflect on the historicity of these very ideas.
>
> —Ivan Illich (2008, p. v)

*Dear Reader,*

*The goals of this chapter are lofty and improbable, potentially impossible. It is my intention to unsettle what is perhaps one of the central truths in your lived experience and cultural worldview. My aim is to disrupt your faith, to shake your confidence in something you very likely hold near and dear to your heart, something to which you and I have already dedicated years of our lives. That "thing" which I aim to question is the value of schooling. To do this, I will attempt to tell my story of schooling, holding myself up as a mirror for comparison. I will offer some of my own experiences with teaching and schooling, and how I eventually decided to leave the classroom and question the entire project of schooling.*

*To better understand this marked shift in my own thinking, I will be building on the ideas of someone you've likely never heard of: a fascinating yet overlooked philosopher named Ivan Illich (1926–2002). Born in Austria, Illich was a rebellious Catholic priest, social critic, historian, and author. Illich's arguments against schooling in the 1970s shook the educational establishment, and his ideas are still deeply unsettling to those of us properly "educated" to believe in what Illich called the "ritual of school." And as you can see from the epigraph quoted above, Illich seeks to directly challenge many of our deeply-held beliefs about schools and society.*

*This chapter is in many ways an effort of paddling upstream, against the "common-sense" currents that our many deeply-held social, cultural, and historical biases entail. Following Illich's suggestion, I'm asking you to place a question mark beside ideas that most of us have long internalized as ending with a period—if not an exclamation point—and such a critical approach will no doubt be unsettling. This struggle is, I believe, the intent of this book, and it's a struggle that I gladly embrace. Will you join me?*

*~RFM*

## Growing Up With Public Education

I grew up in a white, middle class household in a small, post-industrial city near Lake Huron in central Michigan. My parents were both educators. In fact, they met in a rural public school in the late 1970s: my mother was a middle-school English teacher, and my father the school's principal. On our block was one of many rows of similar-looking, post-war houses with green lawns and tall trees. Our next-door neighbors were both public school teachers, and their children became teachers, as did I. Needless to say, my parents were firm believers in public schools, and as educated advocates themselves, they believed in the free exploration of interests and ideas across the sciences and humanities. I was raised to pursue my varying interests in drawing, animals, sports, video games, and music, and my parents supported my eclectic interests. My liberal, educationally-oriented upbringing instilled in me a deep respect for education and teachers from an early age. I was taught that public schools are vital to a diverse, democratic society, and that it is through these schools and colleges that everyone can get a shot at living the American Dream.

As you might guess, school started out great for me, as I had two supportive and well-educated parents. In fact, my father was my elementary school principal for a few years before he retired. One can't help but feel at home in a school when everybody there knows you and your dad. Within a few years, though, as I grew into adolescence, schooling changed for me. I developed a growing dissatisfaction with the ways in which "education" seemed to distract or distance me from activities I enjoyed. As learning became more "academic," I lost any personal connection with what I was being taught. My father was well aware of such proclivities, and he was surprisingly supportive of me through these challenges. This might be because my father has studied liberal philosophies of education in the 1960s and 70s. He was more liberal than most educators of that era, actively supporting desegregation efforts as a teacher in the 1950s and later, as an administrator, implementing project-based learning, team-teaching, and "open classroom" concepts as "junior high schools" transformed into middle schools across the U.S.

Nevertheless, my liberal-minded father couldn't help me cope with the boredom and mindlessness that my schooling had become. As Anyon's (1980) work on the "hidden curriculum" of schooling demonstrates, my experience in a middle-class school primarily involved rote learning, and following procedures to get the right answer. Critical inquiry, hands-on learning, or an active development of one's own interests were rare. Most of my distinct school memories involve out-of-school activities such as music, sports, and unstructured time with my peers. Beyond these, I do remember the occasional independent project, when teachers would graciously allow us actually choose and pursue some topic or project that we felt compelled to know more about. I distinctly recall researching the Boxer dog breed, presenting a poster I made about Malcolm X, and contributing to our middle school yearbook.

Other than these rare self-directed projects, I avoided most forms of homework while managing to slide by in most classes with okay grades. As a student, I was neither dedicated nor passionate until senior year of high school. Suddenly, I encountered a deeper study of the *humanities*—philosophy, history, sociology, and the arts—and through this, I became fascinated on the wider situations and ethical questions that ground, motivate, and explain human actions. The study of culture, history, economics, and politics all offered a chance to explore why some people lived differently than we do, why some had so much while others had so little, and how we might make the world a better place.

Even then, I never questioned the common-sense notion that success in school guaranteed success in life. My parents were both highly educated, as were many of their friends. To be a high school drop-out in my community seemed to mean one was doomed to a life of struggle. While a high school degree could at one time guarantee a middle class job in the auto industry, by the 1990s only college seemed to provide such job security; by the 2000s, this also proved to be untrue. After graduating from high school and searching for a direction in post-secondary studies, I eventually decided to become a teacher, studying both English and History at Eastern Michigan University. After four years of college and student teaching, I moved from Michigan to North Carolina. Soon, I found a job as a substitute middle school teacher in Chapel Hill.

## Becoming a Public School Teacher

Life as a novice teacher is never easy. Even in a relatively successful and affluent community, teaching middle school students was a tremendous challenge.

I remember the question that swirled in my head day after day: *How can I make our 46 minutes together meaningful? What do middle schoolers need to know about literature and North Carolina history? What do I know about these subjects? How can I translate my own intellectual passion for the humanities to these young people?*

Like most teachers, I started by imitating the pedagogical approaches that I had seen my own teachers and professors employ: students seated face-forward in rows, lectures via overhead projector with note-taking and limited discussion, weekly quizzes based on the textbook, the occasional group work activity or project. But these approaches quickly proved problematic. Students were often bored and could only recall a limited amount of content. Behavior issues were rampant, and I spent more time keeping my students quiet and focused on our books than I did teaching. Worst yet, I was disturbed by how our school seemed to perpetuate inequities: the majority of children of privileged, educated backgrounds mostly did fine, while those from lower socioeconomic backgrounds—mostly students of color—tended to be less successful.

Frustrated by this situation, I yearned for professional development workshops. Soon, I began a part-time Master's in Education at the University of North Carolina. Influenced by my studies, I adopted a new philosophy of education best described as "teaching for social justice" (cf. Ayers, Hunt, & Quinn, 1998; Christensen, 2009), a belief that schools often perpetuate inequality, but that with the appropriate curricula and pedagogies, all students have the chance to learn and succeed in school and society. Such an approach immediately transformed my teaching praxis. In history, I revamped our study of the U.S. Civil War by engaging students to create historical fiction characters, while they constructed multigenre writing projects about the human impact of the war from various vantage points. Students' flourished, often crafting lush stories full of historical details of Civil War medicine, music, spies, and the Underground Railroad. They were proud of the work they created, and was I—recalling my own personally-fulfilling inquiry projects.

I also created interdisciplinary English Language Arts units that attempted to engage students through a combination of culturally-relevant pedagogy (Ladson-Billings, 1995), critical literacy (Shor, 1999), and eco-literacy (Orr, 1994). I encouraged students to avidly read books of their choice, while I organized thematic studies of topics and issues that engaged students' lives and communities. For example, we studied the theme of food, which began with students writing about their own lived experiences and tastes that developed into food memoirs. Then we read and discussed Pollan's (2009) young readers version of *Omnivore's Dilemma*, which my students had written a grant to purchase for this unit. Meanwhile, we visited local, sustainable farms, and students developed projects exploring food cultures, family recipes, and ethical debates around eating meat and organic labeling.

Or we studied fracking, a critical political-economic issue for North Carolinians at the time. We critically read and discussed various media representations of the issue, compared with table readings of Arthur Miller's *An Enemy of the People* (1951/2010). Students were urged to draw connections between the play and the issue of fracking, particularly the conflict between the economy, the environment, and society. Students then used the play as an anecdote for composing op-ed articles about fracking, and some even had these published by local news outlets. With these new pedagogies and approaches driving my work, most students thrived in their reading and writing as it took on new meaning and relevance.

## Questioning My Role as a Teacher

But not everything was ideal about this scenario. At the same time, I felt a growing sense of doubt about my work as a public school teacher. I found that the good work I and some of my colleagues seemed to be doing was increasingly undermined by the problematic discourses of standardization, curricular mandates, and accountability measures from both the state and the local district (Taubman, 2009). A growing movement toward testing and quantitative measurement of teaching and learning "outcomes" was drastically reshaping any qualitative understanding of education as dialogic, social, or holistic. What administrators and educational "experts" expressed that they knew "what works" in education, and if we all followed their "best practices," all students would learn—and therefore succeed. Staff meetings became exercises in statistical analysis. Here, joy was never mentioned, and justice was framed in the narrow language of psychometrics: "growth," "accountability," and "achievement gaps" were only legible as standardized test scores.

Personal experience had taught me to doubt these claims, as well as the underlying assumption of progress via educational attainment. Many of my friends and colleagues resisted. When possible, we employed various forms of what Scott (2012) has referred to as "everyday resistance," such as foot dragging, feigned ignorance, and hidden forms of insubordination against standardization. Occasionally, we even spoke out, organizing letter-writing campaigns and efforts to block state and local reforms that increased standardization and testing. Unfortunately, we found no political allies for our fight: Democrats and Republicans supported the "test-and-punish" policies from No Child Left Behind to Common Core and Race to the Top.

Politicians concurred that learning could be taught and tested, and that the results of high-stakes tests were fair and meritocratic. I felt a growing sense of complicity with an institution that, no matter how hard I tried to push against it, treated students as numbers, sorting and selecting them in ways that replicated the classed, raced, and gendered disparities of the wider society. In fact, it seemed that the testing and standardization of schools were not aberrations but naturally arose from schooling itself.

Finally, after taking to the streets of Raleigh in 2013 as part of massive NAACP-led protests against statewide cuts to public education in North Carolina, I began to question what exactly we were fighting to support. Decades of data suggested public school classrooms had become more segregated since the 1990s (Orfield & Eaton, 1996), and that desegregation, affirmative action, and open college enrollment efforts had in fact done little to address structural inequities in American life. In fact, as Marsh (2011) suggests, the belief in education as a way of addressing wider socio-economic problems turned out to simply be a myth. Were we, as teachers and proponents of public education, simply reinforcing these myths? What could more money for public education actually achieve? I even began to question my own assumptions related to teaching for social justice within a system of rigid, competitive, compulsory schooling.

Beyond the myths of equity and justice via educational attainment, I also came to question whether public schools as *institutions* could ever be democratic, liberatory, or oriented to justice in any way. Could schools ever do more than serve the interests of the institutions and their managers, the states and politicians that funded them, and those who controlled the wider political economic interests? What if schools weren't actually failing, as many of the public narratives seemed to indicate? What if they were doing *exactly* what they were designed to do?

Having spent ten years as an intermittently successful teacher, and with such questions clearly in mind, I decided to leave the classroom in 2014 in order to pursue a doctorate in English and Education. It was my hope that full-time graduate studies, along with some distance from K-12 schools, would offer me time and support for researching and writing more about the problems, questions, and dilemmas that decades of teaching and schooling had unearthed. I had no idea where these questions might take me.

### *Finding Ivan Illich*

Now, as a Ph.D. candidate working with teaching pre-service English teachers and undergraduate writing classes at the University of Illinois at Chicago, I continue to question the relationship between education and society. Over the past four years, I've sought to better understand what role—if any—state-run schools might play in addressing the pressing challenges that we currently face. Two years ago, while preparing for my comprehensive exams on this very question, I found myself searching for new approaches to the vexing problem of schools and society. Recommended by a former professor, I finally picked up Ivan Illich's classic 1971 text, *Deschooling Society*. I had little idea what to expect, but I soon couldn't put it down.

Simply put: *Deschooling Society* blew my mind. Avid readers know the experience of finding a book that marks a definitive before/after signpost in one's life and worldview. *Deschooling Society* did this for me, causing me to forever think and speak differently about questions that I have wrestled with since adolescence. Mouth agape, occasionally laughing or furrowing my brow, I found myself relentlessly underlining, circling, and annotating the slim, tattered paperback. While I had encountered many critiques of education and its relationships with society, I was completely unprepared for Illich's scratching critique of schools and what he often calls the "myth" of education.

Though few readers of this collection are likely to be familiar with Ivan Illich, I will do my best to offer a brief introduction on his philosophy of education before discussing the possible applications for schools and society. In short, I believe Illich offers perhaps the most radical and unsettling vision of education, one which warrants significantly more attention from students, parents, and educators, though such attention will urge us to consider some very uncomfortable questions about our lives and work. According to education historian Joel Spring (1975), Ivan Illich is an essential theorists of "libertarian education," which posits that "any successful radical change in a society partly depends upon the changes in the character structure and attitudes of the population" (p. 9). Therefore, any "radical pedagogy," according to Spring, must therefore involve "new forms of socialization that will encourage non-authoritarian and revolutionary character structures" (p. 9). While this definition fits my radical educators, Illich's anti-education stance in highly unusual.

Yet, unlike other proponents of libertarian education such as Paulo Freire, Illich's critical scholarship against schooling has since faced what Gabbard (1994) calls a "discursive exclusion" among educational scholars and academics (p. 173). According to Gabbard (1994), this silencing is due to Illich's rejection of the taken-for-granted, messianic notion that schools are a vital, ultimately pastoral social institution that can be reformed. While myriad scholars and education philosophers have offered critiques of schools, their answers to the problems of school and society must still be wrapped up in either supporting, improving, or transforming the school. Discursively, one is simply not allowed to call for the *dismantling* of schooling writ large and demand an end to education as we know it. Hence, most educators no longer read or speak of Illich.

*Deschooling Society* was composed of a number of essays Illich penned for and out of a series of seminars involving Illich and various colleagues (include Paulo Freire) taught at CIDOC in the late 1960s and early 1970s. These *ciclos*, organized under the title "Alternatives in Education," sought to understand the relations of education and learning in an age of drastic social upheavals, amidst postcolonial revolutions, civil rights protests, and counterculture influences. In the end, Illich and some of his colleagues (Goodman, 1964; Holt, 1964; Reimer, 1971) argued that the current approach to ever-expanding education via modern schooling, especially in the Global South, must be challenged as an imperial project of social engineering.

Context clearly shaped Illich's rhetoric. By the end of the 1960s, schools and universities faced a burgeoning crisis in legitimacy, as did the wider social structure. As Illich (1978) argues, "compulsory schooling has lost its social, its pedagogical, and its economic legitimacy" (p. 69). By this, Illich means that schools no longer "blind[ed] its participants to the divergence between the egalitarian myth its rhetoric serves and the rationalization of a stratified society" (Illich, 1973a, p. 3). Certainly this was wishful thinking, for we've seen vastly more money, time, and emphasis put into education in the United States and around the world since Illich first began calling for deschooling. But this is not to diminish Illich's claims. Nearly fifty years after the publication of *Deschooling Society*, I argue that we need to hear Illich's now more than ever. The current schooling project is both socially and economically unsustainable. Following Illich, I've come to believe that smaller, cheaper, less authoritarian institutions that are at once more humane, empowering, community-based, democratically-organized, and open to all must replace the trillions spent on state-run schools and colleges. Admittedly, such a position is unpopular among parents, politicians, and educators, even less popular today than when Illich's proposed it.

Yet history has also vindicated many of Illich's claims. After roughly one hundred years of free and compulsory public education in the U.S. and other industrial nations, Illich's argues that schools have continuously failed in their promise of creating meritocratic outcomes or democratizing opportunity for students, as liberal-minded proponents had long promised. In fact, according to Illich, schools have actually further entrenched social divisions among social classes by masking the conflict between haves and have-nots, transforming it into one of "earned" accomplishments via the supposed equality of educational opportunity. Both the winners and losers of the schooling game—the graduate and the drop-out—come to accept the notion that their successes and failures were deserved.

What's more, Illich (1971) argues that as the peculiar institution of schooling has rapidly expanded, it transformed education from a few years spent in a one-room schoolhouse into a vast, totalizing institution that has come to constitute a "comprehensive monopoly" (p. 102) over young people's lives and learning. Illich, along with critical education scholars (Bowers, 2001; Esteva & Prakash, 2014; Prakash & Esteva, 2008), view the spread of schooling as a particularly destructive aspect of neocolonialism. Since the mid-twentieth century, the "ritual" of schooling has now spread across the globe in remarkable similar ways—for instance, one would be hard-pressed to find a society in existence today that hasn't come to "value" formal education by enforcing some form of mass, age-specific schooling that mirrors American industrial model of classrooms, desks, teachers, textbooks, curriculum, and grades.

Both materially and ideologically, Illich's claim that schools have come to be the all-powerful social institution in our society, the contemporary church for a secular society, is even truer today than when he first wrote his controversial critiques. Increased consumption of education has also exacerbated "educational scarcity," driving up the value of higher and higher forms of education. "Learning thus becomes a commodity," Illich (1973b) writes, "and, like any commodity that is marketed, becomes scarce" (p. 59). Deeming some pupils proficient and others deficient year after year leads to educational scarcity and commodification within a competitive system of supply and demand. Within this supposed scarcity, schools retain social power as arbiters of knowledge, with teachers function as middle managers. Here, one can see how Illich equates modern schools with the former power of the church, and teachers with clergy members, who held the secretive power of the scriptures and salvation before the reformation. Yet, according to Illich, no recompense can be administered via institutional authority, as any such effort still endorses the original "neediness" of the individual, as well as the (illegitimate) authority of those empowered by the institution to do so.

Schools are not necessarily problematic, according to Illich, but mass education has grown too far beyond its natural limits such that it has become a "counterproductive" institution. As Illich scholar Mitcham (2002) writes, counterproductivity is an ur-concept of Illich's scholarship that describes schools as well as other common targets of Illich's criticism such as the Catholic Church, modern medicine, energy consumption, and automobile travel. In essence, *counterproductivity* is the result of institutions that have too rapidly expanded past the point of sustainability or success. The goals we originally attempt to achieve through these ever-expanding tools end up being sub-verted by the tools themselves. Illich (1978) describes this ironic problem as the "*negative* externalities of modernity," examples of which include the fol-lowing ironies: "time-consuming acceleration [via cars], sick-making health care, stupefying education" (p. xii). Anyone who has spent time in a class-room cannot deny counterproductivity at work in modern schooling, with students who reject the supposed "gift" of compulsory education.

As with other counterproductive tools, schools as they continue to exist today are in no way "convivial tools," by which Illich (1973b) means that schools are not easily used, openly available to all, nor are they free to use when and how the user chooses. To better understand Illich's distinction, compare, for instance, a public library or park to a public school: parks and libraries reso-nate with conviviality in that they are open to almost everyone while imposing no obligation of use upon us. On the other hand, thirteen years of school are compulsory by law, and by custom for many. Moreover, schools are not openly accessible to all—adult learners or visitors, for example—nor are they easily used for the particular purposes of the user in that one's attendance, curricu-lum, level, and movement are heavily managed by teachers and administrators. While learning—and schools of a particular form and character—could con-ceivably be organized to fit Illich's conception of conviviality, there's no doubt that such a move would significantly unsettle our notions of education in both theory and practice. It would likely also reshape our experiences of youth and institutions, as well as the socio-political structures.

## Schools, Needs, and the Hidden Curriculum

One of Illich's central claims continues to run contrary to mainstream thinking: that schools are not *dependent* variables, directly reflecting the socio-political contexts in which they operate. Schools *qua* schools inculcate a modernist, industrial subjectivity, and hierarchical social division *by design*, and therefore they cannot be reformed to do anything else. In other words, the "problems" we might diagnose about schools represent characteristics that Illich claims are inherent to such a problematic institution, regardless of whether we try to reform them or not. Schools cannot solve our society's wealth inequities or racial disparities because, Illich claims, they were designed to exacerbate such hierarchies, while protecting themselves under a mythic facade of neutrality.

Schools are a deeply problematic contemporary global phenomenon according to Illich, and no matter where they exist, they operate in remark-ably similar ways: "All over the world schools are organized establishments designed to reproduce the established order, whether this order is called revolutionary, conservative, or evolutionary" (1973a, p. 2). Under these supposedly different political orientations lies an authoritarianism which is ultimately served by both the logic and outcomes of schooling. To apply Freire's (1970/1993) terminology to Illich's point here, state-run schooling can only yield "banking education," while "problem-posing" can only occur non-compulsory, informal learning arrangements outside of state control.

Breaking with other radical educational thinkers such as Freire, Illich claims that such a socio-economic shift would necessitate an abandoning of compulsory schooling altogether. Illich's "phenomenology of school"—that "the age-specific, teacher-related process requiring full-time attendance at an obligatory curriculum" (1971, pp. 25–26)—remains universally applicable regardless of socio-political context. The surprising implication here is that, according to Illich, schooling is not an ancillary problem that can be improved by reforming society. Accordingly, a turn toward a multicultural liberal democracy or an egalitarian socialist society would not dislodge the oppressive, hierarchical, alienating logic inherent in the school, nor could schools as such become the vanguard of such a cultural change. Instead, Illich's fundamental claim is that we must question presumed "need" for education, itself a historical idea.

Perhaps one of Ivan Illich's most significant insights about education involves his sociological analysis of the "hidden curriculum" of schooling. Such a concept, taken up since by others in educational studies,[1] focuses not on what schools *overtly claim* to teach, but on what is latently learned by those enculturated into the institution. By this, Illich (1973a) describes the "ritual aspects of schooling … the structure underlying what has been called the certification effect" (p. 7), or "the structure of schooling as opposed to what happens in school" (p. 8). Illich claims that the socialization of young and old toward an alienated life is especially pronounced in modern institutions such as schools, and that formal education in particular was training for a passive life of consumerism.

Such training, according to Illich, occurs in two primary ways. First, state-run schools function as monopolies, sapping the time and vitality of youth and along with massive resources of the wider society. The daily grind of lessons, year after year, and the never-ending homework and high-stakes testing leads to an aversion to learning: Why read books unless they're assigned? Why write unless it's graded? Additionally, Illich problematizes the role of public schools that serve as the all-powerful body for certifying knowledge and bestowing qualifications in the form of diplomas, which thereby confirm differing levels of social stratification to those who succeed accordingly. "The hidden curriculum," Illich (1973a) writes, "teaches all children that economically valuable knowledge is the result of professional teaching and that social entitlements depend on the rank achieved in a bureaucratic process" (pp. 8–9). Degrees certify or reify schooled learning, confirming power and authority over the educational have-nots.

When I taught middle school, I observed counselors, educators, and parents regularly reinforcing this myth by projecting value onto further consumption of educational products: high school and higher education. Posters were hung in the hallways state-provided posters of bar graphs contrasting lifetime earnings by education levels. Rather than discussing the social or ethical problem with such inequities, most simply bought into the logic of competition and certification: consumption, growth, certification, meritocracy. This skewed vision of learning, with diplomas conferring one's hierarchical status, undermines informal learning and the self-taught, further reinforcing the sense that anything worth knowing and learning must be approved by a school.

Beyond Illich's (1971) groundbreaking indictment of schooling in modern society in *Deschooling Society*, his solutions to the problem are equally disruptive. Illich provocatively rejects the notion of educational "reform" via child-centered methods, including Montessori methods or Waldorf Schools, and even the more radical "free school" concept championed by anarchists. Instead of arguing for a reform of schooling via alternative curriculum or pedagogies, Illich presents *schooling* as inherently problematic, arguing, "the contemporary crisis of education demands that we review the very idea of publicly prescribed learning, rather than the methods used in its enforcement" (p. 65). Unlike most education theorists, Illich (1978) believed that school reform efforts lead to "a proposed escalation of education in which each step threatens more subtle and more pervasive social control" than current schools do (p. 69). While such claims may lack justification, there is no doubt that Illich's anti-reformist stance against schooling is at once a curious and controversial position, even today.

Upon reflection, while I may not agree with all of Illich's critiques, they have clarified to me why I regularly felt alienated from the labor of my own learning. Illich offers a strikingly clear message: "Schools have alienated man [sic] from his learning" (1973a, p. 11). Like all schooled students, I showed up each day to do work that others assigned and supervised, moving from place to place when bells rang; it was this specific relationship that also alienated me from my work as a teacher, teaching repeated sections of the same lessons to age-specific students year after year. Moreover, the "hidden curriculum" Illich accurately describes became "unconsciously accepted by the liberal pedagogue," me, frustrating my "conscious liberal aims, because it is inherently inconsistent with them" (1973a, p. 9). When I pondered how different teaching would be if students weren't required to be there, or if they had at least true power to "elect" to take the classes and subjects that truly interested them, I was beginning to think more and more like Illich. Furthermore, such a non-compulsory relationship would reshape students' views of the curriculum, grades, or standardized tests if they could actually choose whether or not to attend or submit themselves to such programs. Illich's arguments take the "opt-out" movement's narrow rhetoric against standardized testing and zooms out to implicate the entire institution of formal education.

## *The Three 'D's' of Deschooling*

What then is to be done about schools? After Illich targets mass schooling as a fundamental sociological problem, he then argues that it must be dismantled in three particular ways. First, schools must be *disestablished* through a repeal of compulsory attendance laws. This would start from a repeal of compulsory education laws, making it illegal for the state to require school attendance (Illich, 1973a, p. 19). His argument here is that, just as church attendance was secularized to allow individuals the freedom of—and from—religion, so too must the state remove the even greater requirement of years of compulsory school attendance. Additionally, Illich calls for a political movement for legislation banning discrimination against those who lack schooling or educational credentials. Again, the point here is to break the authoritarian hold on that schools have of legitimized learning via mandatory education. Schools could certainly continue to exist in Illich's vision for the future, but not as the dominant, state-run, educational behemoths we see and experience today; like contemporary churches in the U.S., myriad choices would exist for individuals and communities.

The second argument for dismantling schools is *deprofessionalization*. Such an argument has long made career educators and teachers unions incredibly uncomfortable, for it seems to undermine our livelihoods and entire way of life. For Illich though, the role of "professional" educator becomes problematic in that it creates an unwarranted power differential, and unquestionable hierarchy for certifying "learning," and therefore promotion and success. According to Illich, teachers, doctors, lawyers, and any other service-oriented professionals and their institutions don't actually aid people in the way they think—rather, they dis-able by taking away the legitimacy of people and communities to care for themselves. Furthermore, he idealistically sees educators in a deschooled environment freed from the top-down constraints of the state-run school, able to teach in a freer, freelanced way. Many teachers and students experience this stark difference daily as they suffer through manda-tory classes, curriculum, and testing during the day, followed by the joys of coaching sports teams or sponsoring student-initiated clubs after school.

Finally, Illich's third argument against schooling comes via *deinstitution-alization*. Akin to his claims against professionalization, Illich's problem with schools is part of his much wider critique of modernity, or life in an industrial society overrun by bureaucratic, managerial ways of being. Citizens are left powerless in the face of dramatic technological advances, left to live impotent lives in which institutions and machines administer learning, health, and hap-piness. Furthermore, according to Illich, both capitalism and communism endorse and perpetuate this bureaucratic, managerial logic, and therefore neither politics is sustainable nor humane. Only the mass abandonment of institutions as we know them can offer us a way out, especially compulsory education as this is where we are indoctrinated into the myths of modernity.

Illich's calls for a radical disestablishment following the secularist logic of severing ties between the church and the state—in this case, freeing students from mandatory school attendance, thereby opening up all sorts of alternative educational potentials.

Separating learning from schooling is perhaps one of the most import-ant insights of Illich's deschooling argument. As Illich claims, learning is an active, individual process that occurs best outside of formal, institutional settings and relationships: "Most learning is not the result of instruction. It is rather the result of unhampered participation in a meaningful setting" (Illich, 1971, p. 39). Illich's definition of learning is consistent with various contemporary, anthropological approaches to "situated learning" and "new literacies" (Gee, 2012; Lave & Wenger, 1991; Street, 2003), as it harnesses the notion that learning happens all the time, in active social situations rather than in classrooms or intentional curriculum-based instruction. Furthermore, such an approach questions the myth that explicit teaching leads to learning. We can certainly all think of the myriad invaluable things we learned without the need of schools, textbooks, or quizzes! Most of us already know that we learn by doing, and that, as Springer (2016) suggests, "the best learning happens 'through the soles of our feet'" (p. 262) rather than in a classroom.

## *After Schools: Considering Illich's "Alternatives in Education"*

Beyond schools as institutional settings run by certifying professionals, Illich advocates for a view of education as moving toward something more organic, active, mutual, and spontaneous: Illich writes of his personal, anarchistic phi-losophy of education in this way:

> I believe that only *actual* participation constitutes socially valuable learning, a participation by the learner in *every stage* of the learning process, including not only a free choice of what is to be learned and how it is to be learned but also a free determination by each learned of his own reason for living and learning—the part that his knowledge is to play in his life. (1973a, p. 16, my emphasis)

To accomplish such a radically *deschooled* conception of learning, Illich (1971) imagines the formation of alternative educational formations via ad hoc "learning webs" such as peer matching, tool sharing, and skill acquisition via tutoring. Essentially, Illich's primary vision of learning is that it happens unplanned throughout one's life course—in homes, neighborhoods, communities, and workplaces. If anyone wanted to learn something, to have access to the tools or concepts necessary to learn some discreet thing that eluded them, or to assemble in the company of peers for learning, than they should be able to do so.

When Illich describes people looking to finding others who wished to discuss a book or topic with them via computers, he certainly couldn't possibly have foreseen how the internet and advanced computer technology could have made this infinitely possible in the twenty-first century. Indeed, we've all learned and taught ourselves a great many things via the use of YouTube instructional videos, online recipes, how-to websites, or conversations with family and friends. Tool sharing is another important aspect of deschooling for Illich, along with opening up industrial processes for individuals to explore. Such an "open-access" approach to the tools and technological means of production could individuals further break down the hierarchies of professions and career opportunities that had previously been awarded by schooling.

Illich's discussion of what exactly he means by *learning webs* is somewhat vague and highly idealistic, and critiques are certainly warranted. Illich's main point, related to this definition of learning mentioned earlier, is that freed from compulsory schools, children would be able to take on more active, meaningful, hands-on roles in their families and communities: caring for loved ones, helping plan and tend gardens, learning productive skills such as bike mechanics and building, or participating in creative pursuits such as acting or music. No longer constrained by age-specific classrooms and sorted into discreet grades and subjects, youth would be able to connect with elders of various ages, interests, and abilities. That said, skeptics have certainly questioned the potential for "learning webs" to devolve into further social stratification between haves and have-nots, or expressed fears over how children would be raised or looked after with most contemporary American families engaged in high levels of work outside of the house.

Furthermore, critics wonder what might become of an already deeply divided society. Illich's response, in his essay "After Deschooling, What?" (1973a) is that the crisis of schooling "raises the deeper issue of the tolerability of life in an alienated society" (p. 11). He goes on to explain that an effort toward deschooling cannot work alone to break the grips of modernity and a consumption-oriented economy. Abruptly ending schools while leaving an already isolated, alienated, bureaucratic society in place would be potentially catastrophic. Could we even imagine a large-scale, anti-schooling and alternative political-economic movement taking shape? This is an especially complicated question, given the fact that critiques resembling Illich's are today more often heard from right-wing advocates through their calls for vouchers, charter schools, expanded support for private schools and homeschooling, and the de-professionalization of teachers and teacher education (Ravitch, 2013). "Deschooling," as Illich noted, "does make strange bedfellows" (1973a, p. 20). Beyond his scathing critiques and vehement rhetoric, Illich doesn't offer a coherent political program, unlike Freire's more revolutionary Marxist politics. In the end, reading Illich carefully, one finds he is not against education or learning; instead, he argues that disestablishing state-run schools is essential for developing more convivial, autonomous, sustainable ways of living and learning.

## My Shifting Thoughts on (De)schooling and (Mis)education

Coming to terms with Illich's ideas is likely unsettling for most any teacher, parent, or student to make. Unlike most educational philosophers, teachers, parents, students, and politicians, Ivan Illich's challenging critique does not call for education reform: to improve schools by making them more effective, democratic, culturally-affirming places to learn. Nor does Illich seek to occupy and transform schools as a contested public space, as many Marxian educators and critics of Illich suggest (Freire, 1970/1993; Gintis, 1973). Illich's central claim is that schools are a very recent, peculiar, problematic invention that inculcates subjects into the logics of modernism, managerialism, and industrialism. Based on notions of progress, schooling is training for an alienated, highly-stratified life and labor. Those who succeed or fail in school both tend to succumb to the logic that learning is top-down, that hours of satisfactory attendance leads to certifications, and that these qualifications equate to knowledge and skill. Both the graduate and drop-out, according Illich, are maimed by this process—both coming to see themselves as successful or not in relation to their schooling.

After reading Illich, and taking seriously his controversial arguments about schooling, many are left confused or dispirited. Some, no doubt, simply reject his conclusions about the "ritual" of education as either hyperbole, heresy, or both. Those of us willing to entertain Illich's critiques are left wondering what might be done with the problems that his critiques pose for us. Some supports have moved toward homeschooling or unschooling their children and themselves, but such options are neither easy nor without their faults. Like many readers, I find myself too hopeful about the possibilities of teaching and learning to simply walk away from education altogether.

As such, I find myself agreeing with much of education critic Neil Postman's (1973) response to Illich's work, "My Ivan Illich Problem." In it, he writes:

> You see what a problem Illich is. He not only makes one feel conservative and obtuse: he also makes one wonder about the value of past efforts and future plans. Am I part of the problem? Does my work obscure the real issues? Every time I actually help a school to improve on its treatment of children, do I also help to perpetuate the hidden curriculum? (1973, p. 140)

Some readers would likely agree with Postman's points about the impact of Illich's ideas. Later, Postman goes on to call Illich a "mystic" (p. 141) and a "utopian" (p. 142), claiming that despite Illich's valuable impassioned pleas against schooling, his deschooling proposal simply "ain't gonna happen" (p. 145). Again, likely a common sentiment for readers today. Yet, in the end, Postman does find some important and redeeming value in Illich's critiques, and here I think he offers us an important, pragmatic approach toward making sense of Illich and his deschooling rhetoric.

Postman claims that we should interpret Illich's hyperbolic deschooling vision "as a basis for evaluating practical innovations and experiments," in such a way that Illich's proposals "can be transformed into a measure of whether or not some specific innovation is moving in the right direction" (p. 146). Postman frames his Illich-inspired evaluation for alternatives to education with the following three questions:

1. Will the innovation make resources more widely available?
2. Will it tend to deemphasize the importance of teaching as against learning?
3. Will it tend to make students freer, and their learning less confined? (p. 146)

Postman's rubric may seem like a reformist approach to Illich's ideas of deschooling, which rests on the claim that the institution of schooling cannot be reformed. Yet what I appreciate about Postman's point is that he refuses to dismiss Illich and his radical demands while acknowledging the essential need to question of the modern conflation of learning and schooling.

Together, Illich's radical arguments for deschooling and Postman's practical criteria for how our educational projects, could help us better assess how our daily lives and personal relationships might work to resist the authoritarian, hierarchical ideologies of schooling. Consider where we might find (and create) everyday examples of the sort of radically "convivial" spaces that Illich once called for: playgrounds, skateparks, museums, libraries, or online video games and listservs. And consider how we might begin to view these non-compulsory learning spaces as a hopeful educational alternative, a bottom-up learning space that "prefigures" what learning could look like without teachers, curriculum, or grades, and one that happens to exist, as anarchists are fond of saying, "within the shell of the old" (Graeber, 2009). I have written elsewhere (Mayo, 2018) about my recent work as a writing tutor and researcher in an urban university's writing center, and how I see this space as a clear example of a convivial learning space existing alongside of wider authoritarian structures. Moving forward, we should find, create, and support myriad others such alternatives, with both Illich and Postman helping evaluate such efforts. I believe we might best prepare ourselves for a deschooled future—should we ever want one—if we paid more attention to these open, creative, empowering, and already-existing alternatives to education and relationality that surround us.

In a world that may finally be, in Ivan Illich's words, "all schooled up" (1971, p. 23), it is a hopeful sign that convivial learning arrangements might actually exist all around us. I urge the readers of this chapter not only to explore Illich's writing and ideas—as they've been sorely overlooked by educational scholars for decades—but also to begin seeing our taken-for-granted notions of schooling and learning through a critical, Illichean lens. That is, following Illich's lead, to begin questioning the previous certainties about the educational "needs" of ourselves, our students, and our children as they relate to schooling, learning, and living.

## Note

1. This term was originally coined by education psychologist Philip Jackson in his book *Life in Classrooms* (1968). Beyond Illich, many others have explored the concept (cf. Anyon, 1980; Giroux & Purpel, 1983; McLaren, 2015).

## References

Anyon, J. (1980). Social class and the hidden curriculum of work. *Journal of Education, 162*(1), 67–92.

Ayers, W., Hunt, J. A., & Quinn, T. (Eds.). (1998). *Teaching for social justice: A democracy and education reader*. New York, NY: New Press.

Bowers, C. A. (2001). *Educating for eco-justice and community.* Athens: University of Georgia Press.

Christensen, L. (2009). *Teaching for joy and justice: Re-imagining the Language Arts classroom.* Milwaukee, WI: Rethinking Schools.

Esteva, G., & Prakash, M. S. (2014). *Grassroots post-modernism: Remaking the soil of cultures* (2nd ed.). London, England: Zed Books.

Freire, P. (1970/1993). *Pedagogy of the oppressed.* (M. B. Ramos, Trans.). New York, NY: Continuum. (Original work published 1970)

Gabbard, D. A. (1994). Ivan Illich, postmodernism, and the eco-crisis: Reintroducing a "wild" discourse. *Educational Theory, 44*(2), 173–187. doi:10.1111/J.1741-5446.1994.00173.X

Gee, J. P. (2012). *Situated language and learning: A critique of traditional schooling.* New York, NY: Routledge.

Gintis, H. (1973). Toward a political economy of education: A radical critique of Ivan Illich's *Deschooling Society.* In A. Gartner, C. Greer, & F. Riessman (Eds.), *After deschooling, what?* (pp. 28–76). New York, NY: Harper & Row.

Giroux, H., & Purpel, D. (Eds.). (1983). *The hidden curriculum and moral education: Deception or discovery?* Berkeley, CA: McCutchan Publishing.

Goodman, P. (1964). *Compulsory mis-education and the community of scholars.* New York, NY: Vintage Books.

Graeber, D. (2009). *Direct action: An ethnography.* Oakland, CA: AK Press.

Holt, J. C. (1964). *How children fail.* New York, NY: Pitman Press.

Illich, I. (1971). *Deschooling society.* London, England: Marion Boyars.

Illich, I. (1973a). After deschooling, what? In A. Gartner, C. Greer, & F. Riessman (Eds.), *After deschooling, what?* (pp. 1–28). New York, NY: Harper & Row.

Illich, I. (1973b). *Tools for conviviality.* London, England: Marion Boyars.

Illich, I. (1978). *Toward a history of needs.* New York, NY: Pantheon Books.

Illich, I. (2008). Forward. In M. Hern (Ed.), *Everywhere all the time: A new deschooling reader* (pp. iii–v). Oakland, CA: AK Press.

Lave J., & Wenger, E. (1991). *Situated learning: Legitimate peripheral participation.* New York, NY: Cambridge University Press.

Marsh, J. (2011). *Class dismissed: Why we cannot teach or learn our way out of inequality.* New York, NY: Monthly Review Press.

Mayo, R. (2018). The everyday anarchism of peer tutoring. *The Peer Review, 2.* Retrieved from http://thepeerreview-iwca.org/issues/relationality-si/the-everyday-anarchism-of-peer-tutoring/

McLaren, P. (2015). *Life in schools: An introduction to critical pedagogy in the foundations of education* (6th ed.). Boulder, CO: Paradigm Publishers.

Miller, A. (2010). *An enemy of the people: An adaptation of the play by Henrik Ibsen.* New York, NY: Penguin. (Original work published 1951)

Mitcham, C. (2002). The challenges of this collection. In L. Hoinacki & C. Mitcham (Eds.), *The challenges of Ivan Illich: A collective reflection* (pp. 9–32). Albany, NY: State University of New York Press.

Neill, A. S. (1960). *Summerhill: A radical approach to child rearing.* New York, NY: Hart Publishing.

Orfield, G., & Eaton, S. E. (1996). *Dismantling desegregation. The quiet reversal of* Brown v. Board of Education. New York, NY: The New Press.

Orr, D. W. (1994). *Earth in mind: On education, environment, and the human prospect.* Washington, D.C.: Island Press.

Pollan, M. (2009). *The Omnivore's dilemma: The secrets behind what you eat.* New York, NY: Dial Books.

Postman, N. (1973). My Ivan Illich problem. In A. Gartner, C. Greer, & F. Riessman (Eds.), *After deschooling, what?* (pp. 137–147). New York, NY: Harper & Row.

Prakash, M. S., & Esteva, G. (2008). *Escaping education: Living as learning with grassroots cultures* (2nd ed.). New York, NY: Peter Lang.

Ravitch, D. (2013). *Reign of error: The hoax of the privatization movement and the danger to America's public schools.* New York, NY: Knopf.

Reimer, E. (1971). *School is dead: An essay on alternatives in education.* Harmondsworth, England: Penguin Education.

Scott, J. C. (2012). *Two cheers for anarchism: Six easy pieces on autonomy, dignity, and meaningful work and play.* Princeton, NJ: Princeton University Press.

Shor, I. (1999). What is critical literacy? In I. Shor & C. Pari (Eds.), *Critical literacy in action* (pp. 1–30). Portsmouth, NH: Boynton/Cook.

Spring, J. (1975). *A primer of libertarian education.* Montreal, Canada: Black Rose Books.

Springer, S. (2016). Learning through the soles of our feet: Unschooling, anarchism, and the geography of childhood. In S. Springer, M. L. de Souza, & R. J. White (Eds.), *The Radicalization of Pedagogy: Anarchism, geography, and the spirit of revolt* (pp. 247–265). London, England: Rowman & Littlefield.

Street, B. (2003). What's "new" in new literacy studies? Critical approaches to literacy in theory and practice. *Current Issues in Comparative Education, 5*(2): 77–92.

Taubman, P. M. (2009). *Teaching by numbers: Deconstructing the discourse of standards and accountability in education.* New York, NY: Routledge.

# *Epilogue*

# Everyone Knows Whose Side I'm On: Teachers, Students, and the Struggle for Freedom

JAY GILLEN

I laughed out loud the first day at my new assignment. My teacher and mentor, Bob Moses, had said that when he begins work with a new class of high school students, he needs them to understand that he is not the policeman in the room. His job is not to catch the students when they break the rules or to prevent them from loitering. His job is to help them do math. I laughed because my current assignment is at a jail school, so there really are policemen in the room—well, guards, anyway. They're enforcers. I'm clearly not. It has made things much simpler.

I love working at this jail for adolescent girls, because here at the very bottom of the structures of control, the absurdities of schooling are exaggerated and almost impossible not to see. The A's, C's and F's on report cards. The points taken off for mistakes. The pretense that knowledge divided into "subjects" and time chopped up into "periods" and "semesters" are somehow essential strategies for human beings to learn. I said that these structures are "almost impossible" not to see, because although the absurd is etched in bold relief, many of us are still so enculturated to schooling that we may miss what is right before our eyes.

Scene: The morning staff meeting. Teachers sitting around a conference table. Each teacher has the daily list in front of them with the guards' annotations of the girls who are still at the jail or who arrived overnight.

Mr. Lawson:  I see Stephanie is on suicide watch.
Ms. Gaines:  Only level II, though.
Mr. Lawson:  Does that mean she has a dedicated guard?
Ms. Gaines:  No, you have to be level III.

Mr. Strong:   They moved Jackson from Unit A to Unit B. Probably because she was fighting yesterday with Mulvaney.

Ms. Gaines:   She's been fighting in every unit they assign her to, and she refuses to do any school work.

Mr. Strong:   Maybe we should give her a contract?

Mr. Davis:    I can draw one up. But we have been told not to promise rewards until the night staff verifies that a girl deserves one. The guards feel undermined if a client gets a reward from Education, even though she is being non-compliant in the residence.

Ms. Gaines:   Then how will the contract work?

Mr. Davis:    Oh we do it the same way. If they avoid incidents and comply with all teachers' instructions, they get a second phone call per week and a bag of chips. But we don't tell them whether they qualify. We just report to the residence, and let the guards give the reward if they feel it is still warranted.

Ms. Gaines:   Is Jackson really going to stop fighting for a bag of chips at the end of the week?

Mr. Davis:    We are complying with the directive not to give arbitrary treats without connection to a behavioral plan, so chips are really quite significant to the girls now. Scarcity is a motivation.

Jackson did not stop fighting. She also began to cut herself with a paper clip that she had stolen from her case manager's office. This should be information for us—information about strategies that may not be working. But, instead, it led to a directive extending the prohibition against using paper clips in the classrooms and residences to now include the offices.

As a teacher, I must not undermine the guards, whose primary responsibility is the "safety" of the girls. Ordinarily, of course, being grabbed, handcuffed, thrown in a wagon, and then placed in a locked room would seem like abduction, not safety. But state-sanctioned abduction and forced confinement is the very definition of "safety," or at least of "security" in this setting. This imposition of physical control interpreted as protection of a young adult is no different from the supervisory rituals of schools. Jail may be driving the young person crazy, but we are not responsible for the child's sanity, only for preventable physical harms while on the premises.

The idea of school "safety" creates many paradoxes. I worked once in a neighborhood of Baltimore with the city's highest murder rate and a high rate, also, of sexual abuse. Despite these facts, the middle school where I taught was, in many ways, wonderful. One day a week was devoted to year-long projects that often involved trips near and far. Teachers and parents ran the school, rotating the directorship among the staff. All students lived within a mile, but even neighborhood children who weren't enrolled could play basketball and games on the playground in the afternoon and early evening. Ten or so years into the life of the school, however, as the founding ethos of risk-taking and shared learning began to wane, a staff member became anxious that if something happened in the playground during those hours, there might not be sufficient adult supervision to "ensure safety." And so, a directive was issued that children would no longer be allowed on school grounds after dismissal, and instead would need to "go play in the neighborhood."

Clearly, the solution was more dangerous than the problem. How is requiring students to play in unsupervised space off school grounds safer than unsupervised play *on* school grounds? But the solution, of course, had the signal benefit of removing the burden of liability from the school and its employees. For me, the real problem with the directive is that it removed power from the children—the power to choose where they felt safest or most alive, or just happy.

What's made clear by this example is that the logic of schooling is essentially the logic of jails. Safety and security are procured through iterative processes of physical exclusion and limitation, until the opportunity for harm in the bounded area has been reduced to a minimum. The boundaries—jail bars, school grounds, admission to "selective schools," suburban jurisdictions patrolled by their own police forces, etc.—are essential for our educational structures, and, in fact, teach children how to live in late capitalist America.

Growing up in America is a series of lessons about property: where you are allowed to be, what gives you access, who will *not* have access. Whoever owns a person, place, or thing controls it. Students own very little. Prisoners even less. Mastering the lessons of schooling increase your opportunities to own things. This pecuniary motive gets drummed into students again and again throughout schooling, though usually this idea is understood in terms of the importance of education for the purpose of gaining employment.

In our math classes at the jail we try to teach and learn something different about the importance of education. The purpose of education to me is freedom, and the freedom struggle is about the full expression of our humanity individually and collectively. And we also try to teach and to learn that mathematics and other abstract symbolic representations of the human experience have generally been the property of people who can afford high quality education for their children. Therefore, we must fight to make sure that knowledge of mathematics is not treated as something scarce, not as a privilege that only the rich have access to, but that it—like all other knowledges—should be held in common as a shared birthright of all races and classes.

This view of knowledge as part of the commons puts us at odds with the founding principles of schools and jails—principles that are ingrained in things like grades, test scores, sentences, probations, judgments. How to live within that contradiction is the lesson that we must study. Theory helps by setting up terms and imaginative structures that influence the stances we and others become willing to take up. Words and ideas perform symbolic actions, no less real because they are symbolic. Sometimes symbolic actions feel easier to perform, since no physical obstacles get in the way of your ideas. You can think what you like. But the contradiction must also be solved concretely. You must choose when to speak out loud as opposed to just thinking, or writing in your journal, or talking with a colleague privately at the bar. You must choose when to open your door to your students, even though that physical movement carries a symbolic weight of expressing solidarity. That is, the concreteness of holding the door open, instead of shutting it, is an idea that has moved from the strictly symbolic plane to a physical plane, and suddenly the symbol can be taken seriously in a new way.

At my last school, the principal and some of the faculty were bothered by students arriving late to class. A plan was "agreed on" that all teachers must lock their classroom doors when the late bell rang. This would require that late students to be locked out of class, and they would need to go to the office to "get a pass" which they could then present back at the classroom for admission. But, of course, this would happen only after an admission of one's lateness had been recorded in the great reckoning book for lateness to be punished at some later time. Like jail, much of our work in schools centers around policies that compel compliance or address non-compliance through some form of discipline and punishment.

Unfortunately for me and for this "agreed on" policy, I have a principle that students coming to learn should be allowed into class, even if they are late. It's a principle based on the idea that learning takes precedence over most things. I may be wrong; a case can certainly be made that learning to be on time is more important than learning math, or that learning to live by our society's norms is more important than any particular learning (lateness conceived here as disrespectful to everyone already present and working). I am happy to engage in respectful dialogue about this question, especially in respectful dialogue that includes students as equal partners in decision-making. But I am not happy to look through the window of the locked door at the late student asking to be let in, and send them away arbitrarily, without a prior, thorough, respectful, inclusive discussion of the policy. It is possible that being strict about consequences for lateness is in the student's best interest. But it is also possible that the locked door breaks trust, disincentivizes bothering to come to class, is read by the student not as loving, but simply as unfriendly. The issue that I am raising is not about what the rule should be.

The issue is what the relationships should be among those who make or are made to follow those rules. Far too often in American schools the relationships between teachers and students are assumed to be the relationships of power that already exist in the society. But those relationships are unjust, and so we are faced with a decision.

The question for public school teachers is this: How do you live by what you believe in, given that the function of public education is to reproduce a social and political structure that you *don't* believe in?

We will save a lot of time, energy, and good will if we begin answering this question with a cold, hard, fact: you must choose. You can't have it both ways. It is not possible to please the authorities at the same time as you live by your values, because the *job* of the authorities is to enforce conformity to values that contradict your own.

The cold, hard, fact certainly does not require you to be open or public about your choice. You may well need to disguise your values and intentions, like a spy behind enemy lines. But you cannot feel guilt or shame when you fail to reach your principal's value-added benchmarks, or when you end up two months behind on the mandated curriculum. At least, you must not feel guilt or shame thinking you aren't a "good enough teacher." Maybe you aren't a good enough spy to disguise yourself sufficiently. But the idea that you would value *yourself* based on the enemy's measures defines a weakness of resolve that we cannot afford. The enemy's measures are poisonous, insidious weapons that are arranged against us and that we must not mistake for anything close to what we ourselves value.

You must choose. You will either work to support your students and their families, or you will work to make the system run more smoothly, but you can't do both. The smooth functioning of the system works against your students, dividing them from the wealth, security, and power that high caste families direct consciously and intentionally to their own children. On the other hand, collaborating with families and communities in the successful education of students in poverty means developing the power of those students to challenge arrangements that oppress them; it means giving them the tools to succeed not by the standards of the oppressor, but by their own yet-to-be imagined standards.

The difficulty teachers face in schools of poverty today begins with the illusion that our work could somehow be "reformist" rather than insurrectionary. The still unquestioned ideology of public education persuades almost everyone that schools and school systems can be managed so that they will somehow deliver high quality education to all children regardless of their caste status. Therefore, almost all factions tend to identify the source of educational dysfunction in bad curriculum or bad principals or bad school boards or bad governors or bad Secretaries of Education or bad teachers or maybe bad unions or bad corporations that are milking the system.

But even the most efficient and enlightened management of schools and school systems will fail to address the absurd inequity in access to political and economic power that has made our "democracy" a plutocracy instead. Our school systems are plutocratic, not democratic, at every level: the schools of the wealthy teach children how to wield power. The schools of the poor teach children how to put up with what little they get; the schools of the middle classes teach children that the poor deserve their poverty and the rich deserve their wealth, so that although you are only average, at least you are not destitute.

Teachers who believe they are educating children for democracy must be clear, as Dr. Vincent Harding often repeated, that they are teaching in a system of education that does not yet exist, a paradox at the root of the thousands of personal crises that radical teachers face.

Yes, students can benefit from your teaching. Yes, no one's fate is determined entirely by their circumstances. Yes, many people who work in schools do a lot of good, teach all kinds of great things, open doors for students, create environments of warmth, love, safety, intellectual challenge, creative openness, political consciousness, and on and on.

But even the most wonderful teachers are constrained by the function of public education, which is only nominally to educate, but pragmatically is to maintain the nation's caste structure. It is absurd to imagine that any one teacher or even any group of teachers could undo the history of race, class, gender, and war that has led us to where we are today. A culture's system of education inevitably brings children up into the culture they actually live in, and our culture is poisoned, so our children are inevitably sickened by schools. You can try to mitigate the effects of testing, but the children are tested. You can try to overcome the social violence of educational sorting, but the children are sorted. You can believe that all things are possible for all children, but all children will not graduate from high school or from college or be safe from violence or from hunger or from incursions into their families by the brutal police state and its use of walls and cages.

When a principal or department head or some other functionary announces a new mandate or intervention from the district, we all have the same immediate reaction: "What do they want me to do? How will I make it look like I am doing it?" My friends are the teachers who are hopeful, who believe that much good can be done, but who take these directives as so much manure to be shoveled in order to clean the barn for the real work. The teachers I don't like to be around are the ones who pretend that the functionaries must be directing useful interventions and who pretend to look for "good ideas" in the mandates. They don't mean it. They are lying. They just want to keep their jobs, and pretending to respect the bosses is how they expect to do it.

But I am writing about what happens beneath these outward roles that we display. Most of us are forced into a doubleness, into a kind of "bad faith" existence, and our question is how to deal with it. We speak the official policies with our mouths, and *live* with a doubleness in our hearts. There are the cynics, the ones I don't like and for whom I do not write, who believe nothing will ever change, but still pretend for the sake of their employment. But much more important are the rest of us who say we will do the stupid things we are mandated to do, while in our hearts we know that we will try to do what is best for our students. This is also a doubleness, and it can ruin us unless we are very clear. It can ruin us because, being good people who disdain lies and deception, we imagine (often not quite consciously) that we can have it both ways, that we can do what we tell our bosses we will do while at the same time doing what we know is right. But we cannot have it both ways. We must choose.

In our jail, the girls are starved for music. They aren't allowed electronics of their own, and have very limited access to commercial radio stations in their living quarters. At the school, though, we have computers for "educational purposes." Though the state filters the school networks aggressively, the students have found some workarounds that allow them access to the music they crave, often, of course, quite underground artists and songs. Teachers are required to sign explicit statements that we will forbid the girls from listening to music on the educational computers, and that if we find a girl violating the no music policy, we will require them to stop. If they disobey, we are instructed to unplug the computer from the outlet.

There is little question in my mind that access to music is of enormous educational benefit. Even if it were not, who am I to prohibit access of a human being to their cultural ground and motive force? I violate the policy of the school systematically. The girls listen with headphones so that all the adults, guards and co-teachers, can pretend not to hear. They negotiate sharing the machines, so that everyone gets some music time without my direct intervention. When someone's music is turned up too loud, or when they forget to hide the music website behind some more innocuous looking screen, I give a quiet reminder that "music is not allowed," and everyone immediately pretends to comply. But sometimes there are disputes about whose turn it is, and the disturbance shows up on the video feeds in the warden's office. Sometimes the guards report the violation. I am reprimanded and reminded of the policy. Maybe I will face a serious consequence at some point, if and when I get a new, more aggressive principal. But my choice is clear. I must conspire to help win surreptitious access to music.

What are the consequences of choosing? One of the consequences is the realization that you work for the students and families, not for the principal and district. Your money comes from the district, but your accountability—or more accurately, your responsibility—is to the students. You answer to the community.

This division between the economics of the problem and the ethics of it follow from the choice you must make. The interests of the people who pay you are not identical to the interests of the people whose children you teach. This question of interests is disguised in our society, can only be read in a text that is badly smudged and scribbled over. For example, it used to be obvious that interests diverged when the education of black children was determined by school boards and mayors who were all or mostly white. But now many school boards and city halls "look like" the children they "serve." It does not follow from this surface resemblance, however, that school boards and communities desire or need the same things. Maybe their interests are closer. Maybe not. But they are distinct. And the interests of people outside and "above" the school boards and mayors are emphatically unchanged from fifty years ago: to maintain a caste status that is devastating for our children.

Therefore, you must understand who you work for, who you answer to, no matter who signs your check. And you must be willing to lose the check— lose the check *without* giving up the work.

Here, of course, is an almost impossible challenge. You have bills, debt, student loans, families, obligations. You can't afford to lose the check. But let's look at the historical context. First the context of unions. In labor organizing, isn't this question—who signs the check vs. whose side you are on—the question of solidarity? Unions are effective if workers stick together, even when the bosses try to starve them, hire scabs, lock them out. Workers' rights were not won and are not won unless the moral, ethical, and political consciousness of the collective is strong enough to confront the immediate economic realities and to project an economic future that is humane and inspiring.

Second is the context of the freedom struggle. Fannie Lou Hamer returned to the plantation where she worked, where she lived, after going to try to register to vote. Her employer demanded that she go back and retract her registration. Her reply was, I didn't go to register to vote for you; I went to register for myself. She was thrown out of work and out of her home. Thousands of sharecroppers, day laborers, and domestic workers were denied even emergency food distributions, but they continued to resist because they chose to rank their long-term political, economic, and even spiritual interests above the short-term biological interests that the white supremacists thought they would choose.

Runaway slaves, similarly, had to choose the unknown possibilities and the dangers of freedom over the known limitations of captivity. It was not the common choice. Far fewer enslaved personas risked running away than settled for trying to align their interests with the slaveholders. For many, the runaways' choice read then as foolish, doomed, even selfish. Today, of course, their choice reads as heroic.

Idealistic teachers must similarly choose the unknown and risky possibilities of freedom over the known limitations of "the system." Your socially constructed, intersectional privileges, or lack of privilege, will operate as always to protect you and make you vulnerable in many complex ways. Such choices necessarily provoke opposition, even from one's own kind. You will go further than your peers will feel comfortable going. Authorities and reactionary factions will punish and isolate you. They will make you doubt yourself; they will present convincing evidence that idealists are doomed; they will appeal both to your self-interest and also to group solidarity. But you will need to think better than they do.

Your isolation from the institutional culture of schooling is actually a version of *inclusion* in the culture of your students and their families, because the oppressed are isolated from the dominant culture by definition. You will find possibilities for connection with your students, and those connections will be more real and lasting than the false belonging of domination and arbitrary power. Idealism is not necessarily unrealistic. Idealism and realism are not opposites. Some ideals become realities, and even when they don't, they should. The ideal of undoing racial division is not sullied by the difficulties of making it a reality, and in fact many "realities" have changed because of idealists' persistence. The end of slavery was an ideal of the abolitionists, mocked as unrealistic by the dominant majority for a hundred years. Now, the alternative has become unthinkable. And though your immediate self-interest may seem to depend on going along to get along, it must remain at least conceivable to you that in the longer term your self-interest may actually depend on your integrity.

In the radical, youth-run Baltimore Algebra Project—an extension of the Mississippi Theater of the Civil Rights Movement—we situate our idealism, initially, within structures we call "crawl spaces." A crawl space is both a partly hidden or protected location where you might receive some cover from powerful attacks; but it is also a place to practice difficult skills that you are not yet ready to display for a broader public—a place to crawl while you are still learning to walk. In Mississippi, the 1957 Civil Rights Act created a crawl space for voter registration work. Although local and state police regularly interfered with and jailed civil rights workers, the Civil Rights Act allowed federal officials to "turn the key" and get the workers back out on the street. They did not yet have enough power to succeed in registering very many new voters, nor could the federal government actually punish the local and state authorities. But the civil rights workers had a crawl space to raise up the question of voting, to study the reactions of the enemy, and to try to understand what would be needed in a next, more aggressive phase.

Similarly, the Algebra Project finds a crawl space in math literacy. Everyone says that math and science are key to twenty-first-century education and employment. The structures and resources needed for effective math and science education in poor communities are nowhere to be found. But math literacy workers—young people who *do math* in those communities—have a crawl space to work in. They can try things out; they can challenge authority to an extent; they can raise up the question of access to structures and resources; they can learn how to organize. They can do these things because they are working in the field that everyone says is important—math education. The Algebra Project, for example, has stayed alive for almost 20 years by doing math and activism at the same time, literally putting millions of dollars into the pockets of young people for sharing math knowledge with peers while they challenge the educational status-quo with sit-ins, test boycotts, and demonstrations.

Many potential crawl spaces exist. Teachers choosing to be on the side of the young people probably need to find one and see if it helps to grow the work they are trying to do. It may be a unit of study. It may be a sports team. It may be a school/community project or collaboration. It may be a committee. It may be a school board sponsored program or initiative, an after-school club, or a community-based organization not under the aegis of the school system at all. Any one of these structures can function as a starting point for organizing work.

The idea is that you begin innocuously. You're just doing something fun and interesting with young people. We do peer-centered math. You might be putting on a play, or making a video, or researching lead paint. But the young people will run up against a boundary, a property line, where some authority tells them explicitly (or tells you to tell them) that they are going too far. Our young people want smaller classes, and paid jobs tutoring math after school. Your students might decide through their theater work that they need more time to rehearse, or money for a set, or they might decide to challenge an injustice treated in the play they're performing. Someone in authority might get mad or irritated at them or at you.

This dynamic creates a drama of its own. Drama garners attention. Young people can begin to think and act on their own behalf, and you can support them. This is the crucial moment, where you choose who you work for. Usually adults in these circumstances turn away from the confrontation with the institutions of patriarchy and white supremacy. We usually resign ourselves to the defeat, and prepare the young people to resign themselves, too. But you can make a different choice. You cannot guarantee success, and you certainly shouldn't think of jumping into the role of savior. But you can simply say, "I support you. I'll continue to support you. I'll share ideas. I'll see if I can find allies. I'll be open and honest about whose side I'm on if that's helpful to you. If the authorities come down on me, I'll tell them frankly what ethical or political principles I live by, and we'll have to see how long I can last, but I'll share all the information I have with you, and we'll try to figure out the best path forward together."

You don't necessarily have to break an explicit rule or violate an explicit policy. You don't have to speak on behalf of the young people. You may be able simply to accompany the students when they go to challenge a principal or a board member or a politician. When the adult turns to you to "control" the students, you can invite the students to respond on their own behalf. You will probably be attacked for abdicating your responsibility, and maybe, in some circumstances, you will get a bad evaluation. But in this scenario, you haven't actually violated a policy; you have simply taken a side.

Often this kind of dynamic results in learning for everyone involved. If you keep your head, you can often avoid getting fired or transferred; the students' genuine interest and investment in a particular field of work can camouflage its political nature. Of course, challenging authority and boundaries is political and everyone knows it. But student engagement in positive things is what everyone says we need, so it confuses the enemy when drama develops out of young people as agents of their own learning. You can't avoid being labeled as a troublemaker when you choose sides. But the kind of trouble you make sometimes puts the authorities off-balance, and this may open up opportunities for you to buy some more time and space. Often, for example, it turns out that students who have been labeled "disruptive" find positive roles in this kind of crawl space, and even enemy adults are willing to be bought off with the exchange: "You take kid A, B, or C off my hands, and I'll let you play your little games with students pushing for more say in their own lives." Often, students read more, pay more attention in class, even test better when they understand themselves to be involved in a struggle for their own educational well-being. We're not surprised, but the authorities are; we take advantage of their momentary bewilderment, and skirt by for a time or two.

Still, we might lose our jobs. No guarantees. I confess that my thirty-year-old personnel file is thickened with a leavening of disciplinary actions, proposed terminations, and stern letters from principals and deputy superintendents. But I have always overcome the system's attacks, because my superiors have never been able to find a single student or parent who sees me as anything but helpful. I am far from being a star teacher of any kind—zero charisma, un-cool, middle-aged white guy. But I work hard every day to teach things, and everyone knows whose side I'm on. The bureaucrats and administrators think we work for them. We don't. We work for the students and their families. We are in league with our community. We aren't the police. We dig in deep and stay put for as long as we can. We learn.

# Contributors

**Deborah Bieler** is an associate professor in the English Education program at the University of Delaware. She is a former high school English teacher and writing center director whose scholarship, teaching, and activism focus on the preparation and retention of equity-oriented secondary English teachers. She is the author of the book *Staying to Talk, Talking to Stay: Equity-Oriented Interactions and Retention in Schools*. Her work has also appeared in journals such as *English Education, English Journal, Teachers College Record, Teacher Education Quarterly*, and *The New Educator* as well as in co-authored chapters in *Innovations in Pre-Service English Language Arts Teacher Education* and *Diversifying the Teacher Workforce: Preparing and Retaining Highly Effective Teachers*. She has received the National Council of Teachers of English Promising Researcher Award, the University of Delaware Trabant Award for Women's Equity, and the Conference on English Education Research Initiative Award.

**Mikela Bjork**, after graduating from Smith College, began her teaching career as a Kindergarten Teacher's Assistant in her hometown of Charlottesville, VA. She then moved to Brooklyn, New York, where she received her Masters degree in Special Education and worked in an inclusive high school math and science classroom for five years. Inspired by the strength and resilience of her students, as they worked within a system that seemed in many ways to work against them, she began her journey as a doctoral candidate, receiving her PhD from The Graduate Center, City University of New York in 2017. She currently works at the University of Redlands, teaching pre- and in-service (special education) teachers, as well as doctoral students. In addition to issues around social justice in (special) education and (dis)ability studies, Mikela is interested in the intersections between public health and education, narrative inquiry, and the hidden curriculum of heteronormativity. When she isn't teaching, you might find her bird watching with her almost 2-year-old son or practicing inversions on her yoga mat.

**Kevin Christopher Carey** is an interdisciplinary teacher-scholar (English/ Rhetoric PhD, Russian Literature MA) in the Department of Communication Arts at the University of Waterloo, whose work focuses on higher education and its discontents. Drawing on rhetorical theory, institutional histories, critical pedagogy, and philosophy, his research examines tensions between the progressive aims and the conservative functions of higher education. He has written about critical thinking discourses as constitutive rhetoric, and he is currently investigating the materialist underpinnings of liberal arts discourses. As a teacher, Kevin is interested in collaborative inquiry with students, as well as developing power sharing relationships in the classroom.

**Brian Charest** is an assistant professor at the University of Redlands. He is a former public high school teacher who has taught in both Chicago and Seattle. He's worked in a variety of educational settings with students of diverse backgrounds and identities. Much of Brian's university teaching has involved community-based work of some kind, where students in his courses work closely with local community-based organizations, schools, practicing teachers, and residents in "real world" settings. Brian draws on the traditions of community organizers to help teachers learn the skills and strategies to be strong advocates for themselves, their students, and the communities in which they live and work.

**Alex Corbitt** was a middle school English Language Arts teacher for five years in the Bronx, New York. He is now a doctoral student at Boston College's Lynch School of Education. His work focuses on culturally responsive teaching, identity, literacy, and education technology.

**Sarah J. Donovan**, PhD, is a junior high English language arts teacher and adjunct professor in middle and secondary education. She wrote *Genocide Literature in Middle and Secondary Classrooms* (Routledge, 2016) and the young adult novel *Alone Together.* Dr. Donovan's work is featured in *The ALAN Review, The Best Lesson Series* (Talks with Teachers, 2018), *Queer Adolescent Literature as a Complement to the English Language Arts Curriculum* (Rowman & Littlefield, 2018), and *Contending with Gun Violence in the English Language Classroom* (Routledge, 2019). She serves as a state representative and board member for The Assembly on Literature for Adolescents of NCTE (ALAN).

**Jay Gillen** has taught and organized in an around Baltimore City Public Schools since 1987. In 1994, after a two-year organizing campaign, he became teacher-director of the new Stadium Middle School, the first community-controlled public school in Baltimore in many years. Working with graduates of the Stadium School, Gillen developed the peer-tutoring Baltimore Algebra Project (BAP) in 2001. Students working for the BAP as math literacy workers and student organizers have earned more than $4,000,000 since then. The BAP became entirely student-run in 2009, and is looked to around the country as a model for structuring student power in a sustainable way. In 2009, Gillen returned to full-time math teaching, co-teaching with BAP graduates to create near-peer learning communities for high-school students having trouble with math. Today, he teaches at the Waxter Juvenile Detention Center for Young Women, and is helping to develop a Peer-to-Peer Youth Enterprise Incubator, which has a goal of creating 200 knowledge-based peer-to-peer jobs serving 1,000 students in Baltimore by 2019. Gillen is the author of numerous articles, and of the book, *Educating for Insurgency: The Roles of Young People in Schools of Poverty*. A companion volume, tentatively titled, *Uprooting Education: From Crawl Spaces to a Youth Economy* will be published in 2019.

**Noah Asher Golden** is an assistant professor in the Attallah College of Educational Studies at Chapman University and is a former secondary level English teacher and literacy coach in New York City. His scholarship investigates the identity enactments and (re)positioning practices of minoritized youth, and is situated within critical and sociocultural approaches to literacies research and teaching/learning practice. His scholarship has appeared in *English Education, Equity & Excellence in Education, Urban Education, Teaching Education, Educational Media International, Knowledge Cultures*, and *English Journal*.

**Matthew Homrich-Knieling** is a middle school English Language Arts teacher in southwest Detroit. Matthew is especially interested in learning and practicing culturally and linguistically sustaining pedagogy, transformative justice, and activist pedagogies. He is the faculty adviser for an after-school student activism club. Additionally, Matthew is a co-founder and organizer with MIStudentsDream, a coalition of educators, students, parents, and community members in metro Detroit that organizes for immigration justice as a component of education justice. Matthew's work has been published in publications such as *Teaching Tolerance, Voices from the Middle, Education Week*, and *Literacy & NCTE*. Matthew's teaching, writing, and organizing is centered around a vision of schools and communities as spaces of justice, liberation, and healing. *The views in his co-authored chapter do not necessarily reflect the views of his employer.*

**Will Hudson** is the sixth grade teacher and middle level coordinator at the Children's School in Oak Park, Illinois. Previously, Will taught Kindergarten through 5th grade English as a New Language in public schools in Texas and Illinois where he served as an advocate and occasional translator for immigrant children and their families. He is currently active in various grassroots organizations in his community that focus on immigrant rights, leadership development, and access to educational opportunities for under-served children and families. Will's work is inspired by his ongoing journey as an anti-racist and his belief in the potential for people and communities to take care of one another. In his spare time he enjoys hiking, growing and arranging flowers, reading, and taking an occasional nap.

**Glynis Kinnan** has a BA in English from Grinnell College and a PhD in English from the University of Illinois at Chicago. She was a lecturer at the University of Illinois at Chicago until 2005, when she became an English teacher at Oak Park and River Forest High School in Oak Park, IL. She lives in Oak Park with her husband, three dogs, and one cat. She has practiced Buddhism for 20 years.

**Avi Lessing** teaches English, coaches teachers, and directs plays at Oak Park and River Forest High School just outside of Chicago. He writes fre-quently about education, and his classes and plays have been featured by National Public Radio. Currently, he is working on a book about the con-nection between experience and relationships in school. Avi is grateful for his wife and two children, Bindi, Raiva, and Rafi.

**Russell Mayo** is a doctoral candidate in English at the University of Illi-nois at Chicago, where he works as a graduate instructor of First-Year Writing and English Education. Russ's research examines the relationships between literacy, education, and society. His dissertation is an ethnographic study of social literacy practices of a large, urban university's writing center. His work considers the ways in which non-classroom literacy spaces offer potential models for "deschooling" learning and social relations. Russ is also interested in how anarchist pedagogy and social theory might help communities and institutions move toward social, economic, and environmental mutuality and resilience. Russ holds a Bachelor's from Eastern Michigan University and a Master's of Education from the UNC-Chapel Hill. He formerly taught mid-dle school English and Social Studies in Chapel Hill, North Carolina.

**James McCoyne** is an English teacher at Young Women's Leadership Charter School of Chicago, where he also serves as the staff sponsor for the National Honors Society, yearbook, and literary arts magazine. He is a grad-uate of the University of Illinois at Chicago where he earned a Bachelor in the Teaching of English with a minor in Sociology. James comes from a family of teachers and activists, which has shaped his perspective on education and soci-ety. As a teacher, he strives to educate through a social justice pedagogy. In his free time, he enjoys drawing, reading, and visiting art museums and galleries.

**Kate Sjostrom** is a lecturer and assistant director of English Education at University of Illinois at Chicago. Her research focuses on writing teacher identity development in the context of recent education reforms, as well as on the potential for teacher-writing to build teachers' professional advocacy. She is especially interested in the power of narrative—as both critical thinking tool and mode of expression in K-College classrooms, and as both method and product of academic research.

**Angela Whitacre de Resendiz** is the third grade teacher at The Children's School, a progressive K-8 elementary school outside Chicago, Illinois. She has a degree in Women's Studies from San Diego State University. She was involved in several women's health and anti-racist organizations there before moving to Mexico where she began her teaching career and started a family. She grew up with a teacher and social worker and has always believed the key to teaching is building relationships with children. She lives with her two beautiful children and husband in Chicago and frequently returns to Mexico City to visit family and friends. She used to enjoy reading, spending time in bookshops, dancing ballet folklorico, and watching mysteries. Then she became a parent and progressive teacher and now spends her time finding resources and quality children's literature for the kids in her life.

**Samantha Young** is the co-founder of Preschool Prodigies, an online learning platform for teaching music to preschoolers, and a former high school English teacher. In her seven years of teaching, she instructed 10th and 11th grade English, served as 10th Grade Team Leader, a member of the Instructional Leadership Team, and English Department Chair. During this time she helped lead: curriculum development in preparation for four different high stakes standardized tests, the implementation of a Race to the Top Partnership Zone Turnaround initiative, an iPad 1:1 school wide technology initiative, and action research study regarding blended learning in the literature classroom.

## sj Miller & Leslie David Burns
GENERAL EDITORS

Social Justice Across Contexts in Education addresses how teaching for social justice, broadly defined, mediates and disrupts systemic and structural inequities across early childhood, K–12 and postsecondary disciplinary, interdisciplinary and/or transdisciplinary educational contexts. This series includes books exploring how theory informs sustainable pedagogies for social justice curriculum and instruction, and how research, methodology, and assessment can inform equitable and responsive teaching. The series constructs, advances, and supports socially just policies and practices for all individuals and groups across the spectrum of our society's education system.

Books in this series provide sustainable models for generating theories, research, practices, and tools for social justice across contexts as a means to leverage the psychological, emotional, and cognitive growth for learners and professionals. They position social justice as a fundamental aspect of schooling, and prepare readers to advocate for and prevent social justice from becoming marginalized by reform movements in favor of the corporatization and deprofessionalization of education. The over-arching aim is to establish a true field of social justice education that offers theory, knowledge, and resources for those who seek to help all learners succeed. It speaks for, about, and to classroom teachers, administrators, teacher educators, education researchers, students, and other key constituents who are committed to transforming the landscape of schools and communities.

Send proposals and manuscripts to the general editors at:

sj Miller              sj.Miller@colorado.edu
Leslie David Burns    L.Burns@uky.edu

To order other books in this series, please contact our Customer Service Department at:

(800) 770-LANG (within the U.S.)
(212) 647-7706 (outside the U.S.)
(212) 647-7707 FAX

or browse online by series at:

WWW.PETERLANG.COM